The Spider Dance

Contemporary and Historical Paganism

Series Editors

This series seeks original work on contemporary and revived Pagan religious traditions around the world, as well as re-examinations of ancient polytheistic religion from new perspectives. Contributions are invited from diverse disciplines, including religious studies, popular culture, musicology, anthropology, sociology, ethnography, and feminist philosophy of religion.

Published

Being Viking
Heathenism in Contemporary America
Jefferson Calico

Constellated Ministry
A Guide for Those Serving Today's Pagans
Holli S. Emore

Forthcoming

Albion's Sage for the New Age
John Michell, Radical Traditionalism and the Myth of Sacred England
Marleen Thaler

The Pagan Revival
A Documentary History of Modern Paganism, 1700–1950
Edited by Robin Douglas

The Spider Dance

Tradition, Time, and Healing in Southern Italy

Giovanna Parmigiani

equinox

SHEFFIELD UK BRISTOL CT

Published by Equinox Publishing Ltd

UK: Office 415, The Workstation, 15 Paternoster Row, Sheffield, South Yorkshire S1 2BX
USA: ISD, 70 Enterprise Drive, Bristol, CT 06010

www.equinoxpub.com

First published 2024

British Library Cataloguing-in-Publication Data

A catalogue record for this book is available from the British Library.

ISBN-13 978 1 80050 512 4 (hardback)
978 1 80050 513 1 (paperback)
978 1 80050 514 8 (ePDF)
978 1 80050 589 6 (ePub)

Library of Congress Cataloging-in-Publication Data

Names: Parmigiani, Giovanna, author.
Title: Title: The spider dance : tradition, time, and healing in southern Italy / Giovanna Parmigiani.
Description: Bristol, CT : Equinox Publishing Ltd., 2024. | Series: Contemporary and historical paganism | Includes bibliographical references and index. | Summary: "Based on ethnographic research among contemporary Pagan communities in Southern Italy (Salento, Apulia), The Spider Dance challenges (uni)linear ideas and experiences of time and temporality by showing the interconnectedness of alternative historicities, healing, and place-making among persons engaged in reviving, continuing, or re-creating traditional Pagan practices. The relevance of The Spider Dance is not limited to a description of particular Pagan groups and practices. It also makes some key practical and theoretical contributions to the anthropological study of magic, of contemporary religions, of "historicities," and to scholarly debates around complementary medicine and "well-being," in Italy and abroad"-- Provided by publisher.
Identifiers: LCCN 2024014001 (print) | LCCN 2024014002 (ebook) | ISBN 9781800505124 (hardback) | ISBN 9781800505131 (paperback) | ISBN 9781800505148 (epdf) | ISBN 9781800505896 (epub)
Subjects: LCSH: Occultism--Italy. | Paganism--Italy. | Tarantella--Italy.
Classification: LCC BF1434.I8 P39 2024 (print) | LCC BF1434.I8 (ebook) | DDC 299/.940945/7--dc23/eng/20240522
LC record available at https://lccn.loc.gov/2024014001
LC ebook record available at https://lccn.loc.gov/2024014002

Typeset by S.J.I. Services, New Delhi, India

Contents

Preface

Figure 1. Dancing pizzica at the Torre del Serpe, on the Adriatic sea. Photo credit: Carolina Parmigiani

The protagonists of this book are Southern Italian contemporary Pagans and New Age practitioners of the Salento area of Italy, the place where I have been conducting my fieldwork since 2011. This monograph is the result of a two-year long ethnography with a particular group—*il cerchio,* the circle—and their friends and acquaintances. While I studied a relatively small community (of less than fifty persons, overall, strictly speaking), the implications of this research are far-reaching, contributing to the current debates not only in contemporary Pagan studies, but also in the anthropological study of magic, religion, well-being, and of historicities—i.e., ways to experience and to make sense of time, history, and temporality.

As the anthropological adage goes, anthropologists do not (only) study *the* village, but *in* the village. In this sense, the Salento area of Italy, the southeastern fringe of the Italian peninsula, appears to be a particularly fruitful place for anthropological analyses. As I argued elsewhere, for historical and anthropological reasons, Salento could be considered as an *iperluogo*—a "hyperplace."[1] This notion was developed over the past twenty years by the Italian anthropologist Berardino Palumbo, who used it in reference to Sicily. Following his elaborations on this concept, a "hyperplace" can be described as a "narrative place" or a "place of places."[2] It is a space continuously created and narrated, a "total space of the senses (social, political, emotional),"[3] a place, in other words, where objects and signs of the past, together with poetics, practices, and techniques of the body, are continuously manipulated and reinterpreted in an "endless production of sense."[4]

In this study I concentrate on one aspect, in particular, of the "endless production of sense" of the Salento "hyperplace," and a key one: that of local historicities. Through my participant observation with my Pagan interlocutors, I first witnessed and then learned a specific way to live *temporally* that I called "expanded present" or "presence." This peculiar historicity is at the center of this book, and, I claim, it is not only a useful *descriptive device* to narrate the experiences of southern Italian Pagans. It is also and more importantly, an *analytical filter* that allows to shed some light on

1 Giovanna Parmigiani, "Spiritual *Pizzica*: A Southern Italian Perspective on Contemporary Paganism," *The Pomegranate: The International Journal of Pagan Studies: The International Journal of Pagan Studies* 21, no. 1 (2019): 53–75, https://doi.org/10.1558/pome.37787.

2 Berardino Palumbo, "Iperluogo," *Antropologia Museale* 14 (2006): 45–46.

3 Ibid., 46.

4 Michela Badii, *Processi di patrimonializzazione e politiche del cibo* (Segrate: Morlacchi, 2012), 9.

unexplored dimensions—within and beyond contemporary Paganisms—of the study of magic, the connections between historicities and well-being, and of the epistemological implications of particular ontologies.

In the contemporary world, and in the academic one especially, it is often assumed that all human beings experience, *by default*, time as flowing linearly. Within such a historicity, the past, present, and future are perceived as separated but contiguous, and placed on an imaginary line. On this imaginary line, causes have effects, and the former always precede the latter. While ubiquitous, at least in the modern world, this particular historicity, generally called "linear," is not the only one, nor it is the only one that matters, in the lives of people.[5] In other contexts (or epochs), for example, a cyclical historicity coexists with the linear one—as in what is generally referred to, in popular culture, as the Pagan Wheel of the Year or, more generally, in agricultural societies or contexts. In Salento, among the Pagans with whom I worked, though, I found that the "textures" of time,[6] temporality, and history have additional and peculiar connotations. During my ethnographic work I noticed that my interlocutors experience time as an "expanded present" or "presence."[7] This particular way to live and embody time and space focuses on the *coevality* of past, present, and

5 It is worth noting that there is more than one "linearity," when talking about time. In this book, when I refer to "linearity" I indicate an understanding of time that is unilinear and chronological. On a "diffractive" reading of time, see Karen Barad, "Troubling Time/s and Ecologies of Nothingness: Re-turning, Re-membering, and Facing the Incalculable," *New Formations* 92, no. 1 (2018): 56–86; and on "history without chronology," see Stefan Tanaka, "History without Chronology," *Public Culture* 28, no. 1 (2016): 161–86.

6 Manuela Pellegrino, *Greek Language, Italian Landscape: Griko and the Re-Storying of a Linguistic Minority*, Hellenic Studies Series 89 (Washington, DC: Center for Hellenic Studies, 2020).

7 Rebecca Bryant and Daniel M. Knight point out that "for Husserl, the phenomenology of time-consciousness is consciousness of an "extended present," "an epochal moment that endows experience with its seemingly 'flowing' quality" (Rebecca Bryant and Daniel M. Knight, *The Anthropology of the Future* [Cambridge: Cambridge University Press, 2019], 24). It is worth noting that the

future *within* the flow of linear and cyclical times. Charged of past and future events, the "expanded present" comprises all three temporalities at the same time. Presence is, therefore, different from "mindfulness," not the result of "bracketing" dimensions that are not "in the moment" (past and future). Rather, it is the result of embracing, with a growing awareness, the different dimensions, rhizomes, presences, and connections embedded in the past-present-future coevality of the *qui-e-ora*—the "here-and-now."

This growing awareness that I witnessed ethnographically is the result of many of "body-mind" practices such as Tarot reading, meditations, the use of pendulums, family constellations, and the various magical elements that are usually recognized as belonging to "global" Wiccan and contemporary Pagan communities. Mostly, though, this "presence" among my Salentine interlocutors is achieved through singing, playing, and/or dancing *pizzica*.

Pizzica is a traditional—occasionally ecstatic—music and dance, performed in this particular area of Italy. In the past, it was also associated with specific healing practices related to the (actual or metaphorical) bite of tarantula spiders, a malaise that affected mostly women and that went by the name of *tarantismo*. Now that *tarantismo*, as described in the past by the well-known Italian ethnographer Ernesto de Martino (1908–1965),[8] has disappeared, *pizzica* music and dance have been reclaimed and re-imagined in different ways, mostly as a local identity-marker, as folk-music, and as a touristic attraction. As my fieldwork among the Sisters of the *cerchio* and other Pagans and New Age practitioners in Salento shows, *tarantismo* and the performance of *pizzica* today are also re-appropriated in their spiritual

---

notion of "expanded present" that I use in this book does not necessarily refer to nor place itself into a phenomenological understanding of "presence."

8 Ernesto de Martino, *La terra del rimorso: Contributo a una storia religiosa del Sud* (Milan: Il Saggiatore, 1976 [1961]).

dimensions, outside the Catholic Church, in a form of what could be called *spiritual neotarantismo*.

My Pagan interlocutors, as a matter of fact, associate *pizzica* with their spiritual practices. They do so through an understanding and experience of "self" as unbounded and within a "neo-animist," relational framework through which they experience and understand the world and their presence in it. *Pizzica* is the *filo* (thread, web), the guiding light, and practice of the *cerchio*. *Pizzica* is its common ground, language, and medicine. In spite of all the differences among the members of the group, the one element that the circle shares is a strong relationship with *pizzica* and with the land of Salento. Some of my interlocutors dance it, some others play it or sing it. It is for all of them a way to connect with themselves, with each other, and with that particular land—including its human, more-than-human, and other-than-human inhabitants. *Pizzica* is often part of their getting together—when they want to hang out and have some fun, when they need to meditate, to be healed, to communicate at non-verbal, *sottili* (thin) levels, when they need to recharge, to process thoughts, to celebrate, to pray, to get grounded, to receive insights and guidance from "spirits," to sort things out between them. Moreover, and especially, *pizzica* is considered a healing spiritual practice. Associated with the experience of the "expanded present," *pizzica* allows for a "presence in history," to tweak de Martino's expression, in a way that, by going beyond commonsensical understandings and experiences of time, it is believed to promote well-being.[9] In other words, dancing *pizzica* and accessing the "expanded present" allow contemporary southern Italian Pagans to conceive of and live their lives from the point of view of the persons they are, and are meant to be, but that they are not yet—i.e., to focus on their own "becoming."

9 Ibid.

In line with the "expanded present" historicity, this book is written (mostly) in the present tense, and it does not organize ethnographic data and vignettes in a linear way. While some readers might perceive this as unsettling, the rupture of the linear flow of narration (and of the reader's expectations) parallels the shift in the experience of time and temporality that the "expanded present" cultivates. This is evident also in the relationships between the main text and what can be found in the footnotes. Differently from other academic books, in my text footnotes not only supply glosses but are themselves loci of many academically oriented, in-depth analyses and trajectories—adding other layers and textures to the main narrative. Readers, therefore, can read and approach this text in different ways—all coeval, but not necessarily accessible linearly—according to the level of specific engagement they choose to have with academic debates, language, and frameworks. As destabilizing as it might appear, at first, I believe eventually all this delivers what it promises: a textured, lived, embodied experience, and description of other ways to inhabit time and to approach our "ways of knowing."

Given the topic of the book and of my research, my personal voice and experiences are put in the foreground in the following chapters, the auto-ethnographic dimension of this book is dovetailed with the experiences and voices of my interlocutors. As an anthropologist who could be considered as "having gone native," I thought that my presence in the text was both the most ethical and the most effective choice for this book. First, my "presence" in the text does not set me apart from my interlocutors. Moreover, it openly situates my positionality *vis-à-vis* my readers. Finally, it allows me to overtly use myself, *in my relations with my interlocutors,* as an instrument of knowledge. After all, I believe, this is what anthropology is about.

The chapters are organized in conversation with some of the *Major Arcana* of the Tarot decks. By providing a narrative and a commentary on the "Fool's Journey"—that is, a metaphor for the human journey on Earth—these particular cards are believed to offer a trajectory that is both individual and general, context-specific and universal, historical and mythical. Here again, I wanted to honor the experience of my interlocutors, and narrate our stories through the stories that they use: Tarot, as divination instruments, bend time and space, and offer healing narratives, for my interlocutors, in the *qui-e-ora* of a reading.

Chapter 1, Il Matto/The Fool introduces the reader to my fieldwork, current debates around contemporary Paganisms, and magical practices. Chapter 2, Il Mago/The Magician addresses *pizzica* as a spiritual practice, in conversation with *tarantismo* and the land of Salento. Chapter 3 La Papessa/The High Priestess focuses on the "expanded present" historicity. Chapter 4, L'Imperatrice/The Empress, and chapter 5, La Temperanza/Temperance, provide examples of how, by adopting the "filter" of the "expanded present," this research illuminates unexplored dimensions in the anthropology of religion, magic, and well-being. Moreover, it sheds some light on the relationships between historicities, personhood, and ways of knowing.

All the names in this book, are pseudonyms. All translations, if not otherwise specified, are mine.

This research would not have been possible without the help of many (human and non-human) persons who, in different ways, supported, challenged, provoked, encouraged, and cared for me and this creative enterprise.

My heartfelt thanks go, first of all, to the Sisters of the *cerchio.* I will be forever grateful for what you taught me and for the continuous and supportive encouragement I have been receiving from you, from the first time I met you. Thank you for being in my life, and for the compassion, intelligence, and *bellezza* that you share with the world. I want to thank Antonella, Cristina, Debora, Enza, Rossella, Valentina, Monica, Caterina, Giuseppe, Vincenza, Maria

Teresa Pino, Ada, Nino, Gianfranco, Rita, Luigi, Brigitte, Cinzia, Maria Antonietta, Ilaria, Anna Maria, Alessandro, Andrea, Umberto, Angelo, Gino, Adele, Norma, Nora, Donato, Fabio, Claudio, Morgana, Luna, Annette, Marisa, Eunice, Zaira, Martika, Carolina, Davide, Elide, Giancarlo, Annalisa, Steven, Stefania, Rino, Andrea, Consuelo, Tina, Stefania, Salvatore, Barbara, Klejda, Maddalena, Oriana, Arjeta, Fabio, Giuseppe, Antonio, Luigina, Enrica, Mary, Michele, Loredana, Lorenzo, Sara, Lucia, Fiore, Fabio, Adriano, Alessandro, Rosamarina, Virginie, Elena, Fabio, Claudio, Nicoletta Nuzzo, Vito Cannazza, Corigliano, and the Villa and the Barocci families. You all, in different ways, directly or indirectly, contributed to the realization of this book. Life is brighter, thanks to you.

I am especially grateful to Equinox Publishing, for believing in this project. A particular thanks to Chas S. Clifton and Scott Simpson for their support, trust, and commitment associated with the birth of this book, and for the patience and encouragement throughout the process.

I want to thank all the persons who, in different ways and occasions, have engaged with part of the text or arguments of the book: your feedback proved to be critical for the realization of this monograph. My deepest thanks go to Charles Stewart, Stephan Palmié, Michael Jackson, Annalisa Butticci, Valentina Napolitano, Michael Herzfeld, Danielle Widmann Abrahams, Todne Thomas, Manuela Pellegrino, Veronica Buffon, Helen Berger, Helen Cornish, Caroline Tully, Bron Taylor, Sabina Magliocco, Francesca Ciancimino-Howell, Michael Strmiska, Stefania Palmisano, Amy Hale, Davide Marrè, Mary Balkon, Natalia Schwien, Brenda Prescott, Nora Williams, Vivianne Crowley, Holli Emory, Graham Harvey, J. Christian Greer, Elizabeth Rovere, Charles Stang, David Abram, N. Fadeke Castor, Sravana Borkataky-Varma , Matthew J. Dillon, Hadi Fakhoury, Mimi Winick, Michael Ennis, Shiraz Hajiani, Barakatullo Ashurov, Michael Ferguson, the "Transcendence and

Transformation" seminar, the "neo-animism" group at HDS, Corey O'Brien, Gosia Sklodowska, the CSWR staff, Sabina Izzo, Salvatore Giusto, Gianluca Trezzi, Lauren Sawyer, Annie Mesaros, Kelsi Morrison-Atkins, Joseph Kimmel, Enrica Colazzo, the audiences of my papers, and, in particular, to the students of my courses at Harvard Divinity School. Thank you all for taking the time to read and listen to my work, and for your valuable and thoughtful comments.

A special thanks to Harvard Divinity School: in particular to the "Transcendence and Transformation" Initiative at Harvard's Center for the Study of World Religions, directed by Charles Stang, the Program for the Evolution of Spirituality, directed by Dan McKanan, the Program in Science, Religion, and Culture directed by Ahmed Raghab, and the "neo-animism reading group," led by Mary Balkon, first, and Natalia Schwien, after. Thank you for supporting my scholarly interests, and for creating space for intellectually inspiring conversations and people.

Thanks also to the colleagues and students at the ILCS at the University of Connecticut and to the colleagues and students at Bryant University.

Thanks to Paolo Zerbini for the cover image of this book. Most importantly, I want to thank my husband, Giovanni Bazzana, and my son, Beniamino. Thank you for your patience, support, understanding, and thorough engagement with my work and personal transformations.

Finally, I want to thank the land of the Massachusetts and of Salento: you both welcomed me, a foreigner, with great generosity and acceptance.

May you all be blessed.

Chapter 1

Il Matto/The Fool

[Keywords: beginning, trust, the here-and-now]

Figure 2. A cat at Santa Maria de Finibus Terrae (Our Lady of/ at the End of the World). Photo credit: Giovanna Parmigiani.

You walk and sweat. You have been trying to dance pizzica for a good hour, and you still feel overwhelmed by the sound of tambourines pulsing through your ears, stomach, legs, and feet. You were just introduced to their pizzica: a pizzica that you listen to with your feet, dance to with your mind, and comprehend in your belly. You feel overwhelmed and vulnerable: exposed, bare. You never danced before, and you just discovered the emotional intimacy of dancing, its communicative power. Puzzled, you wonder what information you disclosed to your dancing partners and how exactly it happened. Your mind floats. It wanders without dwelling: your mom's chemotherapy, the eyes of your dying grandmother, your husband and son on the other side of the Atlantic Ocean, the spousal and parental consequences of your planned one-year long fieldwork, the reasons that made this difficult choice a necessity.

The night is ripe of sea mist, and you follow, light-headed, the elegant and unfailing gait of your pizzica teacher, trying not to concentrate on your own uncertain steps. She invited you to the apartment of one of her friends, and you docilely follow her there, through the empty, dark, and narrow streets of Otranto – the many centuries-old city of Salento, at the far south-east of the Italian peninsula.

You know at a certain level that this might be a delicate "first encounter" with some of the women you decided to follow for your research, but you are surprised to find out that you do not really care about your work in that precise moment and about the possible consequences of a bad start. You taste the air that smells of the sea, of a harbor, of a place without winters. While the mid-October wind caresses your skin and soothes your disquiet, you follow your pizzica teacher and your thoughts, knowing that the only way to deal with both is through acknowledging their presence, and your own presence, in the present – in your present. This is your one certainty when everything else feels like spinning. You follow your pizzica teacher and knock at the door of a stranger: seconds later you are welcomed by a warm smile, a pair of vivid eyes, and by the elegant moves of Idrusa's hands.

***

This is my story, a story that I own. While it is not every story, it is also a story, a tale that might speak to its readers about some aspects of their own stories: of our common being-in-the-world, of our common "presence," our common "staying," "dwelling" across time(s).

In Salento, the "heel" of the Italian boot and the place where this story unfolds, locals wisely use *staying* as a synonym of *being*. "*Sta bau a Lecce crai, vagnoni*!" for instance, is the dialectal form for "I am (stay) going to Lecce tomorrow, folks!" *Sta(u),* I stay, *sta bau,* literally "I stay going." As this example shows, staying does not imply passivity, stillness, or lack of change, here. Rather, it entails movement, transformation, action—a particular form of action: sensorial, aesthetic, temporal.[1] In this *active staying,* for the Salentinians I met, lies a key to inhabiting history, to well-being, and to specific political engagements. This is their way to experience time and temporality: one that is at the core of their understanding of who they are and of how to live a happy life. This presence, or "expanded present," is their door to access well-being—a door that, thanks to them, I learned to open, too.

Between 2011 and 2022 I spent more than four years in Salento, more than two of which researching a group of women—the "Sisters of the *cerchio*"—and other contemporary Pagan and New Age practitioners. During my ethnographic research—which included extensive participant observation, interviews, and the collection of life-histories—my interlocutors and I shared our lives: everyday events as well as extraordinary ones. I went grocery shopping, drank beer, shared stories with them. I met their families, cooked with them, drove them to doctors' appointments. I

1 As for the Tarot card of the High Priestess, that will be addressed in chapter 3 in connection with my detailed presentation of the "expanded present" or "presence" historicity that I found in Salento among the contemporary Pagan community I have worked with, where the (lack of) action of "staying" does not entail passivity. Rather, it is very much linked to an ethos of "receiving."

also attended their rituals, made interviews, received initiations, danced to their "traditional" *pizzica* music, and learned of a central feature of their spiritual experiences and practice: the "expanded present" historicity. The last is a goal of many of their ritual practices, but it is achieved mainly through the "interpretation" of a specific aesthetic (both "sensory" and "artistic") engagement: by dancing and/or playing "traditional" *pizzica* music.[2] This music, linked to the rituals of *tarantismo* of the past, is *il filo*, the web, thread, that connects the spiritual experiences of the Sisters of the *cerchio* and of many of their friends.

***

I sit at Idrusa's table – a bottle of Tenent's Super lager beer in front of me and some spicy cashew nuts. Viola, my pizzica teacher, is engaged in a WhatsApp chat with a man she is dating, and switches from that conversation to the one with us with the same gracefulness with which she moves from the table to the couch and back. The small living room is neatly furnished but still retains the allure of a vacation apartment: I can feel, lingering, the relieving almost-like-home feeling that comforts sun-burnt northerners struck by the Salento sun after a mid-August day spent at the

2 In using the verb *interpret* (meaning both understanding *and* performing, possibly understanding *while* performing), I follow Michael Lambek, "The Interpretation of Lives or Life as Interpretation: Cohabiting with Spirits in the Malagasy World," *American Ethnologist* 41, no. 3 (2014): 492, on the topic of spirit possession, who writes: "Indeed, I want to invoke "interpretation" in the sense of what actors *do* with a script or character, or musicians with a score. . . . It is in this sense that I see the Malagasy spirit mediums I describe below: interpreting a particular royal ancestor from the Sakalava repertoire not only through active states of possession in which they embody and personify him but also as they live with him in the course of their lives and as those lives become that living with. Living as and with the ancestor constitutes their interpretation of him no less than does his public manifestation for their audiences, consociates, and interlocutors. Indeed, the interpretation of the ancestral character in, and through, and as the medium's life is simultaneously an interpretation of the ancestor's public significance and the means by which culture or tradition is refracted and reproduced as it is worked through, supplemented, and no doubt changed by each successive generation."

beach. Idrusa, our guest, is sitting at one of the corners of the faux-leather couch, close to the window. The night is dark, and her eyes are looking at something invisible to us, while, lost in her thoughts, she shuffles some cards.[3] *She touches every single one of them as if they were the skin of a lover, feeling and filling with her fingers imaginary rifts and valleys. "I am learning to know them, to make them my own," she mutters, answering a question that I was sure I had not uttered. I smile and slightly blush, feeling like a kid discovered right as she was making mischief. "I already have a connection with my carte delle fate –fairies' cards–, but this is a birthday present from the Sisters of the cerchio and it's the first time that I use them," she continues.*

***

Il cerchio—the circle—is the informal name that the women who are at the core of my ethnography give themselves. A fictive kinship informs the group. As a matter of fact, beyond personal and spiritual interests and practices, this circle is first of all a group of women who call themselves, reciprocally, "Sisters." To signal the non-biological aspect of this kinship, in spite of the fact that only a minority of them know English well, they call each other by the word *Sister,* and not the Italian *sorella,* or the dialectal *soru.* Some of these women might call other people "sis" or "bro," but, since the latter are not considered sisters or brothers by the other members, they are not treated as part of the circle. When I met the Sisters, in June 2015, the circle counted five women, aged from thirty-four to fifty: Viola, Idrusa, Senefera, Fiammetta, and Magenta. Some were married or in relationships; some were single or separated. Some were mothers, and some were not. They all worked but not all

3 The moon was at its first quarter. I did not know this at the time, but I subsequently discovered that Tarot cards should be "cleaned" preferably during a new moon—something Idrusa probably had done a few days before our first meeting. Her caressing the cards, I was told, was her way to "connect" with them.

of them full-time. Most had university degrees although nobody would consider herself "well-off." No one lived in Salento's main city: Lecce. They all came from the southern part of Salento.[4] Very seldom the *cerchio* met as "a circle" or as a "coven"; more often the Sisters met in groups of two or three, variously arranged according to the situations, life circumstances, locations, purposes, rituals, and goals. Moreover, since every Sister was embedded in nets of relationships, often the gatherings of the *cerchio* included outsiders, who also became part of my ethnographic study.[5]

Some six months into my fieldwork, I started to be considered part of the *cerchio* that today counts six women: five Salentinians and me, an Italian "northerner," affectionately called, sometimes, "*la Salentona*."[6] Italians from the north are ubiquitously nicknamed *polentoni*, a word that comes from the word *polenta*—a cornmeal dough, very popular in the past among peasants in the northern part of the country but not traditionally eaten in the south. *Salentona* is a term invented by my Sisters, meaning, quite oxymoronically for them, "a *polentona* from Salento." In spite of the fact that my descent and Italian accent are undisguisedly northern, they

4 The inhabitants of Lecce tend to refer to those who live outside the city as *poppiti*. While mostly rhetorically used in jokes, in my experience, the distinction between "city-persons" and *poppiti* appeared to be tracing, in the past, a cultural and class divide.

5 Through my engagement with the Sisters and the life of the *cerchio*, I encountered about fifty Pagans, in Salento, who are also part of this ethnographic study.

6 My personal ethnographic involvement in the life of the Sisters and in their ritual activities allowed me to better grasp evident and less evident elements of the contemporary Pagan beliefs and practices of the *cerchio*. For important comparisons and discussions on the personal involvement of the religious studies scholar in her ethnographic research see, e.g., Sabina Magliocco, *Witching Culture: Folklore and Neo-Paganism in America* (Philadelphia: University of Pennsylvania Press, 2004); Jennifer Scheper-Hughes, "Mysterium Materiae: Vital Matter and the Object as Evidence in the Study of Religion," *Bulletin for the Study of Religion* 41, no. 4 (2012): 16–24; Susan Greenwood, *The Anthropology of Magic* (New York: Berg, 2009); Haleh Rafi, "The Necessity / Possibility to Re-name: A Spiritual Autoethnography." *Anthropology and Humanism* 46 no 1(2021): 38–53.

believe I do "belong" in Salento: emotionally, practically, and "karmically."[7] And, in a way, I do too.

> You belong here because you certainly were born here and lived in this land in some of your other lives. You feel at home here because this place was your home . . . and your soul knows it. This is probably why you feel *pizzica* so deeply when you dance. Not all of those who were born here in this life can feel it as you do.[8]

The circle is not, strictly speaking, a "reconstructionist" group: it does not aim at practicing a pre-Christian religion as it was practiced in the past. In contrast to many Pagan groups studied in Italy and in Catholic countries, its members do not worship the same gods and goddesses. Rather, their pantheon includes different deities, and they do not conceive "the past" as a distinct reference point.[9] They

7 The use of the word "karma" by the Sisters and other Pagan interlocutors in Salento does not do justice to the complexity of this term in Buddhist and Hindu traditions. It is used, in general, quite superficially: mostly, as a way to refer to the belief in reincarnation—loosely defined and understood.

8 I was told something similar by every Sister of the *cerchio*, in different circumstances. I was born and raised in Lombardy, from parents of north Italian descent. I went to Salento for the first time in September 2011, and I spent almost four years in the last nine in Salento. During my first fieldwork, I studied Salentine feminists (Giovanna Parmigiani, *Feminism, Violence and Representation in Modern Italy:"We Are Witnesses, Not Victims."* Bloomington: Indiana University Press, 2019; "*Femminicidio* and the Emergence of a 'Community of Sense' in Contemporary Italy," *Modern Italy* 23, no. 1 [2018]: 19–34; "Spiritual *Pizzica*," and "'The Witness Is Passing By': *Femminicidio* and the Politics of Representation in Italy," *Italian Culture* 38, no. 2 [2020]: 172–90). From June 2015 I focused on this second fieldwork, dedicating to this project, roughly twenty-four months of on-site presence. During the periods spent in North America, I kept in contact daily with my interlocutors through social media, WhatsApp, and frequent phone calls.

9 On contemporary Paganism in Catholic countries, see, e.g., Francesca Howell, "The Goddess Returns to Italy : Paganism and Wicca Reborn as a New Religious and Social Movement," *The Pomegranate: The International Journal of Pagan Studies* 10, no. 1 (2008): 5–20, and *Food, Festival, and Religion: Materiality and Place in Italy* (London: Bloomsbury Academic, 2018); Parmigiani, "Spiritual *Pizzica*"; Anna Fedele, "From Christian Religion to Feminist Spirituality: Mary Magdalene Pilgrimages to La Sainte-Baume, France," *Culture and Religion* 10, no. 3 (2009): 243–61, and *Looking for Mary Magdalene: Alternative Pilgrimage and Ritual Creativity at Catholic Shrines in France* (New York: Oxford University

are not hierarchical and do not require any particular formal or informal initiation; they do not perform counter-identities *vis-à-vis* their sociocultural and religious Catholic context, nor do they meet regularly or have a high priestess in charge of the rituals. What keeps them together as a *cerchio* is their involvement in particular aesthetic (meaning both "sensory" and "artistic") performances. Specifically, the *filo*—thread—that links the women of the *cerchio* is the practice and "interpretation" of the "traditional" dance and music called *pizzica*, connected with the healing rituals of *tarantismo* (see chapter 2).

Pizzica is the *filo*, the thread, the web, the guiding light, and practice of the *cerchio*. *Pizzica* is its common ground, language, and medicine.[10] In spite of all the differences among them, the one element that the Sisters of the circle share is a strong relationship with *pizzica* and with the land of Salento. Some of them dance it, some others play it or sing it. It is for all of them a way to connect with themselves, with each other, and with that particular land—including its human, more-than-human, and other-than-human

---

Press, 2013); Kathryn Rountree, *Crafting Contemporary Pagan Identities in a Catholic Society* (Farnham, UK: Ashgate Publishing, 2010), and "Localizing Neo-Paganism: Integrating Global and Indigenous Traditions in a Mediterranean Catholic Society," *Journal of the Royal Anthropological Institute* 17, no. 4 (2011): 846–72; José Mapril and Ruy Llera Blanes, eds., *Sites and Politics of Religious Diversity in Southern Europe: The Best of All Gods* (Leiden: Brill, 2013); Angela Puca, "The Tradition of *Segnature*: Underground Indigenous Practices in Italy," *Journal of the Irish Society for the Academic Study of Religions* 7 (2019): 104–24, and "'Witch' and 'Shaman': Discourse Analysis of the Use of Indigenizing Terms in Italy," *IJSNR* 9, no. 2 (2018): 271–84; Stefania Palmisano and Nicola Pannofino, *Contemporary Spiritualities* (Abingdon, UK: Routledge, 2021); Jenny Butler, "The Nearest Kin of the Moon: Irish Pagan Witchcraft, Magic(k), and the Celtic Twilight," in *Magic and Witchery in the Modern West : Celebrating the Twentieth Anniversary of 'The Triumph of the Moon,'* ed. Shai Feraro and Ethan Doyle White (Cham, Switzerland: Palgrave Macmillan, 2019), 85–105.

10 For a comparison, see Incoronata Nadia Inserra, *Global Tarantella: Reinventing Southern Italian Folk Music and Dances* (Urbana: University of Illinois Press, 2017) on *tammuriata* dance, a southern Italian traditional music and dance played in the Campania region of Italy, and, as Inserra shows, internationally, too.

inhabitants. *Pizzica* is often part of their getting together—when they want to hang out and have some fun, when they need to meditate, to be healed, to communicate at non-verbal, *sottili* (thin) levels, when they need to recharge, to process thoughts, to celebrate, to pray, to get grounded, to receive insights and guidance from "spirits," to sort things out between them.

I approached *pizzica* without any previous dance training or habit. In fact, I did not look at myself dancing in the dance studio mirrors or watch the videos of me dancing recorded by my friends for a long time. Partially, this was due to a certain uneasiness in thinking about myself as a dancer. Partially, this was due to Viola's teaching method. She wanted us to learn in the ways "elders learnt"— by watching people dancing, and by actually dancing with people during the classes and, especially, during public gatherings—such as concerts, *sagre* (rural festivals), and spontaneous *ronde* (dancing circles).

This is not always the case. The atmosphere around *pizzica* is quite complicated in contemporary Salento, and, while *pizzica* is very popular, not many share the approach of the *cerchio* to this music and dance. With the popularization of Salento as a tourist destination, for example, *pizzica* started to be danced and taught as a codified dancing style, complete with structured choreographies. While this *pizzica* is artistically sound, visually appealing, and beautifully danced, it is not the *pizzica* that I have learned. Viola's approach to this dance and to its teaching is quite different, in fact, and different are also the ways in which the other members of the *cerchio* live, dance, play, and conceive it. According to my teacher, *pizzica* cannot be defined by a sequence of steps. Rather, it is something that you feel, experience with and in your body.[11] Consequently, learning

11 I heard some, in the Salentine *pizzica* world, distinguishing between the Italian verbs *ballare* and *danzare* (both meaning "to dance") *pizzica*. The latter term refers to a more structured and choreographic approach—and it is used

to dance *pizzica* is not replicating some choreographies but has to do with going through an apprenticeship—one that needs to happen gradually and through relationships (with oneself, first of all, and with others). By carefully watching other people dance, by sensing their type of "energy-sharing," and by dancing with others, *pizzica* novices can be guided through the process of learning the *pizzica* language and, in some cases, of "becoming *tarantate*/i" (*tarantarsi*).[12] As a consequence, for Viola, every dancer develops her own "variation within the structure" and her signature style.[13] The only guidance that she gave during the course I attended was the description of what she calls the "one-two" step—a rhythmic, vertical, well-grounded stomping of the feet regulated by the pulsing sound of the tambourines. This, she claims, is the base of *pizzica*, as it establishes our connection with the Earth, our Mother. For the rest, the only indication Viola gave us in our first *pizzica* class was: "Allow the sound to move through and within you"—easier said than done, at least for some of us. To Viola's surprise, and to mine, despite not having been raised in that context, and therefore not being exposed to this music and dance, I could immediately feel the *pizzica* sounds moving inside and through me. Although I was not able to grasp for a long time some of the relational, aesthetic, therapeutic,

---

by some in a derogatory way—while the former is used to refer to a more spontaneous, non-codified attitude towards the dance (and not mainly nor necessarily "spiritual"). It appears that a folk-theory on the distinction between popular and high cultures informs this distinction between *ballare* and *danzare*: the former is connected with popular culture (and positively connoted) and the latter with "high" culture (associated with "fiction," and deemed to be inauthentic).

12 The term *tarantarsi,* a verb coined by some of my interlocutors but not unanimously accepted by all of them, is a reflexive form, and means "making oneself *tarantata.*" *Tarantata,* as I will explain in detail below, is the term used to describe a woman who, in the past, was thought of having been bitten by a tarantula and who, "possessed" by the spider, was treated and possibly cured by "dancing" the *pizzica tarantata* music. With the exception of the St. Peter and St. Paul festival in Galatina, these healing rituals were mostly private.

13 This element is comparable to the "ritual creativity" of contemporary Pagan pilgrims described by Fedele, *Looking for Mary Magdalene.*

communicative, and energetic implications of this practice, I immediately felt a connection with *pizzica*—and with myself and others through this dance.

***

The doorbell rings, and I am pleased to see the faces of Patrizia and Senefera appearing behind the door. I had met Patrizia at my first pizzica *class, the week before. On that occasion I had felt a sort of energetic flow taking place between the two of us while dancing – as unexpected as it was powerful. While I watch Patrizia greeting Idrusa, my mind goes to that* pizzica *dance and to how we had found ourselves, two complete strangers, hugging as soon as the music stopped. We barely knew each other's names at that point. We did not know anything about each other's life. Nonetheless, that* pizzica *had undeniably connected us. Puzzled by this novel experience (to me) and unsure of what to make of it at first, I had decided that this – our dancing connection – was all that mattered to me about her. The rest of the information we shared over time came effortlessly and did not add any substantial changes to the way we related to each other and to the frequency of our meetings. We met once a week for the* pizzica *class, until spring.* Pizzica *was our language, and, over time, I learned not to be concerned about what information I am disclosing while dancing, with her and others, as long as I feel empowered by the dance.*

There is something freeing, relieving, even moving about sharing the same space, time, and music, and about seeing, accepting, connecting to each other on the basis of what, in other contexts, is not explicitly acknowledged as substantial: the way one smiles, the grace of how one moves through space, the intensity and extension of one's hugs. No education or work "pedigrees" matter, no family status or belonging is considered as relevant, no class or financial information is deemed important, in most cases, by my interlocutors. The latter elements, in fact, are considered mostly as unsubstantial dimensions for choosing with whom to make connections (or not) within the *pizzica* relational space that I have encountered. I was taught by the Sisters that relationships and connections rely, primarily, on "energetic" or "vibrational" similarities, and immaterial, or "spiritual" dimensions. As uncanny as this language seemed to me, at first, I learned, over time, to understanding it as a validation of what I had already known for a long time: some people feel *different* than other. Simply put: some leave me happy and replenished, others, instead, tired and hollow.[14]

Patrizia and Senefera kiss Idrusa twice, one kiss per cheek, and I watch them. Then they greet Viola and me, with two other pairs of kisses. I smile. I am happy to have them here. Their presence in the room fuels me, relieving a bit of my uncanny tension. Senefera's voice and laugh resonate in the room. She is a pizzica *singer and player, and her words are music when she speaks. She always rigorously uses the Salento dialect with her friends. This is a language of intimacy for her, and her vivid expressions are like strokes of colored paint on the canvases of our conversations.* "Cestappaaassu vagnooone!" *[tche-sta-ppAAA-ssu va-*ñÒ*-ne] she says with a rogue smile that immediately melts into a contagious laugh.*[15] *We return the smile. Clearly, there is news in her romantic life, and we are eager to learn the details.* "Tocca facimu le carte!" *[in dialect, "we need to do a Tarot cards reading!"] Idrusa quickly added.*

14 My shift could be considered as an example of "interpretive drift" as defined by Tanya Luhrmann (*Persuasions of the Witch's Craft: Ritual Magic in Contemporary England* [Cambridge, MA: Harvard University Press, 1989]). It is worth mentioning that Luhrmann's first monograph has been controversial, and not always well-received by contemporary Pagan communities. See, e.g., Douglas Ezzy, "Practicing the Witch's Craft," in *Researching Paganisms*, ed. Jenny Blain, Douglas Ezzy, and Graham Harvey (Walnut Creek, CA: AltaMiraPress, 2004), 113–128; Ronald Hutton, "Living with Witchcraft," in Blain, et al. eds,, *Researching Paganisms*, 171–188; Robert J. Wallis, "Between the Worlds: Autoarchaeology and Neo-Shamans," in Blain, et al., eds. *Researching Paganisms*, 191–216.

15 *Ce sta passu, vagnone* can be translated as "Oh, what am I going through, girls!" and in Salento is a dialectal way to express the hardship of a situation that affects the speaker. In this particular context, it is not used literally but as a way to introduce some news in Senefera's dating panorama.

My sisters might be considered witches—*macare* in the local dialect—and since I joined the *cerchio*, I might be considered one too. While occasionally we call each other *macara*, none of us uses this term as an identity marker. The use of the term "witch" among the interlocutors with whom I work does not appear to be specific, and certainly it is not thought of as in connection with other Italian or Italian-American witchcraft traditions. As a matter of fact, I have never heard any direct or indirect references, for example, to Aradia, the Ways of the Strega, Raven Grimassi, or Leo Martello in my fieldwork.[16] Consulting the Tarot using *pendula*, casting circles, performing Moon rituals, celebrating the unfolding and returning of the seasons, engaging in meditations and neo-shamanic practices, channeling other-worldly and non-obvious presences, wisely using and mixing herbs and Bach flower remedies, participating in family constellations, practicing Reiki, working with Aura-Soma specialists, invoking the Ascended Masters of the Seven Rays, undergoing shamanic *curanderías*, developing a relationship with power animals and fairies, following the Magnified Healing practice, calling and making offerings to the orixàs and consulting karmic astrology are some of the spiritual experiences and practices I engaged with, following one or more members of the *cerchio*. While our sisterhood and our relationship with *pizzica* are the elements that define our belonging to the circle, by hanging out with each one of its members and with their networks of friends or clients, I was exposed to many spiritual practices and beliefs, including all the aforementioned ones. As

16 Possibly, this is connected to the fact that my interlocutors did not find it necessary to take on specific (counter)identities in the Salento context. See Charles Godfrey Leland, *Aradia, or, The Gospel of the Witches*, ed. And trans. Mario Pazzaglini and Dina Pazzaglini (Blaine, WA: Phoenix Publishing, 1998); Raven Grimassi, *Ways of the Strega : Italian Witchcraft : Its Lore, Magick, and Spells*. (St. Paul: Llewellyn Publications, 1995); Leo Louis Martello, *Witchcraft. The Old Religion* (Secaucus, NJ: University Books Inc, 1973). See also Howell, "The Goddess Returns to Italy."

it appears from this list of practices, the Pagans with whom I work belong, mainly, to the "eclectic" pole in the "reconstructionist-eclectic" spectrum described by the scholar of contemporary Paganism Michael Strmiska.[17] In other words, they do not belong to closed traditions, and do not try to reconstruct the "old ways." Rather, they approach their own spiritual traditions and the ones of their land with flexibility, accepting and including influences from other experiences, times, and geographical areas. While, in the Italian and Salentine contexts—socially and historically quite different from the northern European and North American ones—issues around cultural appropriation are neither perceived nor framed as in English-speaking countries, they are still important to address, in an analysis of contemporary Paganism.[18]

Similarly to the Pagans described by anthropologists Sabina Magliocco and Sarah Pike,[19] the motivations behind the cultural borrowing and appropriating of foreign spiritual practices, notions, and objects by Southern Italian Pagans revolve more around aesthetic impulses rather than monetary ones, and are central in their quest for "making

17 Michael Strimska, "Modern Paganism in World Cultures: Comparative Perspectives," in *Modern Paganism in World Cultures: Comparative Perspectives*, ed. Michael Strmiska (Santa Barbara: ABC-Clio, 2005), 1–53.

18 On contemporary Paganism and the issue of cultural appropriation see, e.g., Graham Harvey, *Contemporary Paganism: Listening People, Speaking Earth* (New York: New York University Press, 1997); Sarah M. Pike, *Earthly Bodies, Magical Selves: Contemporary Pagans and the Search for Community* (Berkeley: University of California Press, 2001); Sabina Magliocco, "Italian Cunning Craft: Some Preliminary Observations," *Journal of the Academic Study of Magic* 5 (2009): 103–33; Kathryn Gottlieb, "Cultural Appropriation in Contemporary Paganism and Witchcraft" (PhD diss., University of Maine, 2017); Lee Gilmore, "Pagan and Indigenous Communities in Interreligious Contexts: Interrogating Identity, Power, and Authenticity," *The Pomegranate: The International Journal of Pagan Studies* 20, no. 2 (2018): 179–207; Diane Purkiss, "Getting It Wrong: The Problems with Reinventing the Past," *The Pomegranate: The International Journal of Pagan Studies* 21, no. 2 (2019): 256–77; Adam Possamaï, "Cultural Consumption of History and Popular Culture in Alternative Spiritualities," *Journal of Consumer Culture* 2, no. 2 (2002): 197–218.

19 Magliocco, "Italian Cunning Craft"; Pike, *Earthly Bodies, Magical Selves.*

themselves anew."[20] While, differently from other Pagans, in Italy and elsewhere, the Salentine Pagans do not use the term "indigenous" or "native"[21] to describe their spirituality nor understand their positionality as an ethnic minority, my interlocutors do not seem to be aware at all of international debates around cultural appropriation. In truth, they probably never heard this expression.

Following their relational ontologies, they understand personhood as, fundamentally, relational (see chapter 5), and they believe in the unity of the cosmos and in Jungian notions of the collective unconscious. These are enough, from their point of view, to justify their adoption of other traditions, which they understand as a form of cultural appreciation. While the distinction between the latter and cultural appropriation is not always easy to define, as it appears also from the debates within North American Paganisms, it is worth noting that, oftentimes, my Southern Italian Pagan interlocutors adopt foreign traditions as a result of an invitation from (native) practitioners, like in many of the cases here below.[22]

20 Pike, *Earthly Bodies, Magical Selves*, 126.

21 On the meanings and uses of "indigenous," in relation to and beyond the European context, see Bjorn Ola Tafjord, "Modes of Indigenizing: Remarks on Indigenous Religion as a Method," *International Journal for the Study of New Religions* 9 no. 2 (2018): 304–5. In this article Tafjord distinguishes between "three different poles or, better, different modes of indigenizing: between, first, indigenizing in colonial and anti-colonial modes, second, indigenizing in romantic modes, and, third, indigenizing in nationalist modes. There are both analytical and political reasons for making these distinctions and using this triadic scale…They represent three different but related ideological currents. Deliberations on the meanings and uses of "indigenous" and "indigenizing" cannot escape historical and political realities. Scholarship is perhaps more entangled than ever before in broader ideological struggles that involve these concepts."

22 On the distinction between cultural appreciation and cultural appropriation, quite present in contemporary Pagan debates on cultural appropriation, see, e.g., River Enodian, "Cultural Appropriation vs Appreciation: A Primer for Pagans, Polytheists, and Occultists," Patheos, January 15, 2019, https://www.patheos.com/blogs/teaaddictedwitch/2019/01/cultural-appropriation-appreciation/; Gilmore, "Pagan and Indigenous"; Gottlieb,

Viola and the Tarot

There is a particular Mediterranean pinewood that Viola and I call "our" *pineta.* Technically, this is not a public place—according, at least, to the signs that promise dire consequences for those who get past the protective fence. A Dantean warning in the midst of the Mediterranean maquis.[23]

All I have ever experienced, beyond those gates, is far from being infernal. In fact, our *pineta* is a refuge for me: peaceful, grounding, and balancing. Some of my most memorable moments and insightful breakthroughs happened there: often linked to Viola's generous Tarot readings. She sometimes chooses this place to read me her Osho Tarot cards. Sitting in an old children's wooden playhouse that was left in the forest with no apparent reason, she asks questions and delivers advice—in conversation with

"Cultural Appropriation." Is "being invited" into foreign spiritual practices by native practitioners enough to justify the lack of awareness of Salentine contemporary Pagans around issues of cultural appropriation? It is my opinion that it is *not.* While I can certainly confirm that the adoption of foreign spiritual items, practices, and beliefs is, generally, not done superficially and in explicit disregard of Native practices and interpretations, by my interlocutors, I can also positively affirm that the political implications of their adopting foreign practices, in general, is overlooked. My Salentine interlocutors, in general, neither engage in any particularly appropriation-oriented self-reflection on the adoption of aspects of other traditions, nor do they enquire about the political effects of their cultural appreciations. Moreover, they lack a specific awareness about the political implications and responsibility of "allyship." My being new on the field did not allow me to delve into this aspect of southern Italian Paganism, but I intend to do more research on this specific topic in the future. The change in my positionality allows me, now, to explicitly ask questions around cultural appropriation in my conversations with my Salentine informants. As an anthropologist new to this field, I needed to gain my interlocutors' trust, and to build a relationship with them. Now that I have gotten to know my interlocutors and to be known by them, I am in the position of being able to engage them in very much needed research and conversations on the *effects* and *consequences* of the adoption of foreign spiritual practices.

23 Dante Alighieri, *Inferno*, Canto III. See Dante Alighieri, *La Divina Commedia*, ed. Natalino Sapegno. Nuova Italia Editrice (Florence: Nuova Italia, 1955).

the turtledoves, the cicadas, and the silent whisper of the trees. According to Viola, asking better questions is a way to move closer to their answers, and sometimes the latter arrive through the body rather than through the mind. This is why "being in nature" is such an important aspect of our existences.

I think she is right: inebriated by the smell of pines and rosemary, juniper and myrtle, life is undeniably sweeter, and, with Viola and her Tarot cards, the future is definitely not as scary.

Tarot cards are divinatory and meditation tools that foster self-awareness and are used as a way to relate to what I call "expanded present" or "presence": the specific linear *and* coeval historicity—i.e., the way one understands and experiences time and temporality—that I found among my interlocutors. The Tarot cards, allegedly, originated in the northern part of Italy in the fifteenth century and are so important for the women I met and are so entrenched in the weavings of their lives that I decided to use them metonymically to introduce the topics of the chapters of this book.[24] In their current configuration, they usually comprise seventy-eight cards: twenty-two numbered major arcana (from card 0—The Fool—to card 21—The World), and fifty-six minor arcana, divided in four suits. The latter, traditionally, are Pentacles (*denari*, associated with the "Earth Energy"), Wands (*bastoni*, associated with the "Fire Energy"), Cups (*coppe*, associated with the "Water Energy"), and Swords (*spade*, associated with the "Air Energy"). The Major Arcana describe the Fool's journey of self-awareness

24 On Tarot cards see, e.g., Danny L. Jorgensen, *The Esoteric Scene, Cultic Milieu, and Occult Tarot. Cults and Nonconventional Religious Groups* (New York: Garland, 1992); Hong-An Wu, "Tarot as a Technology," *Journal of Cultural Research in Art Education (Online)* 37 (2020): 193–218; Melissa F. Lavin, "On Spiritualist Workers: Healing and Divining through Tarot and the Metaphysical," *Journal of Contemporary Ethnography* 50, no. 3 (2020): 317–40; Marcelitte Failla, "Black Tarot: African American Women and Divine Processes of Resilience." *Liturgy* (Washington) 36, no 4 (2021): 41–51.

and refer to external, karmic forces. The Minor Arcana, instead, deal with more mundane energies. They are numbered in a progression from 1 to 10 for each suit with the addition of sixteen court cards (pages, knights, queens, and kings), four for each suit, that embody some special personal (or situational) traits and characteristics. Each card in the deck has a special meaning in relation to its number and suit, and it is associated with a range of connotations (often summarized in one or more keywords). By drawing cards from the shuffled deck, and by positioning them following particular patterns (spreads), the reader is able to assess the situation connected to the querent's questions and to create a (healing) narrative from the drawn cards. My interlocutors give the card decks specific agency and follow a particular practical etiquette in order to show to the cards respect and gratitude, and to "build a relationship" with them. Since a reading depends both on the cards and on the intuition of the reader, who attributes certain and not other possible meanings to the individual cards read in relationship to the others in the context of the spread, the efficacy of the reading is the result of a joint action: of the reader and of her cards. This is why one is not normally allowed to touch the deck of another person—unless for breaking the deck, if in the position of the querent—and why the deck needs to be "cleaned" every once in a while. There are many ways to do this: with sage, incense, or by using particular crystals, for example. It is advisable to do so during a new moon.

Carlo and **Pendula**

The "mornings after" life-changing experiences and encounters are always moments of truth: they mark our first steps into a new life. Somehow, nothing will be as it was before. Through unrefined emotions and raw imagination, they experientially carry all the potential of a new beginning. The emotional signatures of "mornings after" never fail us: if they signal a shift, it is immediately clear, in spite of all our rationalizations, if the change they carry is or is not a good one.

I woke up a bit emotionally intoxicated—after a dreamful night spent on the upper part of a bunk bed. Carlo, who had slept below me, told me I had talked a lot during my agitated sleep—but my discourses had been unintelligible, even for him, who seems to have quite a skill for deciphering the unknown. The day before I had attended my first *curandería* at Fenice's place. My task was to write down the shamanic journey while it unfolded, trying to remain as close as possible to the words uttered by Fenice, the woman the others called "shaman." Recording the *curanderías* had been prohibited by Fenice's spirits who, instead, allowed for a pen-and-paper transcription. She had asked her spirits to be able to provide mementos of the shamanic visions to her patients, so that they could go over them at a later date and recall all the details of the ritual.

To my surprise, that night I realized that Fenice's vision was not a one-woman experience. Apparently, she was not alone in the shamanic journey, and other participants of the *curandería* could experience it while it unfolded. Carlo, who was not a shaman but a long-term sitter in Fenice's works, particularly surprised me. He seemed to partake visually in Fenice's journey himself, and to be able to make sense of its most obscure aspects.

This first *curandería* was a transformative event for me: it was the first time I have possibly started to feel energetically and decode invisible energies. While my vision skills, as my interlocutors would call them, had not been activated, yet, I realized I had sensed most of the developments of the shamanic journey on my skin—including the pain and suffering that brought the patient to Fenice. It was for me an initiation into a new way of knowing — and a transformative one. A positive and enriching new beginning for me, to be sure.

Carlo, Fiammetta, Alberto, and I, who had spent the night at Alberto's place, decided to head to a crystal shop only thirty minutes away—most of them spent trying to give advice to our host, who was torn between two lines of actions. As soon as we parked the car, Carlo asked for our attention. He reached for the pocket on his shirt and grabbed a small metal cone hanging from a silver chain. "It comes from Budapest," he said with a smile, and started swinging it. Alberto, differently from me, immediately understood the situation, and enthusiastically said "Yes! I am ready! Go!" Carlo, then, placed this object on his heart with his right hand, and raised his left one towards Alberto, holding it up in the air above Alberto's head. He concentrated for a few seconds then released the cone, holding on to the chain. The cone bumped a little bit, while Carlo moved his lips, uttering silent words, with his eyes closed. After a few seconds the cone started to make wider and wider clockwise circles. "No," adds Carlo, "the answer is no!"

Similarily to the Tarot, *pendula* (pendulums) are also divinatory tools, used by my interlocutors to get in touch particularly with the "future" dimension of the "expanded present." They are usually pointed crystals or stones hanging from a chain. Sometimes used with a "radionic table," in general they give "yes/no" (sometimes also "I don't know") answers to specific questions asked by the querent.[25] As with the tarot decks, *pendula* are also believed to have their own agency, and it is advised to develop a personal relationship with one's own pendulum. For example, not every pendulum indicates the "yes" and "no" in the same ways. Some might swing horizontally and vertically; some might move in circles (clockwise or counterclockwise); some might use a combination of the two movements (e.g., swinging vertically to say yes and rotating clockwise to say no). The type of "language" the pendulum uses is the

25 See, e.g., Robin Robertson, "Divination." *Psychological Perspectives* 61 no. 2 (2018): 170–93.

result of both a preference of the pendulum and of the commands of its owner. I was told that one should ask a new pendulum how it prefers to indicate the "yes/no" answers. Alternatively, one can "teach" a new pendulum how to tell "yes" and "no." This process needs a few rehearsals during the first days or weeks of practice, but it is thought to be quite successful. My interlocutors believe that one's higher self or intuition is karmically aware of what we usually call "past," "present," and "future," and that it can access information that one is not consciously aware of. This is why when one interrogates the pendulum by explicitly connecting to one's higher self, one's body instills a micromovement in their arm and hand that makes the pendulum oscillate according to their inner awareness. This, according to my interlocutors, guarantees the exactness and efficacy of the pendulum.

Carmen, Drums, and Circles

Ester and I arrived at Angelo's laboratory on a summer afternoon, without notice. Everything was still and dry around us: the sound of the cicadas appeared to be the only resemblance of life. We parked the car: the heat immediately enfolded us, and the acrid smell of goat skins greeted us. That was tanning day, and we could see, at a distance, the skins lying in the sun to dry. Angelo's cigar left olfactory traces in the backyard, too: an unmistakable proof that he was home. Ester and I had come to visit him and Carmen, and we were glad that our forty-minute drive to this remote town in the southern part of Salento was worth the effort.

Angelo greeted us with smiling eyes and bitter words—a warm, oxymoronic way to tell us that he was happy to see us, of our unexpected visit. "*Diaule siti*!" (You are she-devils, in dialect), he said, trying to withhold a complacent smirk. He was working at his table, patiently fixing goat skins to the frames of the *tamburieddhri* that he sells throughout the summer at his itinerant stand. He follows the numerous festivals that light up the summer Salento nights, and that the Sisters and I enjoy, too, as part of our spiritual and social routines.

Carmen was sleeping downstairs, and we did not want to disturb her. Proudly, Angelo showed us the last present he had just finished building for her: a "shamanic drum." "She will use it for her circles," he added with his signature style: a proud and amused voice, and a shaking head.[26]

Casting circles is a widespread practice among Wiccans, self-proclaimed witches, and within other contemporary Pagan communities. While it is not mandatory or necessary for every ritual, it is believed that it helps protect a space from forces that are not "light" forces or hold a "low vibrational pattern." Casting circles fosters a connection with the energies one wants to contact, and it psychologically triggers an adequate and empowering state of mind. Both scholarly and general literature on contemporary Paganism and Wicca show that the ways circles are cast can differ considerably from tradition to tradition and from coven to coven.[27] Among my interlocutors, and in the *cerchio*, this practice is not fixed. First, there are two main types of sacred spaces: the one generated by expanding one's own *bozzolo di luce* (light cocoon) and the one created on occasions of important rituals that normally involve more than two or three persons.[28] Second, the ways the circle is cast

26 In this context, shaking heads is generally a sign of disapproval.

27 On Wicca, see, e.g., Ethan Doyle White, *Wicca: History, Belief, and Community in Modern Pagan Witchcraft* (Eastbourne; Chicago: Sussex Academic Press, 2016); Chas S. Clifton, *Her Hidden Children: The Rise of Wicca and Paganism in America*, (Lanham, MD: AltaMira Press, 2006); Michael Howard, *Modern Wicca: A History from Gerald Gardner to the Present* (Woodbury, MN: Llewellyn Publications, 2010).

28 The "cocoon" is a visualization technique that has the function of setting a sacred space around one's body. It is said that, by visualizing oneself in a cocoon of white light, one is protected from energies and forces that do not hold high vibrations—i.e., do not belong to the "light." This cocoon can be

differ from sister to sister, and it is not a practice that we discuss in detail together. Unlike other covens, as I mentioned before, the *cerchio* is not hierarchically structured (i.e., it does not have a high priestess who is in charge of the performance of rituals and of the education of novices), it does not require any initiation, nor it is organized around the worship of any specific deity. Therefore, there is no formal transmission of knowledge, nor are there specific, fixed practices, besides *pizzica*, that identify the group.[29] Nonetheless, in spite of the liturgical and doctrinal flexibility, I could notice some commonalities in how the ritual circle is cast. It is performed in solitude by the sister who is leading that particular ritual some time before the other participants arrive. It includes some sort of visualization, the utterance of prayers for protection, and a physical delimitation of the sacred space. The ways these steps are performed, the deities or spirits invoked for protection, and the tools utilized to separate the sacred space of the circle from its surroundings not only differ from sister to sister but also from ritual to ritual. For example, Carmen and Viola prefer using incense and the sound of drums (or singing bowls) to delimitate the space, while Fiammetta, who likes to use her index finger as if it were a wand, sometimes employs *zagareddhre*. These are cords of different colors that can be purchased during yearly festivals of particular Catholic saints in certain towns or villages of Salento (and elsewhere in Southern Italy)—e.g., in Galatina for the festival of St. Peter and St. Paul or in Torrepaduli at the festival of St. Rocco. They are material mementos of the devotion to those saints and are believed to hold some of the energies of the festivals. Usually, Salentinians hang them on their tambourines, on their cars' rearview mirrors, or with paper

visualized as expanding way beyond one's body (e.g., comprising a room, a building, a whole city). Since it generates a circle of light, the Sisters consider it as a way to cast circles. This cocoon technique is preferably used in solitary rituals or in private ones.

29 See Parmigiani, "Spiritual *Pizzica*."

calendars on their kitchen walls. As to the prayers themselves, I was told that sometimes they say the Christian *Pater Noster* prayer for protection, sometimes they utter a mantra or a heartfelt, spontaneous prayer to Kwan-Yin or to the Mother Earth. Those who work with the orixàs ask the elementals, or spirits of the natural place, for protection and invoke the relevant orixà—e.g., Iemanjà if the ritual takes place close to the Mediterranean Sea, or Oxossi if we gather in a pinewood. Since every Sister retains a special connection with certain deities or Catholic saints, they invoke their help, too.

Moon Rituals and Celebration of The Wheel of the Year

I will always remember the last day of my black stiletto boots. I had bought them in a bargain sale, and they had served me well—surviving far beyond the average life of my average shoes. I like to think that their disappearance from my wardrobe happened in a blaze of glory, though. I had started my evening *pizzica* classes not long before that day, and, sweaty and hungry after the class, I was invited by Viola, for the first time, to join her for a group ritual—my first one. I gladly accepted her offer and followed her driving indications: the plan was to meet her at the ritual place. The celebration was happening at a dolmen not too far away from Otranto. While, following Viola's directions, I was counting the gas stations I encountered, before taking a right turn in a dark lane between olive groves, I looked at the clear night sky and saw a wonderful full moon. Luna is a protagonist of many Salentinian folk songs and poems, and, maybe, in that moment I realized one of the reasons of its ubiquity in Salento's popular culture. Since Salento is surrounded by the sea and separated by the rest of Italy by a six-hour drive, the vertical dimension of the sky, in the absence of light pollution, is an important one for many Salentinians. The moon, in particular, is a shining companion during sleepless nights—and a presence with whom one can think through and complain to about the reasons that triggered particular individual insomnias. As the song claims, many are the things that the Otranto moon has been witnessing over time, in the Apulian nights—that are long, and last long.[30]

While I drive, humming the lyrics of that song, I find myself thinking that the length of the Salento nights is comparable to that of the days of a (sweaty and hungry) ethnographer, who often begins her day not knowing where it will end, and who should be always carrying a change of clothing, a toothbrush, and an extra pair of shoes in her car, from that day on.

Not without some unplanned detours, I arrived at the meeting place. I saw Viola's car, and I parked next to it. Viola got out of the car, illuminated by the moonlight. I joined her and followed her steps, feeling my stiletto heels digging holes into the grass and the dirt, and shaking under the pressure of the random rocks that, in the darkness, I was accidentally trampling on. I tried to tiptoe to the dolmen in the middle of the olive grove, where I could see a fire and hear the laughing voices of a group of people. I was starting to feel comfortable in my (wet and dirty) shoes, when I realized that my stiletto boots had to be immolated at the dolmen: one of the heels had gotten stuck somewhere in the earth, leaving the boot crippled, and making my ambulation appear a bit quaint.

There was food, at the dolmen, and some "moon water": I was told that, "charged" with crystals and in the light of the full moon, this water was particularly beneficial to animals, plants, and humans—thirsty ethnographers included. Known and unknown faces had gathered around the dolmen, and I soon started the usual hug-giving and

30 "Luna Otrantina "is a song written by Rina Durante. Three versions of this song have been recorded so far, for example, by Canzoniere Grecanico Salentino, Ghetonia, Rachele Andrioli and Antonio Castrignanò.

hand-shaking routine. I was offered affection and food, attention and smiles, and my limping gait went mostly unnoticed. The group had met some hours before, while Viola and I were at the *pizzica* class, for a full moon ritual. The celebration had ended, leaving behind half-burnt candles and some food offerings. It was now "feasting time." Together with the laughs and the food, this sharing time soon started to include music: some of the attendees picked up their instruments, and the *pizzica* music began. I took off my stiletto boots and I started moving at the sound of the tambourines. I was getting comfortable in my own Pagan shoes—and it is preferred to dance *pizzica* barefooted, anyway.

Moon rituals and the celebration of what in other contemporary Pagan traditions is referred to as "The Wheel of the Year" are key practices for the circle and for many of the interlocutors I met in Salento. Full and new moon days are often important moments for solitary or group rituals. During new moons they typically work on setting intents, and during full moons on "letting go" and on the manifestation of the intents proclaimed during the previous new moon. The energy of full moons, in particular, is experienced as quite strong and powerful, and therefore it is more likely to be celebrated with group rituals (*vis-à-vis* the solitary rituals typical of the new moons). The yearly calendar of celebrations in Salento appears to be more loosely overlapping with, and more flexible than, the one adopted by many English-speaking contemporary Pagan communities and described in detail by the literature on Wicca or contemporary Paganisms. Partly, as in the case studied by anthropologist Kathryn Rountree in Malta, this is due to the fact that the variance in temperatures and climate between Northern and Southern Europe makes the general experience of the seasons different.[31] Partly it is due

31 See Rountree, *Crafting Contemporary Pagan Identities*, and "Localizing Neo-Paganism."

to the peculiar attitude of my interlocutors towards their Salentine social, cultural, historical, and relational context. Similarly to Malta, Italy is a Catholic country, and Salento has been historically a crossroads of peoples: here, though, Catholicism is not considered by the Sisters a "native religion."[32] Unlike Maltese contemporary Pagans, though, the women of the *cerchio* do not feel the need to embody a counterculture, to mark their spiritual belonging visually or to define themselves in reference to Catholicism. This lack of the urgency of assuming a counter-identity *vis-à-vis* their socio-cultural context is one of the reasons why my interlocutors do not define themselves explicitly as Pagans or as witches. Differently from other contemporary Pagan or Wiccan communities, including those in Italy and Spain studied by the scholar of New Age and Pagan spiritualities Anna Fedele, the *cerchio* and the persons that gravitate around it do not explicitly claim to be heirs of particular pre-Christian religions of the area, nor consider, as in the case of Malta, Christianity as their "native" religion. They are indeed fascinated, for example, by the possible connections between Salento and *Magna Grecia*—and therefore between *pizzica* and ancient Dionysian rituals. They talk about Roman religion and about the allegedly Messapic cult of the Mother Earth.[33] Nonetheless, this appreciation of pre-Christian (imagined or actual) religious experiences

32 Cf. Rountree, "Localizing Neo-Paganism."

33 Usually, to support this claim, my interlocutors quote the "Parabita Venuses," two prehistoric female figures made out of horse bones that were found in Parabita, a village of Salento, in the 1960s. On the archaeologist Marija Gimbutas and the (pan-Mediterranean) "feminine divinity" discourse see, e.g., Fedele, *Looking for Mary Magdalene*, 10, 53. What Fedele argues for her interlocutors could be valid also for mine. See also Ruth Mantin, "Theaologies in Process: Re-searching and Theorizing Spiritualities, Subjectivities, and Goddess-talk," in *Researching Paganisms*, ed. Jenny Blain, Douglas Ezzy, and Graham Harvey (Walnut Creek, CA: AltaMira Press, 2004), 147–70; Kaarina Aitamurto and Scott Simpson, "The Study of Paganism and Wicca: A Review Essay," in *The Oxford Handbook of New Religious Movements: Volume II (2 ed.)*, ed. James R. Lewis and Inga Tøllefsen (Oxford: Oxford University Press, 2016), 482–94; Ronald Hutton, *The Triumph of the Moon*, Oxford: Oxford University Press, 1999.

does not translate into anticlericalism, taking political or identity stances against Catholicism or in the explicit political re-claiming of their being "Catholic witches" or of their Catholic heritage.[34] The latter is considered as important as any other tradition, spirituality, or religion that seeks "light" and "love." This applies to forms of spirituality that have been part of the land of Salento as well as ones that have developed elsewhere. All religions and spiritualities that foster "light" are to be respected, since they could prove useful for easing a soul's spiritual path.[35]

If most of my interlocutors distinguish between religion and spirituality (and tend to define themselves as "lightworkers"), it is also true that many of them would well call themselves Catholic, if they had to, and that all of them follow a Wheel of the Year that is, in fact, substantially molded on the Catholic calendar.[36]

However, discourses about the origins and adoption of that specific calendar appear to change positionally and situationally. In other words, when approaching persons who are not Pagans, my interlocutors present their festivals in relation to Salento's specific local traditions (framed as common knowledge and sensorium when in dialogue with

34 In this, they differ from the pilgrims studied by Fedele, in her *Looking for Mary Magdalene*. If there are many commonalities between the world views described in her books and the ones I found in Salento, the discourses (but not necessarily the practices) around Christian heritage are one of the differences among our respective interlocutors.

35 Unlike what Rountree claims for Malta, though, among my interlocutors, cultural *métissage*, although similarly extensively employed over the centuries, is not *explicitly* considered part of their Salentine identity. *Pizzica* is, instead: not much as a set of beliefs, more or less historically appropriated by the Catholic Church, but first of all as a musical and bodily practice (see chapter 2).

36 On "lightworkers" see also Fedele, *Looking for Mary Magdalene*. It is worth mentioning that, for contemporary Italian Catholics, though, what the Sisters of the *cerchio* do and think would easily still be considered as "demoniac" today. As described for contemporary Pagans elsewhere (see Rountree, "Localizing Neo-Paganism"; Strmiska, "Modern Paganism in World Cultures"), my interlocutors are also open to adopting "global" contemporary Pagan rituals, beliefs, and practices.

Salentinians and as a specific Salentine, folkloric trait when in dialogue with non-Salentinians). When approaching other Pagans, instead, it appears that my interlocutors find it very important to think and talk about their yearly festivals in conversation with a popularized, globalized "Wheel of the Year," molded from anglophone contexts—representing an interesting case of glocalization.[37] It appears, in fact, that most of my interlocutors have been encountering global, popular, anglophone versions of Paganism and New Age spirituality and have been integrating them into their world and practices. Maybe counter-intuitively for religious studies scholars, books and bookstores do not appear as the main channels through which my Salentine interlocutors have been in contact with these "global" Pagan and New Age practices—at least, not directly. That is to say, the Salentine Pagans I met do not appear to often share books (although sometimes they do), but they do share their individual knowledge, preexistent and *in fieri*, in informal settings.[38] In fact, given the different background, experiences, and spiritual experiences, the conversations with old and new acquaintances (me included) seem to be at the center of their knowledge-building processes. Those trained in neo-shamanism, for example, share their knowledge in these spiritual practices; those who have special relationships with fairies share their knowledge;

37 With "global Paganism" I refer to a generalist and popularized version of contemporary Paganism that, developed in anglophone countries, populates bookstores and the Internet, with a reach that go beyond anglophone countries and contexts. On this type of phenomena see, e.g., Oliver Krueger, "The Internet as Distributor and Mirror of Religious and Ritual Knowledge." *Asian Journal of Social Science* 32 no 2 (2004): 183–97; Howell, "The Goddess returns to Italy"; Michael York, "New Age Commodification and Appropriation of Spirituality." *Journal of Contemporary Religion* 16 no 3(2001): 361–72. Ross Downing, "Hashtag Heathens: Contemporary Germanic Pagan Feminine Visuals on Instagram." *The Pomegranate: The International Journal of Pagan Studies* 21 no 2(2019): 186–209.

38 The only exception to this patterns, to my knowledge, involves the Book of Enoch, which some of my interlocutors purchased and started to read more or less in the same period.

those who study the Mayan calendar do the same.[39] Rather than organizing reading groups, my interlocutors prefer to attend courses together: from Reiki to Magnified Healing, from bio-dance to Aura-Soma. During these meetings, they make friends outside their own circle, and encounter persons with different spiritual backgrounds and experiences—including Wiccan and "global" solitary Pagans. Finally, the Internet—especially Facebook—has an important role in these glocalization processes. Facebook pages such as: "*La soffitta delle streghe*, "*Le 4 facce della Luna*," and "*Il Giardino degli Illuminati*," in addition to personal pages such as those of the Spiritual teachers Cristiana Caria, Raúl Micieli, and Kryon Lee Carroll, seem to be quite popular and to play a role in how information is received, circulated, and re-framed.[40]

It is my belief that my interlocutors' adoption of either one of the aforementioned narratives in relation to their Wheel of the Year responds to the need to be intelligible to their own interlocutors and has similar performative effects: building relational bridges, so to speak, with the persons with whom they are interacting. Moreover, as forms of "social poetics," these different frameworks allow them to authoritatively navigate power differentials and grant them acknowledgement, recognition, and acceptance by non-Salentine Pagans.[41] These aspects reflect, at a micro-level, an empowering way to inhabit dynamics

39 I found among my interlocutors a few who are fascinated by English language and British culture. Since most of my interlocutors were using "global" Pagan vocabulary before my arrival, it is possible that these anglophiles had a role in the circulation of this type of content.

40 La Soffitta delle Streghe, https://www.facebook.com/soffittadellestreghe/; Cristiana Caria, https://www.facebook.com/CristianaCariaTeacher; Le 4 facce della Luna, https://www.facebook.com/Le-4-facce-della-Luna-499633193481219; Raúl Micieli, https://www.facebook.com/Raúl-Micieli-Metafisica-Saint-Germain-1745187245808695: Il giardino degli illuminati, https://www.facebook.com/Ilgiardinodegliilluminati:Kryon Lee Carroll, https://www.facebook.com/KryonLeeCarroll

41 According to anthropologist Michael Herzfeld, "poetic principles guide all *effective* social interactions. Such a poetics must also correspond intelligibly

that are active at the macro-level and that are connected with the Italian internal north-south divide and, more generally and importantly, with the European one, and with the—perceived or actual—cultural, economic, and political predominance of English-speaking countries, globally. In this sense, being recognized as following a Wheel of the Year that can be superimposed to a "global," mainstream, commercial one speaks to the desire to not being seen as geographically and culturally marginal. It speaks, to the desire to be recognized as an integral part of a movement that, today, at a popular level, appears to be dominated by debates that happen within English-speaking countries.[42] As a consequence, out of respect for my interlocutors and *their* needs and preferences, since this book is written in English and I operate within north American academia, I choose to present their Wheel of the Year in conversation with the "global" Pagan one. In general, the year, among contemporary Pagan communities in the English-speaking world and those who have been influenced by them worldwide, is celebrated in connection to the following calendar of sabbats (seasonal festivals), and relative esbats (coven meetings).[43] Regardless of the many traditions, deities,

---

with local social theory, with indigenous ideas about meaning, and with criteria of style, relevance, and importance."

Michael Herzfeld, *The Poetics of Manhood: Contest and Identity in a Cretan Mountain Village* (Princeton, NJ: Princeton University Press, 1985), xv. See also Michael Herzfeld, *Cultural Intimacy: Social Poetics in the Nation-State*. (New York: Routledge, [1997] 2005).

42 During my ethnography I could observe a tension between my interlocutors' attempts to be in dialogue with global Pagan and Wiccan practices and their widespread skepticism *vis-à-vis* local Wiccan practitioners and rituals. This tension might be worth of further ethnographic investigation.

43 Obviously, given the internal difference of what is referred to as contemporary Paganism, these and the celebrations associated to the different festivities may vary. Among some practicing Wiccans and other practitioners of what could be referred as "global Paganism" it is held that: "While there is no evidence suggesting that any one culture of pre-Christian religious observers enacted all of the festival dates held in the modern Wicca calendar, there is plenty to suggest that all eight festivals occurred on or near significant events held sacred amongst a variety of cultures and across great distances in time."

and rituals evoked during these sabbats by contemporary Pagan groups, it is fair to claim that celebrating the cyclical, seasonal aspect of time is a way for some contemporary Pagans and Wiccans to think, meditate on, experience, resonate with, and live within a birth-death-rebirth cycle.

It is widely assumed, within the "global" version of Paganism influenced by the English-speaking world, that the year begins with Samhain, on October 31st. This festival of Celtic origin is celebrated around the mid-point between the fall equinox and the winter solstice and corresponds, for my interlocutors, to three different festivals: the Day of the Dead (popularily called *il giorno dei morti*), *Ognissanti* (All Saints, November 1st and November 2nd) and, with different nuances, the day of San Martino (November 11th). During those nights, the boundary—or veil—between the visible and the invisible, the living and the dead is considered very thin, and rituals are held in honor of the dead. Samhain is a festival in which many contemporary Pagans reflect on death as a necessary step for rebirth—at various levels: material, psychological, spiritual. This happens also in Salento, among my interlocutors. While a connection between Samhain and the Catholic celebrations of All Saints is quite straightforward, the festival of San Martino needs a bit of contextualization. St. Martin of Tours is celebrated all over Europe, but in Salento this festival is linked to the bottling of the new wine and to the sharing (of the cloak; of time in the hagiography of the Saint; and of food and wine today) of moments of conviviality. On the day of

(J.A. Nock, *Provenance Press's Guide to the Wiccan Year: A Year Round Guide to Spells, Rituals, and Holiday Celebrations* [Avon, MA: Provenance Press, 2007], xii.) In fact, the situation is much more complex than this. On the one hand, there are many religions and spiritualities that go under the contemporary Paganism label that do not follow (all) these holidays. On the other hand, as historian Ronald Hutton shows, the history of the Wheel of the Year in the British and Irish contexts is not linear, nor it is its adoption in the context of the United States. See Ronald Hutton, *The Stations of the Sun* (Oxford: Oxford University Press, 1996) and "Modern Pagan Festivals: A Study in the Nature of Tradition." *Folklore* 119 no 3 (2008): 251–73.

San Martino, Salentinians celebrate the must turning into wine (*mieru,* in dialect, from the Latin *merum*) by organizing social gatherings, parties, dinners among family and/or friends. *Pizzica* is a protagonist of these types of gatherings, too, among the Sisters and their friends.

Among Germanic peoples, Yule is the winter solstice, the shortest day of the year. In this particular period of the year, the minutes of darkness outnumber those of light, and the sun's path through the sky seems to pause in its north-south vacillation (solstice comes from the Latin *sol*=sun, *stitium*=stand still). For many contemporary Pagans and Wiccans, celebrating Yule is a way to think about the moment of pause, quietness, stillness, and dwelling that anticipates rebirth. Just *after* the solstice the number of minutes of light gradually increases, and the light and warmth of the sun slowly and increasingly brings about the rebirth of nature in the spring and summer. The faith in this process is at the center of the celebration of this moment of the year. There is something especially deep in celebrating the power of light on the shortest day of the year, and in experiencing the seeds of rebirth when everything is dead around you, according to my interlocutors. This distinct emotional and spiritual way to experience temporality, which holds together what we usually refer to as past, present, and future, is of key importance for them. While particularly evident during the winter solstice, it informs all the celebrations of the Wheel of the Year and their approach to *pizzica,* everyday life, and spiritual dimensions. It is a key feature of their specific historicity, or way to interpret time, which I call "expanded present" or "presence," and that I will address in detail in the rest of this book.

The *solstizio d'inverno* is a very important appointment for my interlocutors, who sometimes refer to it with the term Yule, and the whole month of December is considered, in a way, a preparation for it. In particular, they celebrate the "days of the Mother" that go from December 8th, the festival of the Immaculate Conception of Mary, to the end of the month, culminating in the celebration of Christmas. In addition to New Year's Eve, they celebrate the festival of Saint Anthony (January 17th), and attend to the many *fòcare* (see below) that are organized during the months of January and February.

The festival popularly known as Imbolc, January 31st through February 2nd, is "the first light in the dark of winter" for many practicing Pagans.[44] It is one of the four "cross-quarter" days (Samhain, Imbolc, Beltane, Lughnasadh or Lammas) that are celebrated in-between the solar festivals (popularly called, today, Yule, Ostara, Litha, Mabon) by Wiccans and other "global" Pagans.[45] This sabbat that celebrates the changing season is associated with fire as a symbol of light and purification, of clarity of mind and intent, and of letting go of attachments and of what does not serve us anymore. It is the first step of natural, personal, and spiritual rebirth. The days are noticeably longer, and nature is preparing for blooming.

In Salento, among my interlocutors, Imbolc is known as the *Candelora* (Candlemas, on January 31st), that is celebrated both with private rituals and by participating, while holding special spiritual "intents," in public traditional festivals called *fòcare*. The latter are organized throughout Salento (and Italy, in general) during the month of January. They are village festivals built around the construction and the burning of a bonfire. Among Salentine *fòcare*, the most important (and biggest) one is that of Novoli. During these festivals, *pizzica* music is played, and the general tone of the event is quite secular, as for every other *pizzica*-related public gathering. If my interlocutors decide to participate in the event, though, they do it with a spiritual intent. On the outside they completely blend in with other participants: they eat traditional food, buy gadgets at the stands,

44 Nock, *Provenance Press's Guide to the Wiccan Year*, 65.
45 Ibid., xii.

dance in the same "squares" (*ballare in piazza*) among other *pizzica* dancers; on the inside, though, they give an explicitly spiritual meaning to their participation in that popular event. At a more personal level, during Imbolc the Sisters "make space" for the new by "cutting out (and burning) dead branches," metaphorically speaking (and sometimes not), invoking renovation, healing, material security, and particular outcomes in their work, health, emotional, and love lives. At the same time, the Sisters try (and ask for help in order) to let go of the attachments to ways of thinking, feelings, personal relationships, sense of lack, and poverty. They write "release" and "invoke" lists and burn them: in doing so they try to let go of their attachments and to *affidare* (entrust) the universe to take care of them, if for their higher good and for the higher good of what is around them. This, together with the summer solstice, is probably the most important yearly event for the *cerchio*.

Ostara, or how is usually called the spring equinox among followers of global Paganism, is celebrated as the festive coming of spring and of fertility, as a way to honor rebirth and the balance of light and darkness. In Salento, as elsewhere, this is a way to welcome the spring, the warm weather, the produce in the orchards.

On May 1st, starting on the last night of April, Beltane is usually celebrated. Fertility is the main theme of this festival, and especially in British and Germanic traditions is associated with the Maypole dance. While the latter is not performed by Salentinians, they sometime call the festival Beltane. More often, though, they called *il primo di Maggio* (May 1st). Abundance, creativity, and pleasures of life are at the center of this festival: a pure celebration of life, in all of its forms. In Salento, among my interlocutors, this aspect of the Wheel of the Year is mostly celebrated by staying in nature, reconnecting with elements and elementals, and by celebrating the sensuous, physical aspect of being alive. This does not happen on one particular day, but it is better described as an overall attitude, spread over whatever occasion is available to them. In this sense also, the traditional picnic of the 25th of April, a national holiday celebrating the liberation from Fascism, or of the 1st of May, the national *festa dei lavoratori* (workers' day), can be suitable occasions for celebrating Beltane. On these occurrences, too, *pizzica* is at the center of the celebrations.

The summer solstice, sometimes known by the Germanic name Litha, celebrates the longest day of the year. It celebrates light, in its fullness, while opening up to the transient nature of abundance and the inexorable movement towards Yule. It is another festival that celebrates the overcoming of polarities and rebalances attachments. There are at least three main festivals celebrated by my interlocutors in proximity of the solstice: San Luigi (June 21st), San Giovanni (June 24th), and Santi Pietro e Paolo (June 28th and 29th). San Giovanni's festival is linked to folk-magic tales and the festival of St. Peter and St. Paul to the public ritual that used, in the past, to gather *tarantate* from every part of Salento (see chapter 2). In the last years, in particular, my interlocutors and I have been organizing a private pilgrimage to the chapel of St. Paul. Starting our walk at 4:00 a.m. from a village of the Grecìa Salentina, we managed to arrive in Galatina very early in the morning to meet those who had been dancing *pizzica* all night long in front of the chapel (more on this in chapter 2).[46]

46 The Union of the Municipalities of the *Grecìa salentina* (*Unione dei comuni della Grecía salentina*) is a consortium founded in 2000 as a result of Legislative Decree 267/2000. The *Unione* comprises the municipalities of Calimera, Castrignano dei Greci, Corigliano d'Otranto, Martano, Martignano, Melpignano, Soleto, Sternatia, and Zollino, and was established after the recognition of a neo-Greek dialect called Griko as a "historical minority language" (Law 482/1999) by the Italian state. On Griko, see Manuela Pellegrino, "'Dying Language' or 'Living Monument'? Language Ideologies, Policies and Practices in the Case of Griko" (PhD diss., University College London, 2013); "I Glossa Grika: Itte C'è Avri—La Lingua GrecoSalentina tra Passato e Futuro," in *Raccontare la Grecia*, ed. Giovanni Azzaroni and Matteo Casari (Martano: Kurumuny, 2015), 1–33; "Performing Griko beyond Death," *Palaver* 5, no. 1 (2016): 137–62, and *Greek Language, Italian Landscape*.

Lammas (in English) or Lughnasadh (in old Irish), celebrated in August (typically around the first day, but it varies), is the festival of the harvest. Physically and metaphorically, it is the time to reap what has been sowed. It is a way to honor and reflect on the past, with gratitude, and on access to abundance. In Salento, this intent is celebrated on the occasion of another "day of the Mother"—*l'Assunta* (Saint Mary of the Assumption) on the 15th of August. Celebrated by Catholics as a religious festival, it is known as *Ferragosto* by the Italian society at large.[47] The parties and gatherings that are organized everywhere become a potential celebrating occasion for the Sisters of the *cerchio*, especially if *pizzica* music is involved.

With the fall equinox, sometimes called Mabon, some contemporary Pagans honor the impending fading of light and the imminent prevalence of minutes of darkness over those of light. It marks a moving into an atmosphere of rest, reflection, and of drawing towards the Sisters' inner worlds that will be at the core of the Samhain season. In Salento, as in Malta,[48] this moment of the year happens when temperatures are still summery, but it is also connected with the beginning of the new activities for the year to come. It is a moment of planning, of setting goals, of sharing among the Sisters and with the universe what they want to "manifest" in the next year. *Manifesting* is a key word for contemporary Pagans and New Age Practitioners worldwide, and it is also an important term for the women I met. They teach the importance of desire and of the act of consciously "imagining" as a spiritual educational practice.[49] In order to "re-learn" how to "desire," they practice and recommend spiritual exercises such as the "compilation of the 101 desires": the writing and reading aloud of a list of

47 The word *Ferragosto* comes from the Latin *Feriae Augusti*, the festival in honor of the Roman emperor Augustus.

48 See Rountree, *Crafting Contemporary Pagan Identities*.

49 Karin Andriolo, "The Twice-Killed: Imagining Protest Suicide," *American Anthropologist* 108, no. 1 (2006): 100–1.

at least 101 desires that adhere to some simple rules. The desires should not be repetitive, should not involve other persons, and should be as precise and detailed as possible. The importance of this exercise does not lie much in the manifestation (i.e., realization) of the desires, rather on learning to "think big," not to self-limit one's own capacity for abundance (more on this in chapter 2).

Gioia and Channeling Angels

Channeling angels and spirits can take many forms: for Gioia, it was something she claims she was born with—and that she had denied for a long time. Only fairly recently she decided to embrace her gifts: she started channeling messages for the wider public—mostly, the words of angels—and to share them on YouTube.

While Gioia is the only person I met who claimed to receive messages constantly and consistently in written (automatic writing) or verbal form (quasi-auditory messages), most of the persons I met—within and without the relational nets of the Sisters—had visual or visionary experiences with angels, archangels, Ascended Masters (see below), and/or spirits of the dead and loved ones.[50] During the first year of my fieldwork, for example, during which I lost both my maternal grandmother and my mother (only one month apart), two Salentine women that do not know each other told me, on separate occasions and out of the blue, that they could see a woman close to me. It was some months before the death of my beloved ones,

50 On "channeling" see, e.g., Cathy Gutierrez, *Handbook of Spiritualism and Channeling* (Leiden: Brill, 2015); Paul M. Helfrich, "The Channeling Phenomenon: A Multimethodological Assessment," *Journal of Integral Theory and Practice* 4, no. 3 (2009): 127–471; Luciano Pederzoli, Patrizio Tressoldi, and Helané Wahbeh, "Channeling: A Non-Pathological Possession and Dissociative Identity Experience or Something Else?" *Culture, Medicine and Psychiatry* 46, no. 2 (2021): 161–69. Adam Klin-Oron, "How I Learned to Channel: Epistemology, Phenomenology, and Practice in a New Age Course." *American Ethnologist* 4,1 no. 4 (2014): 635–47.

and both of my interlocutors described this presence as a sturdy, not very tall woman in her sixties, dressed in a black dress and with her grey hair gathered in a bun. Puzzled, I showed them, separately, a picture of my maternal great-grandmother (among other pictures of elderly women and relatives), and they both confirmed that she was the person they were seeing. They both claimed that she was there to support me, since I would probably lose both my mom and grandma in a matter of weeks—as it actually happened. On another occasion, a couple of months after my mother passed away, I was initiated to the first level of Reiki by a woman who lived in another region and whom I had not met before. While looking at my aura—i.e., at the colored energetic fields that the women I met believed to surround every human, non-human, animate or inanimate being—she told me that it looked like I had recently lost someone whom I very much loved, since she could see their presence near me.

Fenice and Neo-Shamanism

Fenice is called the *sciamana*, or "woman shaman," and I met her through two of my Sisters. She lives alone some kilometers away from Otranto, in a beautiful *trullo*—a house built in stone, in accordance with the architectural style of the area. She is in her seventies, and her freshness, curiosity, enthusiasm, beauty, and irresistible laugh are contagious. She was born in another Italian region and moved to Apulia after many years spent journeying—physically and spiritually. She was initiated to a version of what is referred to as Core Shamanism, a shamanic movement founded by the anthropologist Michael Harner.[51] Similarly to him, she

51 Michael Harner, *The Way of the Shaman: A Guide to Power and Healing* (New York: Bantam Books, 1982). See also Joan Halifax and Julio Mario Santo Domingo, *Shaman: the Wounded Healer*. (London: Thames and Hudson1982). On neo-shamanism, see, e.g., Robert Wallis, "Between the Words: Autoarchaeology and Neo-Shamans" and "Journeying: The Politics Of Ecstasy: Anthropological

works with the spirits of the Shuar people—a branch of the Jívaro people of Ecuador. With the aid of tobacco water, she practices shamanic journeys during which she performs *curanderías* and *chupadas*, she finds power animals and receives messages from the spirits for those who ask for advice and for the group of people who follow her. Fiammetta and I are part of this group, informally called (on WhatsApp) "*la ragnatela*" (the spider web). This name was not chosen in reference to the *tzentzak*, the shamanic spiritual helpers, but to the symbol of the spider/tarantula, so widespread in Salento among my informants, and to an idea of being a *filo*—thread—a "web" of different people, connected "at thin levels" (*a livelli sottili)* with each other. Fenice received training also in other disciplines, religions, and practices, including Crystal therapy, Bach flowers, Hinduism (she spent some years in India, among the followers of Sai Baba), and family constellations.

Family Constellations

My first family constellation was an individual one. Fenice had scheduled my work for a late afternoon, in early September. There were only the two of us in her circular room in the *trullo*, and a bunch of pillows. She traced with some of the pillows a sort of symbolic path that went over the diameter of the room and asked me to stand at one end of the path. She asked me if I was ready, and I said I was. I had no idea of what a family constellation was (I did not want to gather information, beforehand, and to deny

---

Perspectives on Neoshamanism," *The Pomegranate: The International Journal of Pagan Studies* 13 no. 6 (2012): 20–28; Jenny Blain, *Nine Worlds of Seid-Magic* (London: Routledge, 2002); Alex K. Gearin and Oscar Calavia Saez. "Altered Vision Ayahuasca Shamanism and Sensory Individualism." *Current Anthropology* 62, no. 2 (2021): 138–50; Nofit Itzhak, "Making Selves and Meeting Others in Neo-Shamanic Healing," *Ethos* 43, no. 3 (2015): 286-310; Tatiana Buzekova, "The Shaman's Journeys Between Emic and Etic." *Anthropological Journal of European Cultures* 19, no 1 (2010): 116–30.

myself the pleasure of the surprise), and I requested Fenice to explain to me the process. She said that all I had to do, at first, was to answer her questions—possibly fast, without thinking. A bit overconfident, I thought that it looked easy enough to me.

"How old are you?" Fenice started. "Three," I reply. "What color do you see?" "Grey." "How do you feel?" "Worried." "Where are you?" "At the funeral of my grandfather."

"Whaaat?" I think. I was shocked: I had never thought (nor wanted) to recall that buried early memory, and I was surprised to have gotten to that forgotten memory and emotional place in no time, during my first constellation. Things started to look a bit more complicated than I would have thought.

Fenice picked up a pillow and threw it on the other side of the room, and asked me: "Who is this?" I closed my eyes and my body shivered. "It's my grandfather!" I said. I was clearly feeling his energy—one that I used to be familiar with in my very early life, and that I had forgotten. Surprised and emotional, moved by this re-embodiment of the emotions and feelings of my toddler self, I burst into tears. If I looked in front of me, I only saw a pillow. Nonetheless, I could swear on the fact that I could unmistakably give a name to what I was feeling in my body: my *nonno* Alfredo.

I was so happy to meet him again.

Constellations are therapeutic encounters, "a spatial arrangement of a family system in which individuals who are not members of the real family serve as stand-ins for the clients' family members."[52] They are led by a facilitator—Fenice, in my case—and can be either individual or

52 Jan Weinhold et al., "Family Constellation Seminars Improve Psychological Functioning in a General Population Sample: Results of a Randomized Controlled Trial," *Journal of Counseling Psychology* 60, no. 4 (2013): 601–09; see also Jakob Robert Schneider, *Family Constellations: Basic Principles and Procedures* (Heidelberg: Carl-Auer, 2009), and Barna Konkolÿ Thege et al., "The Effectiveness of Family Constellation Therapy in Improving Mental Health: A Systematic Review," *Family Process* 60, no. 2(2021): 409–23.

collective. The latter, in my personal opinion as well as in that of many interlocutors, are the most powerful. Ten to fifteen persons usually attend the meeting that normally is held at Fenice's place. Some of the participants know each other, some do not. The constellation usually starts around 3:00 p.m. and lasts until well after midnight. All the participants and the facilitator sit in a circle. A querent poses a question to the facilitator and to the "field" concerning a past or present issue. Each participant will be in the position of the querent during the meeting, but there can be only one querent at a time. After a very brief presentation of the issue at stake, the facilitator asks the querent to choose, among the participants, a number of persons who stand up and move in the middle of the circle. Usually, one of the chosen persons represents the querent, and the others impersonate family members (alive or dead), emotions, diseases, or feelings. At first neither the querent nor the participants, oftentimes, know who is who (or what). Only Fenice does. Nonetheless, the facilitator asks the querent to move the bodies of the chosen participants within the space of the circle. After this, the constellation begins. The participants who impersonate the (unknown) protagonists of that particular constellation tune in and start moving and talking, behaving according to what they feel like doing or saying in that particular moment—or, as my interlocutors say, since "the field works," (*il campo lavora*) "they follow the energy of the field."

The facilitator, the querent (who, at this time, is only observing and not participating in the action), and the participants look at that representation. The facilitator observes and gradually intervenes in order to explain what is going on and interrogates the querent, asking them to describe what they see and feel. The querent, at first, is a spectator of his own life, but as the constellation unfolds and the family dynamics get clearer, they are guided by the facilitator to take part actively in the representation. By performing particular actions, dictated by the facilitator, the querent is able to understand and to "fix" the issue at stake. Individual constellations work in a similar way, but objects and not persons represent the protagonists of the familiar issue. Since the objects do not move and act, the role of the querent is more active from the beginning, and they are asked to tune in and understand what is going on a less visible dimension.

Amelia: Crystals and Bach Flowers

Amelia is not Salentinian. She came to visit me in Salento for a couple of days, and she met some of the Sisters. She bonded with Fiammetta, in particular, who is always very generous in sharing her intuitive insights with everyone—believers, followers, and skeptics like Amelia. During a dinner at a friend's restaurant, Amelia started to talk about her life: her marriage, her work, her deep sense of exhaustion. Fiammetta offered a listening ear for a while, but then abruptly interrupted and asked Amelia to follow her. They left me and the table in my own company, and came back only minutes later. Fiammetta had a smiling face, and Amelia, who had been talking a lot since the beginning of the evening, was silent. She looked serene, but, clearly, she did not want to resume the narrative on her life.

A couple of weeks later, I received a phone call from Amelia. She told me that she had followed Fiammetta's advice, and that she had been wearing a shungite pendant for the last 10 days. She had felt less worn out, but, a bit worried, she noticed that the crystal was starting to change shape and color, as if it absorbed all the "negativity" that she felt around her. She asked me for Fiammetta's phone contact: Amelia wanted to ask her directly for an explanation—one that probably confirmed her own suppositions.

Crystals, gemstones, and other stones are believed to have healing effects. They are believed to balance internal energies, facilitate bodily and psychological healing, and promote energetic and spiritual awareness. The same is believed for Bach flowers. The latter are considered a natural method of healing associated with the work of Dr. Bach, who lived in England at the beginning of the twentieth century. They [are believed to] "promote and restore the balance between mind and body" The Bach Flower Remedies are made from wild flowers and are considered safe for everybody."[53] Among my interlocutors, crystals and other healing aids and practices (from *Pizzica* to Reiki, from Bach flowers to meditation) are understood in relation to the popularized version of the "chakras."[54]

Pina and Reiki

"*Signorina, a ci sei figghia?*" (in dialect, literally: "Miss, to whom you are daughter?" Meaning: who is your family? A kind way to ask me "Who are you?") An old man asked me—the only human being I encountered in Minervino, one hot July early afternoon. I was headed to the house of someone who was hosting the Reiki initiation workshop I had signed up for. Viola, who had organized the event, had been vague in her directions and, instead of giving me the relevant information (the name, surname, and nickname of the person who owned or lived in this particular house,

53 "38 Bach Flower Remedies," Bach Flower, http://www.bachflower.com/original-bach-flower-remedies/. See, e.g., Craig Molgaard, Elizabeth Byerly, and Charles Snow. "Bach's Flower Remedies: A New Age Therapy." *Human Organization* 38 no 1 (1979): 71–74.

54 On the popular use of the chakra system in new religious movements see, e.g., Jay Johnston, "Theosophical Bodies: Colour, Shape and Emotion from Modern Aesthetics to Healing Therapies," in *Handbook of New Religions and Cultural Production vol. 4*, ed. Carole M. Cusack and Alex Norman (Leiden: Brill, 2012), 153–17; Egil Asprem,"Theosophical Attitudes Towards Science: Past and Present." In *Handbook of the Theosophical Current*, ed. Hammer, Olav Hammer and Mikael Rothstein (Leiden: Brill, 2013), 405–27; Charles Webster Leadbeater, *The Chakras: An Introduction* (New Delhi: Cosmo Books, [1927] 2003); Olav Hammer, *Claiming Knowledge: Strategies of Epistemology from Theosophy to the New Age* (Leiden: Brill, 2001).

the names, surnames, and nicknames of those whom the owner was born from, and the name, surname, and nickname of the person to whom the owner was married), useful to be able to locate the workshop place in case I got lost, she had given me only the address of the house. Therefore, when my navigation system lost connection in the middle of the town, and I got stuck in a series of one-way streets (per usual), I did not have enough information to share with locals to find my way to the Reiki initiation preparation meeting.

The old man was sitting in the shade, at the table of a bar that I was surprised to find open. The heat is almost unbearable at this time of the day in the summer in the Salento hinterland, and the streets are emptier than in the wee hours of the night. In these ghostly hours, locally called *controra*, only weirdos like a northern ethnographer, or people who are, for one reason or another, really motivated to not stay home, are to be found around. An interesting selection of human beings, indeed.

Not surprisingly, when I asked the old man some directions, I was not able to give all the relevant information. He, very kindly, had agreed to help me out in my quest, and really tried hard to understand, at first, what and whom I was looking for. Unimpressed and maybe a bit pitying my performance and lack of information (not to mention, probably, my Northern Italian accent), though, he eventually gave up, and started to try to understand, instead, who *I* was, and whose family's honor I had just wasted with my poor interaction. I finally got to the house where the workshop was to be held, with the help of a serendipitous temporary resurgence of my internet connection, and I was greeted by Viola, Gennaro, and Pina—the Reiki Master.

Pina is not Salentinian: she comes from the Campania region, and was in Salento for her vacation. A friend of a friend of Viola, she had agreed to hold this workshop for Gennaro and me, who wanted to learn and be initiated into

Reiki. I had read of this practice before, but I never had seriously taken it into consideration. Devastated by my mom's death, I was in need of some "healing tool" that would help me cope with my grief, and I took the last-minute organization of this workshop as a synchronicity.

Reiki is also a healing practice, originating in Japan. This name (re=universal, ki=life force energy) and practice were elaborated by Dr. Mikao Usui in the early 1900s.[55] The philosophy underlying Reiki is that the universe and everything in it is made of energy—an energy of expansion, of growth, of love. Love is expansion, and what we mundanely call "love" has in it the seeds of this expansion, growth, fulfillment, and thriving energy. By learning how to channel the ki and to direct it where the connection with this energy is weak or lost (our own body, the bodies of others, objects, situations, memories, places, etc.), one can foster, facilitate, and re-establish the connections with this energy. As a result, one can bring healing, balance, strength, and love where it was lost. In order to become a Reiki master, one has to go through three initiations, one for each level. With every level comes theoretical and practical indications, and the ability to channel, treat, and relate to different aspects of "reality." My initiation ritual followed a weekend of theoretical and practical teachings and culminated with the "opening" of our energy channels. After this "opening" we had to practice self-treatment every day for a month, and we could not eat meat and drink alcohol during that time.

55 On Reiki see, e.g., Dori-Michelle Beeler. *An Ethnographic Account of Reiki Practice in Britain. An Ethnographic Account of Reiki Practice in Britain* (Newcastle-upon-Tyne: Cambridge Scholars Publisher, 2016), "Reiki as Surrender: Evidence of an External Authority." *Journal of Contemporary Religion* 32 no. 3 (2017): 465–78 and "A Reiki Sense of Well-Being." *Anthropology News* 59 no 1(2018): e82–e86; Isabella Ricco, "Searching for a 'new Magical World': The Contradictions of CAM and New Age Therapies in the West." *Anthropology & Medicine* 27 no. 1 (2020): 96–109.

Diana and Aura-Soma

A castle out of the window, a hot tea in front of me, and colored paintings on the walls: it was quite a view, from my table. I was in a café, waiting for the presentation of Viola's book to start. It was afternoon, and the air announced that fall was coming and that the summer warmth was starting to become a memory. The atmosphere in the bar could have been defined as "boho-chic" – a design choice quite difficult to find in Salentine coffee shops. I quite liked it. It was my first time in this particular town of Salento, the existence of which I had learned only by memorizing the surnames of some of the locals I had met: apparently this toponym is quite frequent as a family name, in Salento and elsewhere. I had greeted Viola upon my arrival, and now she was busy talking with her editor. She was wearing a colorful dress, and loose hair. She was so radiant that she glowed.

Just minutes before the start of the presentation Viola came to my table and introduced me to one of her friends, Diana. "I know you!" I immediately said to Diana, while shaking her hand. "I saw you two summers ago at a local festival. You appeared to be working with some colored bottles!" "Yes, I am an Aura-Soma specialist, and I could tell many things of you now, just on the basis of the shade of blue of the coat you are wearing today!" I smiled. I liked her, and, desperately looking for new points of view, I also liked the possibility that she could tell me something about myself that I did not already know.

Aura-Soma is a healing method that uses the vibration of colors, the power of crystals, and natural essences as means to balance one's mind, body, and spirit.[56] It was founded in the United Kingdom in 1984 by Viki Wall, and it uses colored "equilibrium" bottles as both a way to analyze and to treat energetic imbalances. In my experience, an Aura-Soma session starts with the querent choosing four colored

56 See, e.g., Johnston, "Theosophical Bodies."

bottles among the one hundred twenty displayed on a particular stand, lit from behind. These bottles can be of one color or a combination of two. Being that the liquid inside the bottle is a combination of oils over water (mostly), the two colors appear as separated (if the bottle is not shaken). It is believed that the bottles chosen and the sequence in which they are chosen can reveal aspects of the querent's soul in that precise moment: its needs, vocation, challenges, and aids. Not too dissimilarly from tarot cards—to which the Aura-Soma bottles are associated—the Aura-Soma bottles can be used as a meditation tool or as an instrument for self-awareness. In this respect, these Equilibrium Aura-Soma bottles are associated with specific Kabbalistic beliefs (such as the sephirot), and to some Ascended Masters, angels, and archangels (see below)—i.e., there is a link between Aura-Soma and to what is generally called, in these circles, (spiritual) Metaphysics. Similarly to crystal therapy, Aura-Soma bottles can also be used as a healing aid. By rubbing the liquid of a specific bottle (chosen in accordance with the querent's personal choices and reading) over some specific areas of the body (that vary with the bottles), the practitioner allows for the healing energies of colors, herbs, and crystals to work on her chakras, and to establish a healing and harmonious connection between her energetic body (aura) and her physical one (soma).[57] In addition to Equilibrium bottles, an Aura-Soma practitioner can use other medicines, such as "pomanders," "light beams," and "essences."

57 The idea at the base of this practice is that "As we know, colors are simply wavelengths of light. But we also know that we are actually made of light ourselves. As such, our own true vibration is mirrored in various frequencies of color. When we choose colors from among the Equilibrium bottles, we do so because those particular colors 'speak' to us, and we are seeking to understand what it is they want to tell us. So the Equilibrium colors are simply bringing us into the light of our own 'true colors.'" https://www.ronnaprince.com/aura-soma/

Veronica: Spiritual Metaphysics and Theosophy

Veronica is Brazilian-Italian. She is a Reiki Master and a follower of the Goddess Kwan-Yin.[58] It is the Goddess of Compassion who had asked Veronica to come to Italy, and to Salento in particular, to bring her spiritual message: in particular, through the initiation to the Magnified Healing (MH) practice. Through Diana, many of the Sisters of the *cerchio* came to know Veronica, and, with her, the Ascended Master Kwan Yin, and the "violet ray" of which, they believe, she is currently in charge of. Viola, Fiammetta, and Diana were attending a multi-day workshop with Veronica and appeared to be fascinated by the experience. They kindly invited me to join one of the meetings. I gladly accepted the invitation without any questions and without asking too many details about the event, content, and purpose of the meeting.

The room of the private house that hosted the event was cold and humid but crowded. Twenty or so persons were diligently sitting on the chairs tidily arranged in lines. They were preparing pens and paper for their notes, in anticipation of the lecture. I took a seat, and I was given some handouts. Mimicking the others, I got hold of a pen and paper and waited for Veronica to start the lecture. I felt comfortable in this formal learning environment: after all, as an academic, this felt quite reassuring—differently from many other circumstances on the field. With her lovely Brazilian accent and graceful manners, Veronica greeted us and suggested to start right away with the "*decreti*" (decrees). These were prayers that we could find on the handout, and that had to be communally proclaimed and repeated three times. I started reading the text out loud with the other attendees. The text was invoking colored rays, a spiritual being who appeared to be called Saint-Germain, angels, archangels,

58 For Veronica and the Sisters, differently from the Chinese tradition, Kwan Yin is a female goddess.

"Christ Consciousness," and what, with my background in Hebrew, appeared to be the translation of אֶהְיֶה אֲשֶׁר אֶהְיֶה, "I am what/who I am." I was puzzled: what did all these Christian and Abrahamic languages, traditions, metaphors, and anthropology have to do with Kwan Yin, the Chinese bodhisattva of Compassion?

Ascended masters, angels and archangels are some of the aiding forces that are invoked by the followers of the spiritual metaphysics. Ascended masters are believed to be illuminated beings who incarnated in humans through the centuries, and who underwent spiritual transformation and elevation reaching the 6th dimension (and, therefore, "immortality"). According to the spiritual metaphysics I learned from my interlocutors, they are divided into and belong to the Seven Rays—i.e., spiritual energetic forces spread from God (known as the "Mighty I AM Presence").[59] Each ray is associated with a color and connected to a specific "quality" of God. Each one of the Seven Rays is led by a special ascended master called a "Chohan." For example, Kwan-Yin (or Kannon, in the Japanese tradition), is, together with Saint Germain, the Chohan of the 7th ray, the "purple ray," that of "compassion." Kwan-Yin is a particularly important ascended master for my interlocutors, and "she" is worshipped by many of them, in particular since they received the initiation to "Magnified Healing."[60]

Branded as "an ancient healing modality," Magnified Healing was invented in 1983, and was actively exported

59 According to some, there are more than seven rays (possibly, twelve), but they have been not revealed, yet. On Theosophy see, e.g., Olav Hammer and Mikael Rothstein, *Handbook of the Theosophical Current* (Leiden: Brill, 2013).

60 In the words of their practitioners, "In this time of important earth and cosmic energy shifts, mankind now has an opportunity to enter into a creation consciousness. And as Planet Earth is approaching its mutation into a body of light, so too humanity needs to begin its mutation into higher vibratory dimensions. In order to accomplish our ascent into Oneness, we need to heal ourselves at all levels: physical, emotional, mental, etheric, spiritual." See Magnified Healing, https://www.magnifiedhealing.com/. I learned that in Japan Kwan-Yin is not considered as feminine, but as neutral.

worldwide since 1992. Working with energies from "the Source"—otherwise known as God—Magnified Healing is believed to re-harmonize the body, to support mental, physical, emotional, and spiritual healing, and to favor "spiritual ascension." This last concept, quite ubiquitous within New Age spiritualities, postulates that we are currently living in the "third dimension" characterized by materiality, dualism, and the distinction between mind and body. As the ascension process unfolds, though, humanity is transitioning towards higher dimensions—namely, the fourth and fifth dimensions (but there are more). These are characterized by a new way of living in one's own body and in this world (less dependent on matter), and different ways to communicate, learn, and relate to each other.

Viola: Fairies, Elementals and Spirit Animals

Organized by a local sports association, it was advertised as a "meditation in nature" and it was planned to be led by Viola, whom I had met before only after the re-enactment of the yearly pilgrimage of the *tarantate* women in Galatina (see chapter 2). I liked her—and her friends. Moreover, I had never meditated before, let alone in nature, and I was happy to give it a try.

We met in Maglie, in a pinewood. Viola, Fiammetta, and another five women, including me, were there. We had brought yoga mats, water, and mosquito spray for the occasion. The smell of the maquis was inebriating (in spite of the mosquito spray), and the gentle late afternoon wind was cuddling us—who were sitting on our mats, in a circle. At the center of the circle, in front of us, there was a smaller circle of cards. They portrayed some unknown symbols and words: rainbows, arrows, hearts, vertical lines. In the silence that was preparing us for the work, I was immediately drawn to a purple one that showed an arrow that pierced a heart and a star.

Viola started the meditation with a general introduction to the orixàs: gods and goddesses associated with natural elements, the "chief" of whom, apparently, was called Oxalà, the "Father-God, the sky." Each one of the cards in the middle of the circle was representing an orixà.

The meditation was, in fact, a visualization. Viola asked us to tune-in with the elements of water, air, fire, and earth, by evoking some of their qualities and manifestations: the ability of water to make its way even through rocks and obstacles, the transformative quality of fire, the resilience of the earth, and the lightness of the wind. The meditation allowed for long times of "silence," accompanied by the sound of the drum, that Viola played while walking around the circle.

I found the experience of visualizing and reflecting on the qualities of our natural environment quite invigorating, and I was moved by discovering that I, too, was holding some of their qualities, and that I, too, was somehow part of it. While I was immersed in my meditation, and emotional tears were sliding on my cheeks, I felt something bumping on my head: the wind had ruffled the cards, and had lifted one of them, that ended up hitting my head. I opened my eyes, abruptly interrupting my meditation, and I picked it up it was the card of Oxalà. While ignoring the notion of synchronicities and not being used to give "magical" interpretation to events, I, surprisingly, took it as a salutation, a blessing: a welcoming form of initiation by the Father of the orixàs. It felt, indeed, for me (for the lack of better words, at the time), like a kind of baptism.

Those with power animals, fairies and, in general, the "elementals" — i.e., a spiritual force embedded in the various elements and presences in and of the natural environment are important relationships for my interlocutors.[61]

61 See, e.g., Dennis Gaffin, *Running with the Fairies: Towards a Transpersonal Anthropology of Religion* (Newcastle upon Tyne: Cambridge Scholars Publishing, 2012); Sabina Magliocco, "Reconnecting to Everything": Fairies in Contemporary

While this is particularly true for those among them more inclined to pursue and live a shamanic form of spirituality, I find that some sort of connection with the natural environment, Mother Earth, and the non-obvious forces that inhabit it is part of the religious experience of all of my interlocutors. Those who follow the Umbanda tradition and its orixàs are obviously working primarily with the natural environment and its elementals. For my interlocutors, the encounter with the Umbanda tradition happened through their interest in *biotransenergetica,* in transpersonal psychology, with encounters with native practitioners, and, more generally, with the work of Pierluigi Lattuada.

Guido: Astrology and Karmic Astrology

Learning to think "karmically" certainly changed my experience and perception of time: it not only redefined both my origins and my destinations (or *destino,* destiny, see chapter 2), but also my relationships. At first, I only listened and observed the narratives and experiences of the Sisters, but, over time, I learned to make these perspectives my own. The turning point, for me, was my encounter with Guido. He is a karmic astrologer born in another region: he lives now in the north and comes to Salento every year to offer his services to the Sisters and their network. Trained in "classical" astrology, he adopted a "karmic" approach to his readings of the sky and of birth charts. After an hour-long

Paganism," In *Fairies, Demons, and Nature Spirits,* ed Michael Ostling (London: Palgrave Macmillan UK, 2017), 325–47 and "The Taming of the Fae: Literary and Folkloric Fairies in Modern Paganisms," in Feraro and Doyle White, eds. *Magic and Witchery in the Modern West : Celebrating the Twentieth Anniversary of 'The Triumph of the Moon,'* 107–30; Amurabi Oliveira,"Umbanda as Syncretistic Shamanism in Barcelona," *International Journal of Latin American Religions* 4, no. 1 (2020): 123–36; Viola Teisenhoffer, "Assessing Ritual Experience in Contemporary Spiritualities: The Practice of 'Sharing' in a New Age Variant of Umbanda," *Religion and Society* 9 (2018): 131–44; Diana Espírito Santo, "Clothes for Spirits: Opening and Closing the Cosmos in Brazilian Umbanda," *HAU: Journal of Ethnographic Theory* 6 no. 3 (2016): 85–106.

conversation in which he analyzed my birth chart and the one of the sky on the day of my thirty-ninth birthday, he shared some information on my life—something I much needed, at that time. I do not recall the details of the conversation I had with him (Viola still scolds me for not having thought about recording the reading!), but I do remember the one element that changed my approach to time and relationships. According to Guido, by analyzing the birth charts of both my husband and son, it appeared that we had been a family also in our previous lives: a quite comforting perspective for a person who had lost her parents. Placing my "family origins" before my birth was indeed a soothing thought, for a grieving daughter.

Paying attention, daily, to the position of the planets, the phase of the moon, and the astrologic sky is also a widespread practice among my interlocutors, who not only read the horoscopes of their favorite astrologers but also understand it within a "karmic" approach[62]. This is why the complex discipline of "karmic astrology" is of particular importance. Moreover, knowing the movements of the planets and the sky is considered extremely important to assess the "energies" that "work" on and with us towards our "ascension" and the "ascension" of our planet Earth. It is believed, in fact, that the transition towards the fourth and fifth dimensions is encouraged and activated by particular planetary alignments of the type studied by astrology.

By following my interlocutors during my stay in Salento, I could gather information, accumulate hands-on experiences, and connect with persons related to different spiritual experiences that, among religionists, some would label as belonging to "contemporary Paganism" and others

62 On astrology within New Age Spirituality see, e.g., Susannah Crockford. "A Mercury Retrograde Kind of Day: Exploring Astrology in Contemporary New Age Spirituality and American Social Life." *Correspondences* 6 no 1 (2018): 47–75 and also her *Ripples of the Universe* (Chicago: University of Chicago Press, 2021); also Nicholas Campion. *Astrology and Popular Religion in the Modern West: Prophecy, Cosmology and the New Age Movement* (London: Routledge, 2016).

possibly "New Age." There is much debate around definitions of contemporary Paganisms and New Age spirituality. Both these expressions are terms that encompass many diverse spiritual experiences.[63]

Contemporary Paganism is generally considered an umbrella term for "a loosely affiliated group of religions or spiritual paths that share a notion of divinity within nature, typically celebrate both a male and female element to the divine, and in most instances practice forms of divination and magic."[64] Due to its internal differentiation, to the lack of shared beliefs or practices, and to the many different traditions that take on this term, there is no single definition of contemporary Paganism. There are many contemporary Paganisms, in fact, from Druidry to the Goddess Religions, from Witchcraft to Heathenism. This broad definition of Paganism could include spiritualities as different as Hoodoo, Wicca, Romuva, popular "global" versions of Paganism, Suomenusko (Finnish Faith), Dievturība, Rodzimowierstwo, Hellenismos, Kemetism, Canaanite Reconstructionism, neo-shamanism, non-theistic Paganism and, for some, Umbanda and other devotion to the orixàs.[65]

63 For a thorough description of the debates on these topics see e.g., Fedele, *Looking for Mary Magdalene*; Sarah M. Pike, *New Age and Neopagan Religions in America* (New York: Columbia University Press, 2004); Wouter J. Hanegraaff, *New Age Religion and Western Culture: Esotericism in the Mirror of Secular Thought* (Leiden: Brill, 1996), "New Age Spiritualities as Secular Religion: A Historian's Perspective," *Social Compass* 46, no. 2 (1999): 145–60, and "The New Age Movement and Western Esotericism," in *Handbook of New Age*, ed. Daren Kemp and James R. Lewis (Leiden: Brill, 2007), 25–50.

64 Lippy, Charles H., and Peter W. Williams, "Neo-paganism." In *Encyclopedia of Religion in America* (Washington: CQ Press, 2010), 1539.

65 See Kaarina Aitamurto and Scott Simpson, eds. *Modern Pagan and Native Faith Movements in Central and Eastern Europe* (Durham: Acumen, 2013); Yvonne Patricia Chireau, *Black Magic : Religion and the African American Conjuring Tradition* (Berkeley: University of California Press, 2003); Dalia Senvaityte, "The Hunt for Lost Identity: Native Faith Paganism in Contemporary Lithuania," in *The Pomegranate: The International Journal of Pagan Studies* 20, no. 2 (2018): 234–60; Tõnno Jonuks and Tiina Äikäs "Contemporary Deposits at Sacred Places: Reflections on Contemporary Paganism in Estonia and Finland," in *Folklore* 75 (2019): 7–46; Michael Strmiska, "Modern Latvian Paganism: Some Introductory

In the Italian context, as I will point out below, contemporary Paganism is locally understood as comprising two main "branches:" the one locally called *neopaganesimo* and the one referred to as *veteropaganesimo*. Some contemporary Pagans practice in groups, others—possibly, the majority—alone.[66] Some invoke a direct historical connection with pre-Christian cults; others are more nature-oriented and have a more "shamanistic" approach to spirituality. Some worship a pantheon of gods and goddesses, some others just "Mother Earth." Some practice a *bricolage* of different spiritual practices and traditions; others follow strictly one particular set.

In order to make justice to different forms of Contemporary Paganism, including non-theistic ones, in his introduction to the edited volume *Godless Paganism*, John Halstead, a Pagan writer and blogger, proposes to change metaphors, so to speak, to think about contemporary Paganism, today. Instead of talking about this as an "umbrella" expression, he proposes to conceive contemporary Paganism as a "tent."[67] "The problem with the umbrella metaphor," they claim, "is that it implies that there is a single 'center' around which all Pagans gather. Bot no one can agree on what this center is. The reality is that there are multiple centers of Paganism." :The tent metaphor, instead, allows, according to the editor of the volume, to conceive Paganism around "multiple poles and multiple centers": namely, Earth, Deity, and

---

Remarks," in *The Pomegranate: The International Journal of Pagan Studies* 14 no 1 (2013): 22–30; Scott Simpson, "Only Slavic Gods: Nativeness in Polish Rodzimowierstwo," in *Cosmopolitanism, Nationalism, and Modern Paganism*, ed. Kathryn Rountree (New York: Palgrave Macmillan US, 2016), 65–86; Stian Sundell Torjussen, "Hellenismos: Texts in the Contemporary Worship of the Ancient Greek Gods in North America," in *The Pomegranate: The International Journal of Pagan Studies* 22 no 2 (2020): 196–220; Shai Feraro, "Canaanite Reconstructionism Among Contemporary Israeli Pagans," in Rountree, ed., *Cosmopolitanism, Nationalism, and Modern Paganism*, 157–77.

66 See Berger, *Solitary Pagans*.

67 John Halstead, ed., introduction to *Godless Paganism: Voices of Non-Theistic Pagans* (N.p.: Lulu.com, 2016).

Self.[68] While there is no one way to conceive or relate to one or more of these centers, within the Pagan tent (nor it needs to be), Halstead proposes to change metaphors to make space for different Pagan minorities. While I find Halstead's remarks very useful, I realize that they don't necessarily help me answer one of the main questions I encountered in my fieldwork: Is the practice, so to speak, that makes someone a "Pagan" or the "Pagan" that makes a practice "Pagan"? This has been a particularly difficult question, for me, since "Pagan" is not the term that my interlocutors primarily use to call themselves—although it is one that they are comfortable with, when I use it to describe what we do. Moreover, most of the interlocutors with whom I worked are solitary practitioners and do not formally belong to a coven. Even the *cerchio* itself, as I mentioned above, is not particularly structured and does not conform to other, more quintessential, forms of contemporary Paganism. In general, as an anthropologist, I think it is always important to acknowledge self-definitions (or "emic" categories) put forward by one's interlocutors. As in Halstead's edited volume, I believe that this practice is central in order to recognize and give voice to under-represented communities and individuals.

Moreover, it is also a way to challenge possible "gatekeeping" attitudes. Nonetheless, similarly to what I elsewhere claimed for the word "feminist" in my research on feminism in Salento,[69] I choose to broaden the category "Paganism" as to include the practices and beliefs I encountered in Salento. I believe that limiting one's analyses to those who explicitly use the that specific term to define what they do risks concealing more nuanced practices that are nonetheless relevant to the study of contempo-

68 See Halstead, *Godless Paganism*, 3–4.

69 Giovanna Parmigiani, *Feminism, Violence and Representation in Modern Italy: "We Are Witnesses, Not Victims"* (Bloomington: Indiana University Press, 2019), 16.

rary spiritual practices centered on Earth, Deity, and Self[70]. Moreover, refusing to refer to the practices I encountered as Pagan would also explicitly be at cross-purposes with my interlocutors' need to be seen, acknowledged, and perceived as in conversation with "global Paganism," for the reasons I mentioned above. In this sense, it would be disrespectful of the context of my research. Finally, since *pizzica* and the relationship with the land of Salento are the main commonalities among the Sisters and giving the fact that the "Pagan tent" makes spaces for hybrid spiritualities to be included in the category, I decided to write about the *cerchio* as a contemporary Pagan group—an eclectic one that, often, includes New Age elements[71].

70 On this see Bron Taylor, *Dark Green Religion: Nature Spirituality and the Planetary Future* (Berkeley: University of California Press, 2010) and his "Bounding Paganism: Who and what is in and out, and what does this reveal about contemporary kinship-entangled nature spiritualities?," *Journal for the Study of Religion, Nature and Culture*, forthcoming.

71 On contemporary Paganisms see, e.g., Carol Barner-Barry, *Contemporary Paganism: Minority Religions in a Majoritarian America* (New York: Palgrave Macmillan, 2005); Helen A. Berger, *A Community of Witches* (Columbia, SC: University of South Carolina Press, 1999), *Witchcraft and Magic* (Philadelphia: University of Pennsylvania Press, 2006), and *Solitary Pagans* (Columbia, SC: University of South Carolina Press, 2019); Blain, *Nine Worlds of Seid-Magic;* Jefferson F. Calico, *Being Viking* (Sheffield: Equinox, 2018); Clifton, *Her Hidden Children;* Howell, "The Goddess Returns to Italy," "Sense of Place, Heterotopia, and Community: Performing Land and Folding Time in the Badalisc Festival of Northern Italy," *Folklore* 124, no. 1 (2013): 45–63, and *Food, Festival, and Religion;* Ethan Doyle White, "The Meaning of 'Wicca': A Study in Etymology, History, and Pagan Politics," *The Pomegranate: The International Journal of Pagan Studies* 12, no. 2 (2010): 185–207; Anna Fedele, "The Metamorphoses of Neopaganism in Traditionally Catholic Countries in Southern Europe," in *Sites and Politics of Religious Diversity in Southern Europe: The Best of All Gods*, ed. José Mapril and Ruy Llera Blanes (Leiden: Brill, 2013), 51–72, and *Looking for Mary Magdalene;* Greenwood, *Anthropology of Magic;* Harvey, *Contemporary Paganism*, and *Contemporary Paganisms: Religions of the Earth from Druids and Witches to Heathens and Ecofeminists* (New York: New York University Press, 2011); Christine Hoff Kraemer, "Gender and Sexuality in Contemporary Paganism," *Religion Compass* 6, no. 8 (2012): 390–401; Murphy Pizza and James R. Lewis, *Handbook of Contemporary Paganism*, Brill Handbooks on Contemporary Religion (Leiden: Brill, 2009); Luhrmann, *Persuasions of the Witch's Craft;* Magliocco, *Witching Culture*, and "Witchcraft, Healing and Vernacular Magic in Italy," in *Witchcraft Continued: Popular Magic in Modern Europe*, ed. Willelm de Blécourt and Owen

The Sisters of the circle and many of their friends and acquaintances share a neo-animist worldview (see chapter 5), a polytheist cosmology, and they respect, venerate, and have a personal connection with the natural environment—especially the one of their lands of Salento.[72] The worshipping of nature is definitely central in the spiritual experiences of the Sisters, as it is the practice of magic. Nonetheless, unlike other well-studied northern European Pagan communities, this Salentine *cerchio* does not feel the need to define itself in relation to—or in antagonism with—Christianity. As the sociologists of religion Stefania Palmisano and Nicola Pannofino point out, their Italian colleagues have defined the Italian religious landscape as a "singular pluralism," to refer to the peculiar status of Catholicism in Italy, in comparison to other Catholic Countries.[73] While Catholicism remains Italy's main religion

---

Davies (Manchester: Manchester University Press, 2004), 151–73; Mapril and Llera Blanes, eds., *Sites and Politics*; Melissa Harrington, "Reflecting on Studying Wicca from within the Academy and the Craft: An Autobiographical Perspective," *The Pomegranate: The International Journal of Pagan Studies* 17, no. 1–2 (2016): 180–93; Síân Reid and Lee MacDonald, *Between the Worlds: Readings in Contemporary Neopaganism* (Toronto: Canadian Scholars' Press, 2006); Aitamurto and Simpson, eds. *Modern Pagan and Native Faith Movements in Central and Eastern Europe* and "The Study of Paganism and Wicca," in *The Oxford Handbook of New Religious Movements*, ed. James R. Lewis and Inga Tøllefsen (Oxford: Oxford University Press, 2016), 482–94; Rountree, *Crafting Contemporary Pagan Identities*, "Localizing Neo-Paganism," "Neo-Paganism, Native Faith and Indigenous Religion," and *Contemporary Pagan and Native Faith Movements in Europe: Colonialist and Nationalist Impulses* (New York: Berghahn Books, 2015); Jone Salomonsen, *Enchanted Feminism: Ritual, Gender and Divinity among the Reclaiming Witches of San Francisco* (New York: Routledge, 2002); Pike, *New Age and Neopagan Religions*; Strmiska, "Modern Paganism in World Cultures"; Michael York, *Pagan Theology: Paganism as a World Religion* (New York: New York University Press, 2003). Feraro and Doyle White, eds., *Magic and Witchery in the Modern West*.

72 For a comparison, see Kathryn Rountree, "Neo-Paganism, Native Faith and Indigenous Religion: A Case Study of Malta within the European Context," *Social Anthropology/Anthropologie Sociale* 22, no. 1 (2014): 81–100.

73 See Palmisano and Pannofino, *Contemporary Spiritualities*. See also, e.g., Franco Garelli "Flexible Catholicism, Religion and the Church: The Italian Case," *Religions* 4, no. 1 (2012): 1–13, *Religion Italian Style: Continuities and Changes in a Catholic Country* (Farnham: Routledge, 2014), and *Gente Di Poca*

and most Italian citizens define themselves as Catholics, the interpretations of what "being Catholic" means varies considerably.[74] Moreover, the most recent statistical data show that the percentual difference between Italians that define themselves as "religious," and those who define themselves as "spiritual" has considerably decreased from 1998 to 2007 (the year of the last data available)—with a distance of 0.7 percentage points. In 2007, 73.8 percent of Italians defined themselves as "religious," while 73.1 percent described themselves as "spiritual."[75] These data, indirectly, offer important information in support of my ethnographic observations—namely, that a wide percentage of Italians consider themselves *both* "religious" *and* "spiritual." This aspect, applied to contemporary Italian Paganisms, confirms that, differently from other countries, many Italian Pagans, including the ones with whom I worked in Salento, do not seem to feel the need to define their practices and spirituality in opposition to Catholicism.

What is the Italian Pagan panorama, then, beyond Salento? "*Quello che ci unisce è più importante di quello che ci divide*"—What unites us is more important than what divides us. This is the motto of the *Unione delle Comunità Neopagane* (UCP—Union of the Neopagan Communities), an institution founded in 2014 that currently brings together Italian Pagan, Wiccan, and Druid organizations—in addition to other groups connected with contemporary

---

Fede: Il Sentimento Religioso Nell'Italia Incerta Di Dio (Bologna: Il Mulino, 2020); Luca Diotallevi, *Il rompicapo della secolarizzazione. Caso italiano, teorie americane e revisione del paradigma della secolarizzazione* (Soveria Mannelli [Catanzaro]: Rubbettino, 2001); Enzo Pace "La Pocket-religion. Il New Age Nel Sistema Religioso Italiano," *Quaderni di Sociologia* 19, no. 19 (1999): 36–54, and *Le religioni nell'Italia che cambia* (Rome: Carocci, 2013); Simone Martino and Roberto Scalon, *Cattolicesimi nell'Europa-post secolare Uno sguardo comparator* (Rome: Carocci, 2018).

74 Unfortunately, migrants who live in Italy and are not citizens do not appear in the surveys considered.

75 See Palmisano and Pannofino, *Contemporary Spiritualities*; Garelli, *Gente Di Poca Fede*.

Pagan spiritualities.[76] As it is clear from their webpage, UCP does not intend to represent all the various contemporary Italian Paganisms. Rather, its aim is to unite all the groups and associations *that want to work together*, in spite of the differences among them, to make what they call *Neopaganesimo* acknowledged and recognized as a legit religion in contemporary Italy.[77] As elsewhere, the Pagan panorama in Italy is quite variegated, and not so easy to track down. Palmisano and Pannofino identified three main currents to describe contemporary Italian "spiritual" panorama, revolving around one of the following themes: nature, well-being, and mystery.[78] While their work concentrated specifically on new religious movements, Palmisano and Pannofino's conclusions can be useful, if not to depict, certainly to sketch Italy's contemporary Pagan scene. Many of the Italian Pagan spiritualities, as a matter of fact, could fall within these three themes. On the one hand, it is important to acknowledge the presence of solitary practitioners, especially in online settings, and of practitioners of various forms of vernacular magic together with followers of forms of neo-shamanism.[79] In addition to these important groups, there are a number of associations that could be connected to more specific traditions. Among the latter expressions of contemporary Paganism in Italy there are, for instance: Heathenism (e.g., the *Comunità Odinista* and the *Tempio del Lupo*); Kemetism (e.g., A*nhkeperura*); Hellenism (e.g., the *Comunità Ellena Italiana*); Druidry (e.g., *OBOD – Ordine Bardi Ovati e Druidi*

76 L'UCN: L' Unione delle Comunità Neopagane, accessed January 6, 2021, http://www.neopaganesimo.it/

77 While I prefer to refer to contemporary forms of Paganism as "contemporary Paganisms" rather than "Neopaganism," I acknowledge that, in the Italian context, the term *Neopaganesimo* is used in a specific way as to refer to what is not *veteropaganesimo*.

78 Palmisano and Pannofino, *Contemporary Spiritualities.*

79 See Magliocco, "Witchcraft, Healing and Vernacular Magic in Italy," and "Italian Cunning Craft"; also, Puca, "'Witch' and 'Shaman,'" and "Tradition of *Segnature*."

and *Gran Loggia Druidica in Italia*); Wicca (e.g., *Il Circolo dei Trivi*); earth-based spiritualities, and Goddess-centered witchcraft.[80][81] To this long list, one should add also various groups inspired by Esotericism, including New-Age "wellness" practitioners such as those described by Palmisano and Pannofino,[82] and, most importantly, what is referred to as "*Veteropaganesimo*"—or "old Paganism." The focus on the adjective "neo" in *Neo*paganism (New Paganism), in the Italian context, is a particularly important one. While there is a tendency, especially in English-speaking countries, to avoid the term Neopaganism to refer to contemporary Pagan spiritualities, in Italy "neo" connotes *specific versions* of contemporary Paganism *in opposition to* other ones—namely, to "*Veteropaganesimo*." If both *neo* and *vetero* Paganisms are expressions of contemporary Pagan Spiritualities, it is clear that UCP solidly roots its work in the former and not in the latter. Why is this so? Davide Marrè, a journalist and scholar of Wicca and contemporary Paganism in Italy, has eloquently written about this topic, pointing out that Italy already had its own "modern Paganism," way before it encountered the northern European and northern American developments of Neopaganism at the end of the last century. This Italian Paganism was the *Via Romana agli Dei* (The Roman way towards the gods).[83] Otherwise called *Tradizione Romana* (Roman tradition) or *Tradizionalismo Romano* (Roman

80 See Howell, "The Goddess Returns to Italy," and *Food, Festival, and Religion*.

81 See, e.g., Ankhepura, https://ankheperura.weebly.com; Comunita' Odinista, www.comunitaodinista.org; Lyra, accessed January 6, 2021, http://chi-lyra.com; OBOD: Ordine Bardi, Ovati e Druidi, www.druidry.it; Gran Loggia Druidica D'Italia, www.druidismo.it; "Homepage," Cerchio Druidico Italiano, accessed January 6, 2021, www.cerchiodruidico.it; Circolo del Trivi. Associazione di Promozione Sociale, www.circolodeitrivi.com; Antica Quercia, www.anticaquercia.com.

82 Palmisano and Pannofino, *Contemporary Spiritualities*.

83 Davide Marrè, "La tradizione molteplice: viaggio nel tradizionalismo romano," *Athame*, http://www.athame.it/la-tradizione-molteplice-viaggio-nel-tradizionalismo-romano.

traditionalism), the *Via Romana agli Dei* is the main representative of *Veteropaganesimo*.[84] Developed from the works of Arturo Reghini and, partially, of Julius Evola in the first half of the twentieth century, inspired by Western esoteric philosophies as well as by the ancient Roman religion and pantheon, this Pagan religion revolved (and still does) around the ideas of "Italic wisdom" and "tradition." The *Via Romana agli Dei* had connections with Fascism, before, and with right and extreme right political views, later. Today, the legacy of the *Via Romana agli Dei* is still leaning towards the right, politically, and it is still characterized by a high degree of intellectualism and elitism. According to Marrè, currently, *Movimento Tradizionalista Romano* and *Movimento Tradizionale Romano* are the two main exponents of both the *Via Romana agli Dei* and of *Veteropaganesimo*. Both these groups put the ancient Roman cults at the center of their practices, together with the belief in the superiority of the Italic wisdom and culture. Recognizing their spirituality as an ethnic tradition, they refuse to define themselves with the term "Paganism." In line with their beliefs, the *Movimento Tradizionalista Romano* and the *Movimento Tradizionale Romano* have recently become part of the European Congress of Ethnic Religion.

In addition to the aforementioned Veteropagan groups, Marrè mentions also others. On the one hand, there are groups, including the extreme right nationalist group La Thule Italia and the extreme right eco-nationalist social movement of *Doma Nunch* (in the Lombardy dialect,

84 According to Marrè, "The galaxy of *veteropaganesimo*, together with Roman traditionalism, can therefore be enriched with Celtic groups, Germanic ones, etc., which, despite having different views of tradition, pose the question of ethnic identity and reconstructionism at the basis of their spiritual philosophy. In particular, ethnic identity is often perceived as a political claim" (see Marrè, "La tradizione molteplice"). It is worth noting that in the Italian context, given its particular history (and in other areas of Europe, for similar reasons), discourses about ethnicity are often enmeshed with right and far-right politics.

meaning "Only Us"),[85][86] that could be positioned at the "right" of the two *Movimenti*. On the other hand, there are associations such as the *Associazione Tradizionale Pietas* and *Il Cervo Bianco*, which, in their more flexible understandings of tradition and more open approach to other spiritual orientations, can be situated at the "left" of the two aforementioned main veteropagan groups.

Marrè applies a "left-right" paradigm also to place various forms of Neopaganism in his description of the current Italian Pagan panorama, putting solitary practitioners and loosely organized groups on the extreme left, and those more structured closer to the center.

It is important to mention that in 2014 when Marrè's article appeared, this "left-right" division could have been effective to describe the current Italian Pagan picture, but I do not believe today that it is precise and analytically

85 http://thule-italia.comBranded as a cultural association, La Thule Italia seems to directly engage with the topics of National Socialism.

86 Insubria Press, https://insubriapress.wordpress.com/tag/domanunch/. Recently assimilated into the right political party *Fratelli d'Italia,* the *Doma Nunch* movement developed in the northern Italian regions of Piedmont and Lombardy, and in the Ticino area of Switzerland. This area, following a trend set by the secessionist party *Lega Nord* in the 1990s, is referred to as *Insubria,* since this particular geographical area was inhabited, in antiquity, by the Celtic population of the *Insubres*. Interestingly—especially for me, since this is precisely the area of Italy where I grew up—*Doma Nunch* uses the local dialect as a *lingua franca*.

Many of the texts of the aforementioned website are written in dialect. This is not something that I would consider common, and it is clearly a statement in support of their secessionist political goals. The local dialect, which is significantly different from standard Italian and even more dissimilar from the Salentine dialect present in this book, was spoken almost only by elders, when I grew up. In fact, it was mostly passively known by younger generations—including mine—regardless of the social background. For example, my grandparents always spoke to me in dialect, but expected me to communicate with them in Italian. I am, therefore, only passively fluent in the local dialect: I can understand it and read it very well, but I do not speak it well. When my grandparents wrote—something that I, as a first-generation college student, witnessed only occasionally—they always used standard Italian. My parents, instead, were bilingual, but spoke only Italian with me, between themselves and, often also with their parents. Only occasionally my parents communicated in dialect with my grandparents. They never used the dialect in writing.

strong. While more research on this particular topic would be required, it is important to acknowledge that, with the rise of populism in Europe and in Italy, in particular, with the political party *Movimento5Stelle* (Five Stars Movement), the classic distinction between "left" and "right" ceased to be as meaningful as it was before—for citizens as well as for politicians and political analysts. While it did not completely disappear, it started to be an insufficient (but not erroneous) descriptive category. Therefore, I argue that a thorough study of contemporary Paganism and politics, today, should find and adopt *also* other heuristic parameters. This is not to claim that neo-fascist groups or other extreme right groups are not part of the Italian political and spiritual pictures. On the contrary: my claim is that, since the situation today is much more complicated than what a mere "left-right" division could grasp, it is also more worrisome. This is why additional research on this topic is both pressing and urgent.[87]

***

*Idrusa quietly clears the empty beer bottles from the table and adjusts the plate of cashew nuts. Then she takes a seat in front of me. Viola, on my left, smiles, unaware, while texting. Patrizia, on my right, wonders if it's time for a cigarette or not. Senefera is texting, too, without smiling though. Her smile faded as soon as she opened the WhatsApp application on her smartphone. Idrusa looks at me right in my eyes, and I return, in silence, her eye contact. We spend a few seconds without blinking and then she asks me, "*Vuoi?*" [Do you want?]"*

"Sure, thank you," I reply. We both smile.

Idrusa shuffles the Tarot cards with her eyes closed. She mutters some non-intelligible words. Then she opens her eyes and asks me to hold her hand for a few seconds, after making sure I

87 On Paganism in Italy and populism see, e.g., Giovanna Parmigiani, "Magic and Politics: Conspirituality and Covid-19," Journal of the American Academy of Religion 89, no. 2 (2021): 502–29.

am not crossing any of my limbs. Apparently, this would have allowed my energy to flow smoothly, without obstacles. "Since you are not a leftie, now cut the deck with your left hand, please, and think about your question," she says. I do what she just asked me to and return both hands to my knees. I try to verbalize a question in my head, but it is tough crafting a sufficiently precise one. I know it is a difficult period, existentially, for me, a period of extreme hardship: I often feel lost, without perspective, lacking sense, direction, purpose. I put these feelings, rather than their verbalization, at the center of my unutterable question, and I look at Idrusa. She now reassembles the deck and starts spreading all the cards on the table until they form a circle. With slow and elegant moves, she opens a small book on the front cover of which I could read the name of Osho.[88] *Two small parallel lines appear on her forehead while she reads and turns the first few pages of the book. They immediately disappear when she tells me "Let's do this one, the 'seagull wings.' Pick your first card." I follow her indications, and the ones of the other women who apparently momentarily left their preoccupations and joined Idrusa and me in my first Tarot reading. "Just pick the one that calls you, without thinking," Viola tells me. I raise my left hand and start moving it over the circle of cards. I try to silence all my ruffled thoughts, and I realize that in order to do so I have to close my eyes. My hand becomes my eye, and I pick my first card where I think the warm, tingling feeling in my palm originates. I pick my first card without turning it, and I give it to Idrusa, who carefully places it face down, at the center of the table. I pick another six cards using the same technique, and Idrusa places them according to a precise order described in the book. After my seventh card, a V-shaped pattern appears on the table – my first seagull wings interrogation.*

***

Vulnerability. Vulnerability is how anthropologist and folklorist Sabina Magliocco understands the practice of

88 She was using the Italian version of the Osho Zen Tarot cards.

her ethnography among contemporary Pagans in the San Francisco area,[89] echoing Ruth Behar's "vulnerable observer." Vulnerability and, quoting the theologian and scholar of contemporary Paganism Jone Salomonsen, a "method of compassion" characterizes her (and others') work as well as mine.[90] This "experiential" way to approach not only fieldwork but the "extraordinary experiences" encountered on the field is what has been characterizing the ethnographic work of many religionists, and not only of those who study "magic."[91] In fact, this approach has a long story—albeit not always easily acknowledged in anthropology. In the context of studies of contemporary Paganism, while this "participatory" approach has not been the only one used by scholars, it is the one I followed for this research. I chose not to limit myself to adopting a "participant" status, but I tried to engage with my interlocutors by taking them and their experiences seriously. While I had not been interested in exoteric practices before meeting the Sisters, the "extraordinary experiences"[92] that I had while spending my time with my them and their friends and acquaintances gradually became part of my way of being in the world. I therefore "bracketed" my skeptical,

89 See Magliocco, *Witching Culture.*

90 Jone Salomonsen, "Methods of Compassion or Pretension? Conducting Anthropological Fieldwork in Modern Magical Communities," *The Pomegranate: The International Journal of Pagan Studies* 8 (1999): 4–13. On the positionality of the researcher in the study of Paganism, in particular, see also, e.g., Douglas Ezzy, "Practicing the Witch's Craft," in Blain, et al., *Researching Paganisms*, 113–28; Ronald Hutton, "Living with Witchcraft," in Blain, et al. 171–88; Graham Harvey, "Pagan Studies or the Study of Paganisms? A Case Study in the Study of Religions," in Blain, et al., *Researching Paganisms*, 241–55. See also Fadeke Castor. *Spiritual Citizenship: Transnational Pathways from Black Power to Ifá in Trinidad*. (Durham: Duke University Press, 2017).

91 Magliocco, *Witching Culture*, 14.

92 On the anthropology of the paranormal, or "paranthropology," see, e.g., Jack Hunter, "Engaging the Anomalous: Reflections from the Anthropology of the Paranormal." *European Journal of Psychotherapy & Counselling* 18, no. 2(2016): 170–78; Jack Hunter and George P. Hansen. *Engaging the Anomalous* (n,p: August Night Books, 2018); Diana Espírito Santo and Jack Hunter, *Mattering the Invisible* (New York: Berghahn Books, 2021).

and maybe defensive, approach to "spirituality" and to the "uncanny" and tried to experience it "from within." If, as the Sister claimed, their way of experiencing the world could be taught, I wanted to learn it. As a matter of fact, I tried to follow in my own specific ways and as genuinely as I could what the women I met were trying to teach me. This "as-if approach" allowed me, at the beginning of my ethnography, to transcend the dichotomy "insider/outsider" and to adopt an attitude similar to the one explained in depth by Magliocco. To those interested to know whether she (and I) was an "outsider" or an "insider" of the spiritual movement she (or I) studied, she replies (and I, with her), "I am neither and both."[93] Mostly, then, this book is a narration of my many vulnerabilities: the one I experienced as a struggling human being in front of the death of her beloved ones, the one I chose to experience as a novice, on the field, with my interlocutors, and the one I might experience today, as a scholar who could be easily defined by her colleagues as an "anthropologist who went native." While the stigma that went with this expression is not probably as powerful as it would have been some decades ago, I am

93 I believe, in fact, that "The ethnographic perspective is not about being an objective observer of a culture, but rather about containing within one body multiple, simultaneous frames of reference with which to interpret experience, and being able to shift easily from one to the other." (Magliocco, *Witching Culture*, 15). In adopting an approach to the ethnography and study of religion that privileges practices over belief, I follow Jennifer Scheper-Hughes ("Mysterium Materiae," 22) who claims, "I must bracket, for now, the fraught question of whether scholars must adopt or share the beliefs of our subjects (becoming themselves 'insiders'), or instead, whether scholarship is improved if we preserve our 'objectivity' and critical distance. Yet allow me to suggest here that an approach to religious studies that privileges ritual performance over belief, exterior expressions over interior states, and the *material tremendum* over the invisible *mysterium,* is far less concerned to scrutinize the belief (or lack of belief) of the scholar themselves. If religion is sometimes more about 'doing' than about 'believing,' then—in this one respect, for a fleeting moment—there may not be much that distinguishes the 'agnostic' scholar who temporarily assumes devotional postures toward vital objects for research purposes from the life-long 'devotee' bowing down beside them—although it may be likely that in the very next moment a vast gulf divides them."

nonetheless quite aware of the fact that "going native" is still not advisable—and for important reasons. Nonetheless, as a not-so-novice (nor naïve) ethnographer, I realized, after a few weeks on the field, that accepting the possibility of "going native" was not something that I had to simply entertain and tolerate, but it represented the only way, *for me,* to seriously embark in this anthropological study.[94] The risks of being "changed" by the field was not only a risk that I was willing to take, but a necessary step for being able to investigate the topic of my research thoroughly.[95]It was not only a way to respect, honor, and give justice to the experiences of my interlocutors, but using myself as an instrument was the only way for me to understand their world. I strongly believe that I would never have been able to see and describe the transformative dimensions of the "expanded present" historicity and, even less, its implications for the anthropological understandings of magic and the pursuit of well-being that I describe in this book, if I did not allow myself to "go native."

***

"I do not read reversed cards," Idrusa warns me before moving on. I am not sure if she is talking to me or to the cards. Nonetheless, it's time for me to turn the first card I chose. Idrusa is concentrated on my Tarot reading, and, especially, on keeping a connection with me. Viola is still texting, and Senefera and Patrizia chatting. I feel slightly anxious, but I try not to give this detail

94 See Dagmar Wernitznig, *Going Native or Going Naive?: White Shamanism and the Neo-Noble Savage* (Lanham, MD: University Press of America, 2003).

95 On "going native," experiential ethnography, the study of "extraordinary" experiences, and being "changed" in the field see, e.g., Paul Stoller "Ethnography/Memoir/Imagination/Story," in *Anthropology and Humanism* 32, no. 2 (2007): 178–91; Bruce Granville Miller and Jean-Guy Goulet, eds., *Extraordinary Anthropology. Transformations in the Field* (Lincoln: University of Nebraska Press, 2007); Bonnie Glass-Coffin, "Anthropology, Shamanism, and Alternate Ways of Knowing-Being in the World: One Anthropologist's Journey of Discovery and Transformation." *Anthropology and Humanism* 35, no. 2 (2010): 204–17; Joan Koss-Chioino, et al., "Do Spirits Exist? Ways to Know," *Anthropology and Humanism* 35, no. 2 (2010): 131–226.

and its possible implications too many thoughts. I never thought I would find myself in this situation: I had never been attracted to clairvoyance or to the "uncanny," not even remotely. I look at myself "from the outside," and I see a tired woman in a difficult life period with no idea of the direction her life should take. I see a brave woman who faces her discomfort, uneasiness, and pain with integrity and resilience. I see a struggling woman who cannot tie up her loose ends, feels broken, and who asks advice to some cards.

I smile.

Everything, in spite of what I would have imagined, is making sense to me. I never approached inanimate objects as a source of advice before, but I also feel I do not have strong personal opinions on this subject, yet. While reaching for my first card, I recall my Catholic education, and what I was told about these practices and the "demoniac."

I smile and sigh.

I try not to think. Again.

***

There are a couple of elements that I immediately learned when I started to hang out with the women of the circle and with their friends: they are very suspicious of performances that lack spontaneity and firmly believe that "the mind is a monkey." Therefore, since I am a scholar, and clearly quite "mental" from their point of view (which is not always a compliment), at the very beginning of my fieldwork I could feel a lingering yet understandable sentiment of suspicion towards me. The Sisters and my interlocutors were always very kind to me, but I was not included in their more private activities right from the beginning. I was welcomed in many of the activities reserved to their "clients" or "public," but I was not invited to their private rituals or gatherings. It took me a good half year to be fully included in their activities, and eventually, for most of them, my "being mental" became, non-judgmentally, just part of my way of being.

***

"This card, Giovanna, corresponds to the qui-e-ora (here-and-now), the 'take-off' card," continues Idrusa, looking straight into my eyes.

***

The "here" (*qui*) and (*e*) "now" (*ora*) that my women call "*qui-e-ora*" and I call "expanded present" or "presence in the present" is, together with the Sisters, the protagonist of this book. What I call "expanded" present and my interlocutors call "presence" or "*qui-e-ora*," is the particular historicity (i.e., way of conceiving and experiencing time, history, and temporality) in which my interlocutors' quest for well-being and fulfillment takes place.[96] For the women of the *cerchio* and for many of their Salentine friends or clients, being in the *qui-e-ora* is not merely a form of "mindfulness." The "presence in the present," as opposed to the meditating practice so common in the Western world, is not conceived linearly: charged of—"karmic" and "non-karmic"—past

96 On the notion of historicity and on recent development in the anthropology of history see Charles Stewart, *Dreaming and Historical Consciousness in Island Greece* (Cambridge, MA: Harvard University, 2012) and "Historicity and Anthropology," *Annual Review of Anthropology* 45 (2016): 79–94; Matt Hodges, "The Time of the Interval: Historicity, Modernity, and Epoch in Rural France," *American Ethnologist* 37, no. 1 (2010): 115–31 and "Reinventing 'History'?," *History and Anthropology* 26, no. 4 (2015): 515–27; Stephan Palmié and Charles Stewart, "Introduction," *HAU: Journal of Ethnographic Theory* 6, no. 1 (2016): 207–36; and chapter 3. On time and anthropology, specifically, see, e.g., Johannes Fabian, *Time and the Other: How Anthropology Makes Its Object* (New York: Columbia University Press, 1983); Kevin K. Birth, *Time Blind: Problems in Perceiving Other Temporalities* (Cham, Switzerland: Palgrave Macmillan, 2017); Carol J. Greenhouse, *Moment's Notice: Time Politics Across Cultures* (Ithaca, NY: Cornell University Press, 2018); Alfred Gell, *The Anthropology of Time: Cultural Constructions of Temporal Maps and Images* (Oxford: Berg, 1992); Bryant and Knight, *Anthropology of the Future*; Elisabeth Kirtsoglou and Bob Simpson, *The Time of Anthropology: Studies of Contemporary Chronopolitics* (London: Routledge, 2020). See also Barad, "Troubling Time/s"; Helen Cornish, "Spelling Out History: Transforming Witchcraft Past and Present," *The Pomegranate: The International Journal of Pagan Studies* 11 no. 1 (2009): 14–28 and "Fashioning Magic, Fashioning History: the Past and Present of Modern Witchcraft," *Magic, Ritual, and Witchcraft* 16, no. 3 (2021): 389–97.

and future events, it embraces all three temporalities at the same time. Presence is, therefore, not the result of "bracketing" dimensions that are not "in the moment" (past and future). Rather, it is the result of embracing, with a growing awareness, the different dimensions, rhizomes, presences, and connections embedded in the past-present-future coevality of the *qui-e-ora*. This growing awareness that I witnessed ethnographically is the result of many of the "body-mind" practices such as Tarot reading, meditation, the use of pendula, family constellations, of the various "magical" practices that I mentioned above, and of many of the elements that are usually recognized as belonging to "global" Wiccan and contemporary Pagan communities.[97] Mostly, though, this "presence" among my Salentine interlocutors is achieved through singing, playing, and/or dancing *pizzica*. This coevality, I argue, differs from what is referred to as "polichronicity": the latter, while acknowledging the compresence of different time periods in a given "present" and "place," still understands them within a linear framework and is normally linked to specific places and non-ordinary events.[98]

Pizzica is a healing spiritual practice for the Sisters since it allows a "presence in history" to tweak de Martino's expression[99] (see chapter 2) that goes beyond commonsensical understandings and experiences of time. Practicing *pizzica* and other "global" features of Paganism within a historicity rooted in an "expanded present" is "healing" since it allows the women of the *cerchio* to "karmically" conceive of their lives from the point of view of the persons they are,

97 See, e.g., Strmiska, "Modern Paganism in World Cultures"; and Rountree, "Localizing Neo-Paganism."

98 Howell writes that "The theory of 'polychronic' or 'multi-temporal' times and places, used particularly in regard to archaeological sites, posits a site where multiple time periods intersect and overlap . . . These sites are 'polychronic' because different time periods mix, seep into each other, and 'percolate' together . . . like coffee, making (in this case) a stimulating, complex temporal brew." (Francesca C. Howell, "Sense of Place," 46–47.)

99 de Martino, *La terra del rimorso*.

and are meant to be, but that they are not yet—i.e., to focus on their own "becoming."

***

Idrusa's hands caress my first card while my heart beats fast. "Il matto!" (the fool).

A roar rises around me. I do not understand what is happening. Viola moves towards me and hugs me, Idrusa smiles and so do the others, while loudly and enthusiastically cheering for me.

I am puzzled. I do feel like a fool, in fact. Am I? I wonder.[100]

100 The card of the Fool, as I pointed out at the very beginning of this chapter, is associated with new beginnings and trust in life. It symbolizes a joyful appreciation of one's life journey, wherever it leads. It is the "card 0" of the Tarot that are often considered as narrating the story of the "Fool's Journey." For the Sisters of the *cerchio,* this card is an extremely positive card, one that they associate with being in the *qui e ora,* with a positive attitude towards life, and with a well-balanced approach to one's situation. I believe that, at many levels, the fact that I drew this precise card as my first card ever meant a lot to the Sisters of the *cerchio* who, after this reading, felt certain that I could be trusted.

Chapter 2

Il Mago/The Magician

[Keywords: Manifestation, Alchemy, Consciousness, Creativity, Magic]

Figure 3. An offer to the (Adriatic) sea. Photo credit: Giovanna Parmigiani.

June 29th, 4:14 am. I am sitting alone on a bench in front of the octagonal bell tower of the town of Soleto. The air is sweet-smelling. Soft and sugary like a peach, it carries the explosion of abundance of the new solstice. Sugary and sticky like licorice sticks, it conveys the insouciance that summers always promise *and never fully deliver, leaving you at the same time queasy and wanting for more.*

A stray ginger cat comes by: it draws helices around my legs, tossing question marks with its tail. What is this feline asking me? What is it trying to tell me? I wonder how a white-dressed human in the dark of the night might look into its eyes that, better than mine, can see into (many layers of) darkness. The cat is friendly. Trusting its wisdom, I take its friendliness as a sign of approval.

I watch the slow and solemn movements of the cat and notice a tingling feeling at the back of my neck: it irradiates through the top of my head, sketching spirals, and it runs through my spine, leaving a knot in my throat. Maybe, I wonder, similarly to Bodini's men from Cocumola, this knot has the purpose of "reminding me about the heart."[1] *I feel the energy of the bell tower behind me: a liquid invisible light that gets across me and makes me waver.*

***

1 Cocumola is a small town in Salento, and the protagonist of the following poem by the Salentinian poet Vittorio Bodini (the English translation is mine):

Cocumola

Un paese che si chiama Cocumola
è
come avere le mani sporche di farina
e un portoncino verde color limone.
Uomini con camicie silenziose fanno un nodo al fazzoletto per ricordarsi del cuore.
Il tabacco è *a seccare,*
e la vita cocumola fra le pentole
dove donne pennute assaggiano il brodo».

Cocumola

A town called Cocumola
is
like having hands covered with flour
and a little, lemon-green door.
Men with silent shirts tie knots at their handkerchiefs to remember the heart.
The tobacco is drying,
and life is cocumoling* between pots and pans
where feathered women taste the broth.

* [Translator's note: the name of the town is used here onomatopoeically to refer to the sound of the simmering broth].

During my apprenticeship with the Sisters, I underwent a sort of "energy-sensing" training. Everything carries its own energy, according to the Sisters and many of their friends: a peculiar vibrational signature that all humans can learn to recognize.[2] Persons, places, non-human and non-obvious beings, rocks: they all can be felt and comprehended at an energetic level. This can be experienced in different ways and sensed in the physical body, too. It can take the shape of shivers, goosebumps, or of a sort of electricity that runs through the body. It can manifest at the level of the main "chakras" in the form of pressure, mild pain, or through some sort of activation of one of them: for example, cough for the fifth chakra; nausea for the third; headache for the sixth. Acknowledging this dimension of "reality" is of key importance in the spiritual practice of the *cerchio*, and learning to sense and make sense of energetic fields and exchanges is one of the main elements employed to connect with human, non-human, and more-than-human, non-obvious, presences.[3]

I had never framed social interactions or experiences of places in this way before meeting the Sisters. While I definitely felt good in some places and with certain persons and not-as-good in other contexts and relations, my folk-theories on social interactions did not rely on language and images linked to an energy-related semantic field. My acknowledgement of contexts and relations was quite rudimental, so to speak, from this point of view, and I never considered concealing my ignorance to the Sisters. First of all, I was genuinely interested in trying to perceive what they

2 For a comparison, see, e.g., Sabina Magliocco, "New Age and Neopagan Magic," in *The Cambridge History of Magic and Witchcraft in the West*, ed. David J. Collins (Cambridge: Cambridge University Press, 2015), 635–64; Fedele, "Metamorphoses of Neopaganism," and *Looking for Mary Magdalene*; Anna Fedele and Ruy Llera Blanes, eds., *Encounters of Body and Soul in Contemporary Religious Practices* (New York: Berghahn Books, 2011); Howell, *Food, Festival, and Religion*.

3 For a comparison, on the energies of "place," see Howell, *Food, Festival, and Religion*.

were saying they were perceiving. Moreover, since they were way more versed than me in tuning into the "energetic level" of interactions (whatever they meant with it) they could "feel" me and my (lack of) competence in energetic analyses anyway. There was no point in trying to hide it. If some—scholars and non-scholars alike—might feel uncomfortable in dealing with interlocutors that claim to perceive you according to categories that you cannot comprehend, let alone control, I was literally thriving in this situation. I could just be, let go of control, surrender to existence, to presence. To me, not having to explain, describe, define, state, or verbally position myself in relation to the Sisters, to my research, or to what they were teaching me was relieving, even invigorating. I was sincerely trying to learn and did not want to hide anything from them. Since they could feel my openness, apparently, I was accepted by the Sisters with warmth, generosity, and even enthusiasm.

If most of the people I met can distinguish between "positive" and "negative" energies on the basis of the feelings and sensations that they experience, over the years I spent with the Sisters I found that this distinguishing is not the only dimension that could be meaningful in energy assessment practices. If the polarity of energies, so to speak, is quite important and sometimes even obvious, oftentimes what is more easily perceived is the energetic intensity of a person, situation, place, or object—as in my experiencing the Soleto bell tower. In other words, if distinguishing between energies that are "good" or "bad" *in se* and/or *for you* is of importance, sometimes it is the "*tremendum*" (or the "*fascinans*") of these energies that defines them, even more than their particular qualities.[4] What you do, how

4 The theologian and historian of religions Rudolf Otto used the Latin expression "*mysterium tremendum et fascinans*" to refer to the "awe-inspiring mystery" of religious experiences. In the attempt to give a phenomenologically oriented description of religion, he used *tremendum* to refer to the quality of the emotions triggered by being in relation with the "numinous"—or the "sacred," understood as "entirely other." While I do not completely align with such a

you react, or if and how you decide to "stay" in that *tremendum/fascinans* is at the core of many spiritual experiences.

While some of the Sisters speak about "evil" as an agentive force or energy and frame our experience on Earth as a confrontation with it, for most of the contemporary Pagans I met in Salento "good" and "bad" are relative concepts. Framed as results of personal engagements with the dynamics that link "light" and "shadow," they do not consider "bad" energies as necessarily "evil." While they might want to avoid them to make space for less challenging experiences as bearers of their "life lessons" or to strengthen their "boundaries" to defuse them, for example, by visualizing the "light cocoon" that I described in chapter 1, they do not frame unpleasant feelings or circumstances as necessarily "negative." Rather, "bad" energies, in their experience, are understood in a way that is closer to the etymology of the English term: they are *inadequate* and *adverse*, but the discomfort they may trigger is not necessarily hostility. That is, it does not ineludibly have moral connotations. "Shadow," in fact, while often associated with personal limitations and difficult life circumstances, is mostly considered nothing more than hollowness: it does not have any ontological substance other than being the "absence of light."

On the contrary, "light" is considered as the matrix of life in all its forms: a capacious and overarching energy of

---

way to frame religious experience, I nonetheless find the notion of *tremendum* useful to gesture towards the "unqualified" emotions linked to magical experience in the context of a world known "energetically" —i.e., as it is experienced by my interlocutors on the field. See Rudolf Otto, *The Idea of the Holy: An Inquiry into the Non-Rational Factor in the Idea of the Divine and Its Relation to the Rational* (New York: Oxford University Press, 1958). On the notion of *tremendum* see, e.g., Omar McRoberts, "Beyond Mysterium Tremendum: Thoughts toward an Aesthetic Study of Religious Experience," *The Annals of the American Academy of Political and Social Science* 595, no. 1 (2004): 190–203; Stephan Palmié, "Fascinans or Tremendum? Permutations of the State, the Body, and the Divine in Late-Twentieth-Century Havana," *Nieuwe West-Indische Gids* 78, no3. 3–4 (2004): 229–68; Scheper-Hughes, "Mysterium Materiae."

expansion, otherwise called "love."[5] Love is what moves the universe and what moves the lives of "all that it is," including human life on the planet Earth. Love is the destination and destiny, and the essence of the journey of and on this planet, for humans and non-humans alike. Love is presence, is "expanded presence," and the Sisters choose to call themselves in relation to it. They are *operatrici di luce* – light workers – or, sometimes, *guerriere di luce* – light warriors.

Love is what makes the universe and is also what makes us. People, animals, plants, waters, rocks: we are all connected with one another. This belief in the interconnectedness and relationality of the universe is something that informs not only spiritual practices but also the ways Salentine Pagans approach knowledge.[6] In other words, "interconnectedness" and the "love matrix" are not only ontological issues but also epistemological ones for the Sisters.[7] As a result, they also have political implications. From psychology to quantum theory, from religious traditions to philosophy, from literature to biology, human knowledge is read by my interlocutors through a lens that stresses (real or fictional) connections and analogies.[8] While

5 For a comparison, see, e.g., Magliocco "New Age and Neopagan Magic"; Fedele, "Metamorphoses of Neopaganism"; Fedele and Llera Blanes, *Encounters of Body and Soul*; Howell, *Food, Festival, and Religion*.

6 The vast majority of my interlocutors read the "love matrix" within a perspective that resonates with contemporary versions of perennialism, that is to say "is the notion that there is an eternal truth or wisdom which can be accessed and has been expressed in the world by various elements down through the ages" (Colin Duggan, "Perennialism and Iconoclasm: Chaos Magick and the Legitimacy of Innovation," in *Contemporary Esotericism*, ed. Egil Asprem and Kennet Granholm, [London: Routledge, 2013], 99. In this sense, they are in line with other esoteric traditions.

7 See, for a comparison, the literature on "New Animism" or "neo-animism," for example, Graham Harvey, *Animism: Respecting the Living World* (New York: Columbia University Press, 2006), and "Bear Feasts in a Land without Wild. Bears," *IJSNR* 9, no. 2 (2019): 195–213; and chapter 5.

8 On apophenia, or the inclination to see meaningful patterns in random or unrelated objects, events, elements, and circumstances see, e.g., Susan Claudia Lepselter, *Resonance of Unseen Things: Poetics, Power, Captivity, and*

they are very respectful of and open to listening to different histories, experiences, traditions, and journeys, they are not interested in delving into the complexity of distinguishing between schools, interpretations, orientations, contexts, and disciplines. They are not interested in the details that *divide* experiences and practices. They find all this divisive. What they really want to stress is our interconnectedness, our interdependence, and relationality. This is a spiritual as well as a political statement, since one's wellbeing is framed as depending on the wellbeing of those who are around her: nature, humans, spirits.[9]

If every experience is individual and the paths to self-realization are as many as the number of individuals that have been inhabiting and will inhabit this planet, they are not egoistic enterprises: since we are all one, we are co-dependent, and the well-being of one impacts the well-being of others (see chapter 5). In other words, Salentine Pagans really follow the Medieval and Renaissance alchemist principle stated in the hermetic text *Tabula Smaragdina* (Emerald Tablet): "*Verum, sine mendacio, certum et verissimum: quod est inferius est sicut quod est superius. Et quod est superius est sicut quod est inferius.*"[10] Their "spiritual

UFOs in the American Uncanny (Ann Arbor, MI: University of Michigan Press, 2016). On apophenia and magic, in particular, see e.g., Susan Greenwood, "A Spectrum of Magical Consciousness: Conspiracy Theories and the Stories We Tell Ourselves." *Anthropology Today* 38 no 1 (2022): 3–7.

9 For a thorough description of similar attitudes towards the world, see, e.g., Hanegraaff, *New Age Religion*.

10 "It is true, without lying, sure and certain: what is below is like what is above. And what is above is like what is below" (my translation). It is worth pointing out that what is known today with the term "contemporary Paganism" and/or "New Age Spirituality" could be considered as part of a wider and multifaceted phenomenon called (Western) Esotericism. This body of knowledge and of practices is deemed to be the representative of a corpus of theories and systems that, with the unfoldment of modernity, were (and were considered as) "rejected." It is worth highlighting, though, that "rejected," here, is not a synonym of "disappeared." In fact, the dialectic between mainstream modernities and what was referred to as the "occult" has always been central to Modernist discourses, albeit within a framework that wanted to delegitimize, marginalize, stigmatize, and ridicule both the "hidden knowledge" itself and

alchemy," or their transformation journey towards their "true" although "not yet" attained versions of themselves, is not only a personal enterprise but it is a responsibility towards others and all that is.

***

Legend has it that the impressive bell tower of Soleto was constructed in a single night by an army of demons and witches,

---

its followers. The same applies today, and it could be argued that contemporary phenomena such as "conspirituality" are expressions of new ways to frame these debates and tensions. According to Ward and Voas, who first introduced this term, conspirituality is: "a politico-spiritual philosophy based on two core convictions, the first traditional to conspiracy theory, the second rooted in the New Age: (1) A secret group covertly controls, or is trying to control, the political and social order . . . (2) Humanity is undergoing a 'paradigm shift' in consciousness, or awareness, so solutions to (1) lie in acting in accordance with an awakened 'new paradigm' worldview." (Charlotte Ward and David Voas, "The Emergence of Conspirituality," in *Journal of Contemporary Religion* 26, no. 1 [2011]: 104. On (Western) Esotericism see, e.g., Antoine Faivre, *Access to Western Esotericism* (Albany: State University of New York Press, 1994); Colin Campbell, "The Cult, the Cultic Milieu and Secularization," in *A Sociological Yearbook of Religion in Britain,* ed. Michael Hill (London: S.C.M. Press, 1972), 119-36; Kocku von Stuckrad, *Western Esotericism: A Brief History of Secret Knowledge* (London: Equinox, 2005), and "Western Esotericism: Towards an Integrative Model of Interpretation," *Religion* 35 (2005): 78-97; Olav Hammer, *Claiming Knowledge: Strategies of Epistemology from Theosophy to the New Age* (Leiden: Brill, 2001); Christopher Partridge, *The Re-Enchantment of the West: Vols 1 and 2* (London;: T&T Clark, 2004, 2005.); Wouter J. Hanegraaff, *Esotericism and the Academy: Rejected Knowledge in Western Culture* (Cambridge: Cambridge University Press, 2012), *New Age Religion,* and "On the Construction of 'Esoteric Traditions,'" in *Western Esotericism and the Science of Religion,* ed. Antoine Faivre and Wouter J. Hanegraaff (Leuven: Peeters, 1998), 11-61. On conspirituality, in particular, see Ward and Voas, "Emergence of Conspirituality"; Egil Asprem and Asbjørn Dyrendal, "Conspirituality Reconsidered: How Surprising and How New is the Confluence of Spirituality and Conspiracy Theory?," *Journal of Contemporary Religion* 30, no. 3 (2015): 367-82; Asbjørn Dyrendal, "Hidden Knowledge, Hidden Powers: Esotericism and Conspiracy Culture," in *Contemporary Esotericism,* ed. Egil Asprem and Kennet Granholm (London: Routledge, 2013), 210-35, and "Norwegian 'Conspirituality': A Brief Sketch," in Lewis and Tøllefsen, eds., *Handbook of Nordic New Religions,* 268-90; David G. Robertson, Egil Asprem, and Asbjørn Dyrendal, "Introducing the Field: Conspiracy Theory in, about, and as Religion," in *Handbook of Conspiracy Theory and Contemporary Religion,* ed. Egil Asprem, Asbjørn Dyrendal, and David G. Robertson (Leiden: Brill, 2018), 1-18; Parmigiani, "Magic and Politics."

orchestrated by the alchemist Matteo Tafuri – a well-known Apulian philosopher, physician, and astrologer who lived between the fifteenth and the sixteenth centuries.[11]

As I feel the energy of the bell tower I think about the story of Matteo Tafuri, a story of medicine and Inquisition. Celebrated beyond Apulia, he studied in Paris and Spain before returning to Soleto. After traveling around the world, he came home only to live the last years of his life facing accusations of magic and sorcery. He came back to his "Soletum desertum,"[12] *the hometown he had abandoned, only to acknowledge, once again, the distance between the "stars" of his desire and the astrologer himself.*

Sol-eto: his not-yet-delivered promise of insouciance.

Sol-eto: his own, bittersweet, summer Sol-stice.[13]

It's maybe the most important star he followed in that particular journey of his soul.

***

If the winter solstice is the celebration of light in the midst of darkness, the summer one is the celebration of a gap, a lack in the midst of abundance. It is the festival, so to speak, of dissatisfaction, of longing, of a never-fully-delivered insouciance. This feeling of "lack" is a *stella mattutina* (morning star) in the journey of the "fool" in the Tarot, which is the path of all human beings in search of meaning and realization, according to the Sisters. It guides and directs the steps of these "fools" and is the source of their wisdom.

This "gap," that the contemporary Pagans I met call "desire," does not necessarily come from a place of fear, ingratitude, or scarcity. Rather, it stems from a feeling of

11 For this reason, Soleto is currently referred to as "the town of the witches" (in dialect, *macare*).

12 Literally, in Latin, "Abandoned Soleto." This is how the city is mentioned by Pliny the Elder (Plin., *Nat.* 3.11. s. 16). Soleto appears with the toponym "Sol" and "Salentum" in (possibly) the most ancient map ever discovered, dating circa 500 BCE, found in Soleto in 2003.

13 "Sol," in Latin, means "sun." Sol is part of the etymology of the term "solstice" and appears in the insignia of the town of Soleto.

trust, gratitude, and abundance: it is the celebration of our human infinitude. *Desiderare*, the Italian word for desiring, comes from the Latin *de-sidera*, meaning "being away from the stars." It is an alternative to the action of *considerare*, to consider: the ancient practice of observing, studying, and, ultimately, following the "oracle" of the stars—that is, what is *already* set.[14] The summer solstice is therefore, for Salentine Pagans, the celebration of the capacity of our hearts of exceeding expectations, of expanding our horizons and imagination beyond set boundaries: a creative action that comprises multiple dimensions and possibilities and not just "what is." It is the driving force behind our actions, the mark of our being at the core of ourselves, consubstantial with the same "Love" that governs the universe. Something that Matteo Tafuri from Soleto—the astrologer and alchemist, the wise "fool" chased by the Inquisition—seemed to have known quite well.

Desiring is of key importance in the spiritual practice of the Sisters of the *cerchio*, and, I argue, is a *political* practice. It lies at the core of their capacity for inclusion, for understanding, for transforming the world. In her article on protest suicide, anthropologist Karin Andriolo offers a reading of the novel *Elizabeth Costello* by J.M. Coetzee. She claims that the novelist's understanding of imagination may shed some light on suicide as a form of political protest.[15] For Andriolo, "imagining" is an "embodied minding,"—meaning both caring and mental reasoning. "Imagining can penetrate into territories that are impossible for abstract thought," and "engages the body as an experiential and metaphorical site."[16] As I claimed for the feminists I studied in Salento, imagining can be considered a political practice within a Rancièrian understanding of politics centered on

14 On this topic see, for example, the work of Igor Sibaldi, a spiritual teacher followed also by some of the Sisters of the *cerchio*.

15 Andriolo, "The Twice-Killed."

16 Ibid., 100–01.

"sensing" in contemporary Pagan contexts as well.[17] The French philosopher Jacques Rancière suggests that politics is, primarily, a "way of framing, among sensory data, a specific sphere of experience."[18] It is a "partition" of what can be sensed, seen, experienced, and said, which, consequently, can or cannot make space for certain data and subjects to emerge. This "partition of the sensible," or "regimes of perceptions," is what is generally referred to as "common sense."[19] The aim of politics and of art, in this perspective, is a reconfiguration of the sensible. By "sensible," Rancière refers to both what makes sense and what can be sensed.[20] Following such a definition of aesthetics Rancière develops a philosophy that puts the aesthetic and sensory experiences at the center of political action. In particular, he understands democracy as linked to *dissensus* (in Latin, sensing differently). *Dissensus* is the moment in which the experiences "of those who have no part"—those who are not recognized by the majority and are not included in the political "distribution of the sensible"—are inscribed in society.[21] In other words, *dissensus* (which includes both cognitive and affective dimensions) is intrinsically political in as much as it challenges "common sense" by broadening the sensorium at a given time and space. This, I argue, is what happens in the political actions of "imagination," that is, in the political practice of "desiring" among contemporary Pagans: it starts at an individual level and it expands so as to encompass human and non-human lives.[22]

17 Parmigiani, "Spiritual *Pizzica*."

18 Jacques Rancière, "The Politics of Literature," *SubStance* 33, no. 1 (2004): 10.

19 Davide Panagia, *The Political Life of Sensation* (Durham, NC: Duke University Press, 2009), 7.

20 Ibid., 3.

21 Jacques Rancière, *Disagreement: Politics and Philosophy* (Minneapolis: University of Minnesota Press, 1999), 123.

22 In his 2009 book cited above, Panagia explored the possibility of putting the philosophy of Rancière in conversation with the recent philosophical investigations on affect within the so-called "affect theory" or "affective turn." The

Desiring is a form of *dissensus* among the Sisters. Preached and encouraged as something we all should (re)learn to do, it challenges the *status quo* and broadens the boundaries of inclusion.

---

affective turn (see, for example, Nigel Thrift, "Intensities of Feeling: Towards a Spatial Politics of Affect," *Geografiska Annaler: Series B, Human Geography* 86, no. 1 [2004]: 57–78 and *Non-Representational Theory: Space, Politics, Affect* [New York: Routledge, 2008]) has recently given new vitality to the field of the study of the sensory. Following the lead of Deleuze and Guattari, who developed their theories within a Spinozian approach to the study of the body, emotions, and cognition, some scholars started using the term "affect" in order to challenge sociological and anthropological interpretations that stressed dualism, linearity, and directionality over a more rhizomatic approach to the study of society (Gilles Deleuze and Felix Guattari, *A Thousand Plateaus: Capitalism and Schizophrenia* [Minneapolis: University of Minnesota Press, 1987]). See, for example, Yael Navaro-Yashin, "Affective Spaces, Melancholic Objects: Ruination and the Production of Anthropological Knowledge," *Journal of the Royal Anthropological Institute* 15, no. 1 (2009): 1–18 and *The Make-Believe Space: Affective Geography in a Postwar Polity* (Durham, NC: Duke University Press, 2012); Brian Massumi, "The Autonomy of Affect," in *Parables for the Virtual: Movement, Affect, Sensation* (Durham, NC: Duke University Press, 2002), 23–45; William Mazzarella, *Shoveling Smoke: Advertising and Globalization in Contemporary India* (Durham, NC: Duke University Press, 2003), "Culture, Globalization, Mediation," *Annual Revew of Anthropology* 33, no. 1 (2004): 345–67, and "Affect: What is it Good For?," in *Enchantments of Modernity: Empire, Nation, Globalization,* ed. Saurabh Dube (London: Routledge, 2009), 291–309; Patricia T. Clough and Jean O'Malley Halley, eds., *The Affective Turn: Theorizing the Social* (Durham, NC: Duke University Press, 2007); Melissa Gregg and Gregory J. Seigworth, eds., *The Affect Theory Reader* (Durham, NC: Duke University Press, 2010); Kathleen Stewart, *Ordinary Affects* (Durham, NC: Duke University Press, 2007); Panagia, *The Political Life of Sensation*; Teresa Brennan, *The Transmission of Affect* (Ithaca, NY: Cornell University Press, 2004); Danilyn Rutherford, "Commentary: What Affect Produces," *American Ethnologist* 39, no. 4 (2012): 688–91; Rheana "Juno" Salazár Parreñas "Producing Affect: Transnational Volunteerism in a Malaysian Orangutan Rehabilitation Center," *American Ethnologist* 39, no. 4 (2012): 673–87; Andrea Muehlebach, "On Affective Labor in Post-Fordist Italy," *Cultural Anthropology* 26, no. 1 (2011): 59–82; Valentina Napolitano, "The Virgin of Guadalupe: A Nexus of Affect," *Journal of the Royal Anthropological Institute* 15, no. 1 (2009): 96–112; Deborah Gould, "On Affect and Protest," in *Political Emotions*, ed. Janet Staiger, Ann Cvetkovich, and Ann Reynolds (New York: Routledge, 2010), 18–39; Kristyn Gorton, "Theorizing Emotions and Affects: Feminist Engagements," *Feminist Theory* 8, no. 3 (2007): 333–48; and Ann Cvetkovich, *Mixed Feelings: Feminism, Mass Culture, and Victorian Sensationalism* (New Brunswick, NJ: Rutgers University Press, 1992), "Public Feelings," *South Atlantic Quarterly* 106, no. 3 (2007): 459–68, and "Introduction," in Staiger, et al., eds., *Political Emotions*, 1–17.

When the Sisters of the *cerchio* think about desire and dissatisfaction, imagination and *dissensus*, they immediately think about particular figures whom they consider as part of their "land ancestors": the *tarantate*.

***

I sit on the bench and wait for my sisters to arrive at our meeting place while my eyes wander, scrutinizing the sky for an inkling of dawning light. We decided to organize a short pilgrimage by foot to the town of Galatina, "in lumescendo" *(at dawn), on the day of Saint Peter and Saint Paul. This is meant to be a simple ritual of the* cerchio *to honor the solstice, the saints, and, especially, a genealogy of Salento women to whom this day is inevitably connected: the tarantate.*

***

Nicoletta is a Salentinian: born in the southern part of Salento, she spent her youth in Galatina before moving to another Italian region. I met her years ago in Emilia Romagna, a northern Italian region, when I was doing research for another project on Italian feminists. She is not a contemporary Pagan, but she generously offered one of the most interesting descriptions of *tarantate* that I could find: a personal and original one.[23]

23 Nicoletta chose to answer my questions by giving me an text that she wrote on this subject, and forthcoming. Nicoletta Nuzzo, *Una Madre in Comune* (Bedonia: Rupe Mutevole editore, forthcoming). The English translation is mine. On *pizzica* and *tarantismo* see, among many others, Ernesto de Martino, *La terra del rimorso: Contributo a una storia religiosa del Sud* (Milan: Il Saggiatore, 1976 [1961]); Lapassade, *Intervista sul tarantismo*; Daboo, *Ritual, Rapture and Remorse*; Del Giudice, "Healing the Spider's Bite," and "Folk Music Revival"; Karen Lüdtke, "Dancing towards Well-Being: Reflections on the *Pizzica* in the Contemporary Salento, Italy," in *Performing Ecstasies: Music, Dance, and Ritual in the Mediterranean*, ed. Luisa del Giudice and Nancy E. Van Deusen (Ottawa: Institute of Mediaeval Music, 2005), 37–53, and *Dances with Spiders*; Pizza, *Il Tarantismo Oggi*, and "Margini"; Nacci, *Tarantismo e neotarantismo*, and *Neotarantismo*; Laviosa, "Frontier Apulia and its Filmmakers," and "Tarantula Myths and Music"; Minghelli, "Icons of Remorse"; Rossi, *Lettere da*

According to Nicoletta, if Galatina was once a town that produced milk (*gala,* in Greek) and that was associated with the Greek goddess Athena, it sadly became the town of the *tarantate*, that is,

> women who, working in the fields over the summer, were bitten by the tarantula spider and who, from then on, started to behave in an irrational, often unseemly [*sconveniente*], way: from their mouths came out what normally a respectable [*per bene*] woman would never say—swear words, curses, anger, drool... To free themselves from the furor that tormented them they danced to the sound of a tambourine, over fast, pulsing melodies; they danced frantically, taking their clothes off, messy, they rolled over on the ground, reproducing the same movements of the tarantula spider. The families, who were ashamed of all this, and in order to remove them from the nosy sight of the people, asked someone to help them to calm down by playing the guitar and the tambourine at their homes. . . . In the summer the malaise of the *tarantate* increased, and the only remedy was to ask for the favor of their protecting saint, Saint Paul. For this reason, on the day of his feast, from far-away places such as Switzerland, Germany, or other places where they had emigrated, and from towns close by in the province of Lecce, the *tarantate* arrived [in Galatina] carried in a truck, sitting in its open back, already screaming and ruffled and often wearing night gowns. This happened in the morning, very early, when there weren't people around who could see. . . . It might also happen that some of them [i.e., the *tarantate*] would run away in the middle of the street, then it happened that those [men] who were in the bar in front [of Saint Paul's church] could take advantage of that occasion to encircle them, provoking and exasperating them in order to see what unusual stunts or curses they would [i.e., the *tarantate*] become able to perform. . . . The people from Galatina, since they are protected by the Saint, are immune to the tarantula bite, and this probably explains why I have been relieved from putting on such a show. I could not avoid being terrified by their presence. I knew that the *tarantate* were so rabid that it could happen that they could attack you, maybe for something banal that one normally did not notice. One of these banal things that could infuriate them was the sight of the color red.

---

una tarantata; Signorelli, "Il tarantismo"; De Giorgi, *Tarantismo e rinascita*, and *Il Mito Del Tarantismo*; Mina and Torsello, *La Tela Infinita.*

In Nicoletta's narration, *tarantate* are associated with irrationality, turbulent emotions, disruptive behavior, and with the feeling of shame—notably, not of the protagonists but of the observers, who see *tarantate* as passive *vis-à-vis* their own malaise. They are described as frightening, but also ridiculed, and they are somehow blamed for the fact of being related to their hometowns and their inhabitants, who became associated with these messy performances instead of being considered as heirs of ancient Greek culture. Mostly, though, the *tarantate* are seen as somehow subjected to their own bodies: their suffering is considered to be put on public display in a perspective that positions them at the threshold between being affected by *protagonismo* and being socially unfit.[24]

Protagonismo, the Italian for "protagonism," is an ambivalent concept in the Salento context. Generally, it is not thought to be a compliment. Associated with what is understood as a culpable form of narcissism, it is considered the result of behaviors of people who do not know their place, and who, in so doing, both challenge the *status quo* and become an object of ridicule or, sometimes, rage. *Mettersi in mostra*, showing off, in Salento is an expression often used to criticize persons and behaviors, and is a key trope in the particular *genre* of interaction that is the local "gossip." If *protagonismo* is considered the result of giving into a temptation, then showing off is also indirectly considered as a coaxing perspective for many, at the very least. It is therefore not surprising that, in Nicoletta's words, *tarantate* are objects of nosy gazes, of judgment, and even pity. The *tarantate* were powerful and scary because they embodied something repressed, according to both Nicoletta and the Sisters. The Salentine Pagans

24 This understanding of *tarantate* could be read in relationship to what Judith Butler claims as the "destitute other" in"Bodies in Alliance and the Politics of the Street," in *Sensible Politics*, ed. Meg McLagan and Yates McKee [New York: Zone Books, 2012], 121–22).

think differently about traditional interpretations of *tarantate*: my interlocutors believe that the *tarantate* were feared and pitied not because of their maladies, but because they had the courage to declare, through and with their bodies, what many consider tempting but dangerous, suppressed but fascinating: their dissatisfaction, their *dissensus* – in other words, their infinitude. Around the days of the summer solstice the *tarantate* publicly acknowledged, declared, and embodied the infinitude of their desire, the gap that measured their distance from the "stars." The feelings of uneasiness around the *tarantate* and the actions that aim at ridiculing or dismissing them and their message stem from this general suppressed feeling, according to the Sisters. Most of us forget how to connect with our infinitude, fail to recall our being "star seeds." *Tarantate*, therefore, are teachers in our re-appropriation of our desires, and dancing *pizzica* is both a way to honor their teachings and an embodied form of apprenticeship. It is, similarly to what anthropologist Janice Boddy has claimed for spirit possession in Sudan,[25] an embodied way to share knowledge between generations, for the Sisters, and to honor their land ancestors.[26]

A link between the unsettling *tarantate* of the past and contemporary struggles emerges also in the rest of Nicoletta's story, although framed differently. In this part of her text, she focuses on how representations and audiences have a leading role in the way she understands not just the *tarantate*, but her own being a woman.

25 Janice Boddy, "Spirits and Selves in Northern Sudan: The Cultural Therapeutics of Possession and Trance," *American Ethnologist* 15, no. 1 (1988): 4–27, "Subversive Kinship: The Role of Spirit Possession in Negotiating Social Place in Rural Northern Sudan," *PoLAR* 16, no. 2 (1993): 29–38, and "Spirit Possession Revisited: Beyond Instrumentality," *Annual Review of Anthropology* 23, no. 1 (1994): 407–34,

26 For a comparison, see John C. McCall, *Dancing Histories: Heuristic Ethnography with the Ohafia Igbo* (Ann Arbor: University of Michigan Press, 2000); see also Daboo, *Ritual, Rapture and Remorse* on dance, time, and history.

> These are my memories on the *tarantate* . . . In writing, and in particular in poetry, [I can] find the id-skin [*io pelle*] that allows me to expose myself in a defenseless nakedness without being vulnerable. Poetry for me is body . . . the same messy and sorrowful [*dolente*, in Italian it has also physical connotations] body of the *tarantate*, but inside an interior space inhabited by my own gaze . . . for the *tarantate*, by contrast, it is once again by the exposition on the square that their own suffering becomes another condemnation, another judgment. In front of these women who bared their bodies and souls is the innocent dignity of those who suffer again the violation of the gaze of the other. But then the music started, the dance takes control over the narration of a female inexpressible feature, nourishing the gestures of a woman's body who in this way cries her cry of truth.

Significantly, Nicoletta, in her extraordinary sensitivity and not too differently from the Sisters, does not see or put a *qualitative* distance between her own existential experience and that of the *tarantate*. In spite of the socio-economic disparities and the temporal distance, in Nicoletta's narrative what separates her own experience of being a messy and sorrowful body from those of the *tarantate* is *not* much a socio-economic or cultural status, as many of the "classic" interpretations on *tarantismo* tend to focus on, in the description of these phenomena of "spider possession." Rather, what tells Nicoletta apart from them is her not being exposed, by virtue of her inhabiting an interior space, to a gaze that does not empower, that ridicules, that judges her as unfit, that does not recognize either her being a woman or her cry of truth. Significantly, this status of the *tarantate*, so intensely described by Nicoletta, is acknowledged and reinterpreted by the Sisters in quite an opposite way. In the Sisters' words, as a matter of fact, it was precisely the *tarantate*'s visibility—criticized by Nicoletta—that is of inspiration and that makes them "teachers." They believe that the *tarantate* are examples for us since they had the courage of publicly claiming, with the support of *pizzica* music and probably other-than-human energies, the radicality of their quest for infinitude – in spite of what the people could think, and still think, of them.[27]

***

Viola arrives in her red car. Fiammetta, Fenice, and Alberto are with her. They park the vehicle and come towards me. After exchanging hugs, we are ready for our pilgrimage to Galatina. It is just a couple of miles' long walk, but it is a symbolic journey we want to take on foot. The sky is simpering with its dawning light: a perfect, postcard-like sunrise before us. We walk on a small unpaved trail through the Salentine countryside: drywalls on both sides and olive trees, cacti, St. John's wort, fig trees around us. We talk in whispers, smile, yawn, and breathe the Mediterranean maquis. We stop, take a picture, and continue our walk.

***

The Sisters love to take pictures and, I discovered over many months, love to be the protagonists of mine. Apparently, they find that they appear particularly beautiful when I photograph them, and I am happy to capture moments of their lives through my camera or smartphone to reciprocate their generosity. "Beauty is in the eyes of the beholder," I use to tell them. "If it is true that you see yourself particularly beautiful in my pictures, this is only a reflection of my loving gaze: you are beautiful, this is how I see you. Photography, for me, is a labor of love, and focusing on beauty, a necessity."

Taking pictures is not a vainglorious activity for the Sisters, though. It is an act of beauty (*bellezza*), which is both an ethical and aesthetic concept among my Salentine interlocutors. The same goes for its pursuit. *Bellezza* does not

27 The figure of the spider is understood, in many of the Sisters' claims on the *tarantate*, as a "more-than-human" presence. Spiders are treated, both physically and symbolically, as power animals and spirit guides: in their lives, and in those of the *tarantate*, too.

have anything to do with complying with societal expectations on how successful and attractive women should appear. Rather, it is the result of particular energetic signatures, of spiritual endeavors, of specific actions. Beauty lies in places and persons, behaviors and arts, nature and objects. It is a way to inhabit the world, one that is in harmony with nature and the planet. It is a way to follow the morning star that is one's desire.[28] The Sisters' multifaceted understanding of beauty, in other words, resonates with non-dominant and more all-encompassing concepts of "beauty," such as the Navajo/Diné notion of *hózhó*.[29] In

28 Sartwell defines beauty as characterized by longing. In this sense, the "gap," the capacity for "desiring" cultivated by the Sisters could be linked to the pursuit of beauty. Beauty speaks about our infinitude, and living in *bellezza* is linked to our longing for aligning ourselves to our *destino*. In this sense, as I will show in chapter 3, the pursuit of *bellezza* is an important lived experience of the "expanded present" historicity.

29 On the notion of *hózhó* see, e.g., Angela A.A. Willeto, "Happiness in Navajos (Diné Ba' HóZhó)," in *Happiness Across Cultures*, ed. Helaine Selin (Dordrech: Springer, 2012), 377–86; Crispin Sartwell, *Six Names of Beauty* (New York: Routledge, 2004); Michelle Kahn-John, "The Path to Development of the Hózhó Resilience Model for Nursing Research and Practice," *Applied Nursing Research* 29 (2016): 144–47 and "Concept Analysis of Diné Hózhó," *Advances in Nursing Science* 33 no. 2 (2010): 113–25; Vincent Werito, "Understanding HóZhǫ́ to Achieve Critical Consciousness: A Contemporary Diné Interpretation of the Philosophical Principles of HóZhǫ́," in *Diné Perspectives: Revitalizing and Reclaiming Navajo Thought*, ed. Lloyd L. Lee (Tucson: University of Arizona Press), 25-38.

It is important to note that my reference to hóZhó here does not stem neither from acritical and appropriative intents nor from a mere comparative one, but it is meant to be the result of taking decolonial practices seriously and to foster a "world-anthropologies" approach. In *Decolonizing Ethnography*, Carolina Alonso Bejarano, Lucia López Juárez, Mirian A. Mijangos García, and Daniel M. Goldstein point out that "A world-anthropologies approach" tries to think "about social reality from outside the Western paradigm, from the perspective of those on the fringes of modern life and capitalist prosperity . . . it calls attention to the work of non-Western thinkers" (34). It is in this vein that I think about hóZhó as conveying a particularly meaningful paradigm to better understand my ethnographic material. See Carolina Alonso Bejarano, Lucia López Juárez, Mirian A. Mijangos García, Daniel M. Goldstein, and e-Duke books scholarly collection. *Decolonizing Ethnography : Undocumented Immigrants and New Directions in Social Science*. (Durham: Duke University Press, 2019). See also Matthew Schneider-Mayerson, Brent Ryan Bellamy, and Project Muse,

particular, *bellezza* and *hózhó* are similar in their being both a state of being and a way of living "in harmony and balance with oneself, one's loved ones, one's community, the natural world, and the universe."[30] In spite of the obvious differences, *bellezza,* like *hózhó,* is linked to the pursuit of well-being, and it is a spiritual practice – one that the Sisters associate, though, differently from other understandings of beauty, with embracing a particular historicity. Beauty is not understood, in fact, as the longing for a particular moment in our lives – youth, for example.[31] Rather, *bellezza* is associated with being in the "expanded present," and it is considered central in the journey towards happiness. In the coevality that comes from inhabiting the "here-and-now," the *qui-e-ora,* all the dimensions of our souls, lives, and embodiments are connected and exalted. In particular, in the depth of the present moment, *bellezza* lies in one's being aligned with the journey of one's soul – her destiny and destination – and connected with her life purpose.

Among the Sisters, capturing *bellezza* through photography, then, does not respond to an attempt to accumulate memories that chronicle the course of their lives. It does not stem from nostalgia or from the drive to record a fleeting linear time. Rather, this is a practice that has much to do with experiencing time as coeval, rather than (only) linear.[32] Pictures are little pieces in the grand mosaic of the

---

An Ecotopian Lexicon (Minneapolis: University of Minnesota Press, 2019). See also, for the study of esotericism in (post)colonial contexts and for a cognitive approach to the study of cross-cultural (religious) exchanges, Susannah Crockford and Egil Asprem, "Ethnographies of the Esoteric," in *Correspondences* 6, no. 1 (2018): 1–23. See also Martin Holbraad, "The Power of Powder: Multiplicity and Motion in the Divinatory Cosmology of Cuban Ifá (or Mana, Again)," in *Thinking through Things: Theorising Artefacts Ethnographically*, eds. Amiria J. M. Henare, Martin Holbraad, and Sari Wastell (London: Routledge), 189–225.

30 Willeto, "Happiness in Navajos," 379.

31 See Sartwell, *Six Names of Beauty.*

32 It is worth noting that the Sisters' understanding of time and temporality (linear, circular, and coeval at the same time) seems to be in line with the recent comments of the feminist scholar Karen Barad, who writes, "Any

embodiments of a soul. They do not measure the quantity of time. They are mementos of its *quality*.[33] In other words, they are not chronological (from the Greek, *chronos*) but cairological (from the Greek, *kairos*). While chronological time measures the quantity of time, the cariological one focuses on the present, and it is connected to the qualitative dimensions of time.[34]

The connections between beauty, pictures, time, and spirituality emerge also in another dimension linked to digital photography. Photographs, in fact, are deemed capable of recording what our eyes cannot see or perceive, including non-human and more-than-human presences. If the correlation among technology, and what is usually referred to as "the occult" (meaning, what it is hidden), and spiritism is long-standing, the Sisters do not seem to have deconstructed this association.[35] They carefully analyze,

suggestion that the notion of the linearity of time is unsalvageable and ought to be replaced with a new, arguably superior, notion of time would be ironic, since it would be to fall into the logic of progress and supersessionism. What is needed is an understanding of temporality where the 'new' and the 'old' might coexist, where one does not triumph by replacing and overcoming the other. Quantum superpositions and, relatedly, quantum entanglements open up possibilities for understanding how the 'new' and the 'old'—indeed, multiple temporalities—are diffractively threaded through and are inseparable from one another" (Barad, "Troubling Time/s," 69).

33 It is interesting to note that anthropologist David Zeitlyn ("Haunting, Dutching, and Interference Provocations for the Anthropology of Time," *Current Anthropology* 61, no. 4 [2020]: 495–513) also points out the connection between photography and conceptions of time. See also chapter 3.

34 In talking about Benjamin's idea of politics, Kia Lindroos, in fact, argues in favor of a distinction between these two aspects of time: "In Greek, Chronos has the more definite meaning of as a destructive force of time, an objective, measurable time, and a long duration of time … The cairologic approach neither searches for means of measuring or understanding movement through temporal continuity, nor attempts to control the dynamics of time and action through freezing them. Instead, this approach emphasises breaks, ruptures, non-synchronised moments and multiple temporal dimensions." (*Now-Time Image-Space: Temporalization of Politics in Walter Benjamin's Philosophy of History and Art* [Jyväskylä, Finland: University of Jyväskylä, 1998], 11–12.)

35 Apparently, "spirit photography" has been attested since the 1870s c.a., just a few years after the very invention of the daguerreotype.

compare, and decode each shot, looking for orbs (colored spherical bodies of light) and other light configurations, or for some out-of-the-ordinary traces in the pictures. Digital cameras, better than their predecessors, work as enhanced senses for some or as synchronicities' bearers for others. For all of them, though, the practice of recording or photographing is, in a way, a spiritual one, and one linked to historicity, "presence," and, ultimately, to well-being.

Both *synchronicity* and *synchronous* experiences are key factors in the lives of the Salentine Pagans I met. Introduced first by psychiatrist and psychoanalyst Carl Jung, the word *synchronicity* refers to "meaningful coincidences," to "acausal connections" of psychic and physical phenomena.[36] Linked to the "numinous," to his theory of archetypes, and to his psychotherapeutic practice, this notion is thoroughly addressed by Jung in the early 1950s. In his book *Synchronicity: An Acausal Connecting Principle*, Carl Jung traces the genealogy of this term both referring to Western "forerunners," such as the philosopher Arthur Schopenhauer and the physicist Albert Einstein, and to some non-Western philosophies and cosmologies, such as the one related to the *I Ching* divination. While the link between synchronicities and the expanded present historicity in the experience of Salentine Pagans is an important one, it is worth noting that the Swiss psychiatrist distinguishes between *synchronism* (the simultaneous occurrence of two events) and *synchronicity* (the *meaningful*, a-casual, link between psychic and physical phenomena).[37]

36 See Carl Jung, *Synchronicity: An Acausal Connecting Principle* (Princeton: Princeton University Press, 2010 [1960]).

37 In fact, he claims, following Arthur Schopenhauer, that "All the events in a man's life would accordingly stand in two fundamentally different kinds of connection: firstly, in the objective, causal connection of the natural process; secondly, in a subjective connection which exists only in relation to the individual who experiences it, and which is thus as subjective as his own dreams… The causality principle asserts that the connection between cause and effect is a necessary one. The synchronicity principle asserts that the terms of a

Synchronicities, for the Sisters of the *cerchio*, are expressions of *bellezza*, and the path of *bellezza* is one that has synchronicities as milestones. Synchronicities, in fact, are seen as signs of approval: one of the main ways the Salentine Pagans use to verify their "alignment" to their "destiny" or *destino*. The latter, consistent with its etymology, is conceived by my interlocutors as both the *destination* (of our journeys on Earth) and our *fate*: it is the result of something that is/stays already (the Indo-European root *sta-*).[38] In other words, it is linked to the "active staying" (or

meaningful coincidence are connected by simultaneity and meaning." (Jung, *Synchronicity*, 12.)

38 In "Anthropology and Time," Rebecca Bryant and Daniel Knight point out six "orientations toward the future" that they infer from a remarkably close engagement with a vast array of works in anthropology and continental philosophy. "Destiny" appears to be one of these orientations, discussed in relation to fate and providence. It is worth noting that my use of the term *destino* does not fully overlap with such an understanding of destiny. In fact, it complements Bryant and Knights's analyses. In particular, since it is perceived and experienced, albeit sparingly, *in the present* of the "expanded present," *destino*, in Salento, is not mainly approached as an orientation but primarily as an embodied experience—one that goes beyond the actuality/potentiality dichotomy. Nonetheless, Bryant and Knight's focus on the sociologist Theodore R. Schatzki's notion of "teleoaffects" and on his non-evolutionary, open-ended, indeterminate understanding of teleology (*The Timespace of Human Activity: On Performance, Society, and History as Indeterminate Teleological Events* [Lanham, MD: Lexington Books, 2010]) can be of use in framing the experience of the "expanded present" among Southern Italian Pagans. Moreover, the Sisters' notion of *destino* confirms Bryant and Knight's suggestion that "the view in anthropology that destiny is a problem for agency is to confuse final with efficient causes" (*Anthropology of the Future*, 175). In line with a recent neo-Aristotelian trend in philosophy, the two authors of *The Anthropology of the Future*, in talking about destiny, underline that some misrepresentation of the latter stem from a misrecognition of the four causes "at work in the world" (166). While Aristotle distinguishes between material cause (e.g., the wood used to build a table), formal (e.g., the shape of the table), efficient (e.g., the carpenter who builds the table), and final (e.g., the action of dining), Bryant and Knight convincingly argue that, since the Enlightenment, all causes have been reduced to the efficient cause, only (166–67). While this can be useful in certain contexts, it is not in others—as, e.g., in the case of "presence magic" and the expanded present, as described in this book. On the time of divination, Aristotle's categories, and gnosis see Phil Ford, "Diviner's Time," https://www.weirdstudies.com/66

"dwelling") embedded in the wise syntax of the Salentine dialect.[39] For this reason, destiny and *bellezza* are paramount in the "expanded present" historicity of the Sisters.

***

Figure 3a. *Zagareddhre* decorating Galatina for the festival of Saint Peter and Paul. Photo: Giovanna Parmigiani.

39 See, for a comparison, chapter 1 and, e.g., Timothy Ingold, *The Perception of the Environment: Essays in Livelihood, Dwelling and Skill* (London and New York: Routledge, 2000).

Galatina greets us with the smell of pasticciotti, *a local breakfast treat, and we wonder who, among the few in the streets, is a "still" (awake) and who, instead, is an "already" (awake). Some teenagers laugh, the* zagareddhre *man is setting up his stand; the owner of the coffee bar straightens the tables in front of his shop. The closer we approach the chapel of Saint Paul, the stronger the sound of tamburieddhri. It is a tired, weary sound. We hear voices as cries and words we can barely understand.*

The empty bottles on the cobblestone paved street sketch unknown geometries: melancholic vestiges of a festival night that only too recently came to an end. Our eyes blink, sleepy and pierced by the intense light of the morning. We arrive at the chapel of Saint Paul. The air is pungent: it smells of tobacco, of sweating bodies, of the fresh blood of the musicians on the goat skin of the tambourines.

Some women and some men are sitting in the cobblestone street in front of the chapel: they look tired and serious. Their thoughts appear to be elsewhere, in who-knows-what parallel reality; their bodies, though, are completely there, leaning against the wall. Their hair is ruffled, their feet dirty and bare, their gazes veiled. They have been dancing and playing pizzica *all night, asking for their pain to be relieved, their sorrows lifted, their struggles eased. Some wanted to be "healed"; some others generously accompanied the dancers in their healing journey.*[40] *A woman dressed in black knocks repeatedly at the door of the chapel; another one moves her feet following the weary rhythm of the tamburieddhri. A white-dressed man lies on the street. He rolls around and cries. His eyes are big and dark: a kid's face on a grown-up body.*

Viola and Fiammetta stop talking. They silently get closer to the group in front of the chapel of Saint Paul. Their faces are

40 I here follow Daboo, *Ritual, Rapture and Religion*, 252–55, who, by quoting the medical anthropologist James Waldram, distinguishes between "healing" and "curing." While the latter refers to biomedical processes, the former "refers to a broader psychosocial process of repairing the affective, social and spiritual dimensions of ill health or illness" (James B. Waldram, "The Efficacy of Traditional Medicine: Current Theoretical and Methodological Issues," *Medical Anthropology Quarterly* 14, no. 4 (2000): 604. See also chapter 5.

serious, respectful, solemn. They kindly and reverentially greet the women and men, and hug and kiss some. Their movements are slow, their voice low. The musicians accelerate the pizzica *beat. Viola joins the musicians while Fiammetta starts dancing with a young woman they both know. The blood on the tamburieddhri matches the color of the Salentine soil, and I sit on the sidewalk. The energy is dense, and I sense grieving, hopelessness, and pain. I feel deeply moved and powerless. I quietly visualize my light cocoon, and I imagine a giant bubble of pink liquid light enveloping us all, sending light and love.*

***

The festival of St. Peter and St. Paul in Galatina, celebrated on the 28th and 29th of June, used to be the main yearly event for the *tarantate*. In fact, the Salento area of Italy, and specifically Galatina, is known in anthropology for the phenomenon of *tarantismo*, in particular as described by Ernesto de Martino in his 1961 book, *La Terra del Rimorso*.

Tarantismo is a widely studied phenomenon that has been controversial since the Middle Ages. With pre-Roman origins, according to some, it apparently lasted well into the 1980s. As the aforementioned description of Nicoletta made clear, it is believed to have been affecting mostly (but not only) women, and it has been described in the form of mental and physical suffering—sometimes also as a form of "possession"—thought to be provoked by the bite of tarantula spiders and cured through various private rituals and a public one in Galatina. These rituals involved the performance of *pizzica* music, used as a cure or antidote, and associated with a rowdy "ecstatic dance" that could last for hours.[41] They culminated in the yearly public ritual in the chapel of St. Paul. This public ritual,

41 Karen Lüdtke, "'We've Got this Rhythm in our Blood': Dancing Identities in Southern Italy," in *Dancing Cultures: Globalization, Tourism and Identity in the Anthropology of Dance*, ed. Hélène Neveu Kringelbach and Jonathan Skinner (New York: Berghahn Books, 2012), 70n5.

a result of the "syncretism" of the aforementioned healing practice by the Catholic Church over the centuries by associating it with the cult of Saint Paul, was organized on the occasion of the saint's day, a few days after the summer solstice.[42] During this ritual, *tarantate* used to gather in Galatina from the countryside, begging the saint to heal them from their various maladies through this particular "dance of possession."

The most influential study of this phenomenon is still the one conducted in June 1959 by Ernesto de Martino and his équipe that resulted in the book *La Terra del Rimorso.* The success of this book, among scholars and non-scholars alike, cannot be underestimated: his legacy is so important and his fame so widespread in Italy, that, long after his death, it is still an out-and-out protagonist of current debates, practices, and representations of *tarantismo.*[43] As the anthropologist Giovanni Pizza, one of the main contemporary scholars of de Martino and of *tarantismo* observes, among others, de Martino understood *tarantismo* to be a result of a crisis of presence in history. The latter refers to "an individual's loss of referents in the surrounding world, an experience of the self as unreal and unrelated to present circumstances, and ... seen to result, above all, from traumas caused by socioeconomic and natural adversity."[44] De Martino's interpretation was groundbreaking and had

42 See, e.g., Daboo, *Ritual, Rapture and Religion,* 146–61.

43 An example of this is the initiative "*DeMartino50,*" organized fifty years after the death of the Italian ethnographer.There have been works that criticized or expanded the interpretation of de Martino, see e.g., Glauco Sanga, "L'etnografo impaziente," *La Ricerca Folklorica* 67/68 (2013): 35–43. But his legacy is still very central in the approaches towards *tarantismo.*

44 Lüdtke, "Dancing towards Well-Being," 41.

extremely important political implications.[45][46][47] According

45 "Presence," according to Pandolfi, is "an ambiguous concept for de Martino: partially informed by Heidegger's *dasein*, and partially by historicism" (Pandolfi, "Boundaries Inside the Body," 267. See Ernesto de Martino, *Il Mondo Magico: Prolegomeni a una Storia del Magismo*. [Turin: Bollati Boringhieri, 1981 [1948]], and Ferrari, *Ernesto de Martino on Religion*). As Saunders puts it, directly quoting the Italian ethnographer, in several works de Martino discussed a dilemma that he referred to as "the crisis of presence" which he defines as "the existential drama of being exposed to the risk of not being here" ("Crisis of Presence," 324), that characterizes the magic world—where "presence was still a goal and a task, a drama and a problem" (de Martino 1981, 190, my translation). For the Neapolitan ethnographer, cultural institutions such as religious and magical rituals could re-establish presence *vis-à-vis* its crisis and prevent its loss. Within such a framework he understood, for example, the phenomena of *tarantismo*.

See also Saunders, "Crisis of Presence," on Pentecostalism in Italy 1995. In his analysis of Italian Pentecostalism, Saunders argues that "conversion allows the person to fashion not only a new self and identity but also a new relationship to time and history, and particularly a newly affirmed feeling of efficacy as an actor in the historical moment" ("Crisis of Presence," 324). He read some of his ethnographic data on pre-conversion existential crisis within a de Martinian framework, arguing —similarly to Pandolfi— in favor of the adoption in anthropology of the Neapolitan ethnographer's concepts of presence. Significantly, Saunders stresses an understanding of crisis of presence in relation to the production of oneself and to a change in the perception of time, and of one's place into it. On the concept of "crisis of presence" and on its application in contexts different from the ones of *tarantismo* see, e.g., Saunders, "Crisis of Presence," and Sabina Magliocco, "Witchcraft as Political Resistance," *Nova Religio* 23, no. 4 (2020): 43–68.

46 *Tarantismo* has a long history and has been the object of passionate medical and catholic discussions since the Middle Ages. As Giovanni Pizza notes, "The medical profession classified the female bodily performances in three ways: as a disease caused by the venom of the tarantula; as a hysterical mental disorder; and as female fiction. Catholicism on the other hand introduced the figure of Saint Paul and progressively transformed a possession cult into a Catholic cult of the saint. De Martino showed that the medical approach reduced the "symbolic autonomy" of tarantism, that is, it ignored its ritual function. He also argued that local bodily performances of spider-spirit possession should not be considered "subversive" to either medicine or official Catholicism. They were ritual performances in which ceremony and suffering were interwoven. Tarantism then was no longer understood as a mental disorder but rather as a ritual aiming to give a cultural meaning to female existential and social suffering." ("Tarantism and Politics of Tradition," 199–200.)

47 As Lüdtke points out, de Martino's *tarantate* "belonged to what de Martino identifies, in Gramscian terms, as the "subaltern" class. Most of them were, moreover, women, despite well-known exceptions to both cases. These

to him, *tarantate* belonged to what could be called the "subaltern class." This term, reminiscent of the political analyses of Antonio Gramsci, usually refers to the politically, socially, economically, and geographically subordinate position of part of the population, including the *tarantate* women, *vis-à-vis* the Italian state. This peculiar positionality was understood as being both the cause underlying *tarantismo* and the horizon of its cure. If structural dimensions such as patriarchy, extreme poverty, and social invisibility influenced the onset of *tarantismo,* its ritual cure was not dismissed as an ineffective superstition, or a "relic" of the past, by Ernesto de Martino. Rather, against biomedical interpretations of the phenomenon popular at the time, in his analysis of *tarantismo* the healing effects of *pizzica* were validated, by the Neapolitan ethnologist, and considered culturally specific strategies to cope with structural oppression, inequality, and the consequent hardship that people experienced, at an individual level.

The ritual practice described by de Martino disappeared from the public scene at the beginning of this century with the modernization of the region, and *tarantismo* ceased to be performed as a predominantly healing practice while reemerging mainly as a popular culture musical phenomenon. As some scholars have noted, re-appropriations of *tarantismo* (similarly to re-appropriations of forms of "vernacular magic" throughout Italy) emerged in Salento and elsewhere in the country at the turn of the century in conversation with scholarly studies on the phenomenon. In reference to *tarantismo,* these re-appropriations, called

---

afflictions are shown to be inseparable from a struggle against the "larger hegemonic order" and directly linked to inequalities of gender and extreme poverty. In this sense, the magico-religious perspective of tarantism is examined not as an evolutionary relic of primitive thinking, or as proof of psychological instability, but as a culturally specific response to harsh living conditions and traumatic life experiences. The tarantula's ritual is identified as a means of reliving and healing individual and social crises, which threaten to erupt without control. It serves as a historically tested and socially accepted channel of communicating and resolving distress." ("Dancing towards Well-Being," 41.)

neotarantismi, have been read as identity phenomena or as forms of "patrimonialization" (see below).[48] Moreover, they have been linked to the practice of a form of ecstatic dance, possibly fostering well-being, conceived as a post-modern critique of rationalism, or as a version of "*meridionalismo*."[49] Yet, though this may have been the case in the first years of this century, my two-year-long ethnographic research in Salento showed a situation that has somewhat mutated in the last few years. Today, *tarantismo* and the performance of *pizzica* today are also re-appropriated in their spiritual dimensions, outside the Catholic church, in a form of what could be called *spiritual neotarantismo*. This aspect—mentioned *en passant* by Apolito, Pizza, Magliocco, Lüdtke, Biagi, Inserra, Del Giudice, and Daboo,[50] and considered by most of the aforementioned scholars, with a few exceptions, generally (and often in a demeaning way) as a "New Age phenomenon"—has not been the object of explicit, long-term, in depth ethnographic research.[51] This book is an attempt to give scholarly attention to the lives, practices,

48 On *neotarantismi* see, especially, Pizza, "Tarantismi oggi," "Tarantism and the Politics of Tradition," and *Il Tarantismo Oggi*. See also Nacci, *Tarantismo e neotarantismo*, and *Neotarantismo*.

49 See, for example, Magliocco, "Witchcraft, Healing and Vernacular Magic in Italy"; Pizza, *Il Tarantismo Oggi*; Lüdtke, "Dancing towards Well-Being," and *Dances with Spiders*; Del Giudice, "Healing the Spider's Bite," and "Folk Music Revival."

50 Paolo Apolito, "I Beni DEA e il 'fare' le tradizioni," *Antrolopogia Museale* 17 (2007): 12–17; Pizza, *Il Tarantismo Oggi*; Magliocco, "Witchcraft, Healing and Vernacular Magic in Italy"; Lüdtke, "Dancing towards Well-Being" and *Dances with Spiders*; Laura Biagi, "Spider Dreams: Ritual and Performance in Apulian Tarantismo and Tarantella" (PhD diss., New York University, 2004); Inserra, *Global Tarantella*; Del Giudice, "Healing the Spider's Bite," and "Folk Music Revival"; Daboo, *Ritual, Rapture and Remorse*.

51 For example, as Del Giudice writes: "The *pizzica (tarantata)*—sometimes referred to as *tarantella* (but never when Salentines speak among themselves)—the ritual music and dance of *tarantismo*, has become the Salentine New Age rage, as followers quest for cosmic dance, mysticism and magic. Neo-*tarantati* speak of being bitten, and they call themselves *tarantati, tarantolati* or *attarantati*; one finds them on the piazza wherever *pizziche* are played" ("Folk Music Revival," 220).

and experiences of those (mostly women) who today "practice *neotarantismo*" in a *spiritual* perspective. One of the aims of this research, in fact, is to document these additional developments linked to a "spiritual *neotarantismo*." If the identity dimension of *neotarantismo* is not completely absent in the rhetoric of the Sisters of the *cerchio* and of some of this group's friends, the identity dimensions of *pizzica* are neither central nor all-encompassing, and their attitudes toward this local music and dance have taken on nuances that depart from locally acknowledged understandings of *neotarantismi*.

It is worth mentioning that one of the most important aspects of contemporary *neotarantismo*, and much studied, is the yearly event "The Night of the Tarantula Spider. Since 1999, Melpignano, one of the municipalities of the *Grecìa Salentina*, has become known for hosting the musical event known as "*La Notte della Taranta*."[52] Broadcast both on television and online, this event is preceded by smaller ones organized throughout the *Grecìa salentina* over the previous two weeks. During the final concert of the *Notte della Taranta*, local musicians perform variations of the traditional *pizzica* music, often featuring national and international guests. Yet at the dawn of the twenty-first century, *tarantismo* increasingly became understood locally as either a fiction or a synonym for cultural backwardness and was reframed and re-constructed in a new socio-economical and temporal perspective.[53] This particular dimension of *neotarantismo* is clearly linked to the re-appropriation of the identity dimensions of *pizzica* and *tarantismo*, around a fairly recent development of Salento as a preferred tourist destination, and around local re-framings of both the

52 On the *Notte della Taranta* event see, for example, Karen Lüdtke, *Balla Coi Ragni: La Tarantola Tra Crisi E Celebrazioni* (Bari: Edizioni Di Pagina, 2011); Pizza, "Tarantism and the Politics of Tradition," and *Il Tarantismo Oggi*.

53 Lüdtke, *Balla Coi Ragni*, 17.

phenomenon of *tarantismo* and of its anthropological and historical analyses.[54]

This is evident also today in the festival of Saint Peter and Saint Paul in Galatina. Associated in the *past* with the curative aspects of *tarantismo*, it is *today* one of the most important tourist attractions of contemporary Salento. In particular, it is an "anthropological tourism" destination that has developed in this area since the end of the 1990s, especially following the establishment of the annual event called *Notte della Taranta*.[55] As Apolito points out (explicitly referencing Salento and *tarantismo*), through its anthropological tourism, Salento welcomes many young students who have learned about the tradition in their universities' anthropology courses. They gather at local musical and social events variously connected with local traditions, where their presence, linked to a "symbolic market," "is not limited to passive fruition" but generates "forms of participation that sometimes trigger debates, tensions, contestations, refashioning, instabilities, movements."[56]

***

The young man who was crying and rolling over on the ground appears calmer now. Curled up in a fetal position with his eyes closed, he seems to have found some rest. Viola and Fiammetta are with him: they seem not to worry about what just happened. I feel reassured by their composure and I join them. We become a sort of protective barrier around him: sheltering the young man from the noises of the street, the gazes of by-standers, and from the activities of a wakening town. After a little while he is ready to stand

54 Indeed, to summarize, as Pizza points out, "*Tarantismo* today [encompasses] a wide field of actions, representations and practices, conveyed first of all by anthropological rhetoric, both academic and local, by scientific and political and cultural debates that weave together an analysis of *tarantismo* objectified as an historical phenomenon, and, by incorporating a lived *tarantismo* as an identity trait, as an 'origin.'" (*Il Tarantismo Oggi*, 197, my translation.)

55 Apolito, "I Beni DEA e il 'fare' le tradizioni," 13–14.

56 Ibid., 13.

up. I look into his face: his eyes are smaller after so much weeping. Viola and Fiammetta hug him and hold him for minutes, in what feels like a caring, soothing, healing, neverending embrace. Their bodies slowly disentangle, and they exchange smiles. I am introduced to him, Guido. I smile, too, and shake hands. He looks at me, and I notice that his eyes sparkle, now, after the pacifying hugs he shared with the Sisters. He looks at me and claims I am emanating a turquoise light: a kind of aura he says he sees around me. He seems moved by this vision, and I smile, puzzled and slightly embarrassed. He addresses Fiammetta and Viola, a bit bewildered, and asks them: "And she? Where is she coming from?" "I come from Varese, in the North, but I live in the US," I reply. They look at me and laugh. I smile, and slightly blush. Clearly, this is not the right answer to a question that, although uttered in my native language, I had evidently misunderstood.

We decide it is time for a coffee. Guido comes with us, and we all sit at the table of a coffee shop. I sit there and, while they order coffees, croissants, and pasticciotti, *I think about the 2015 festival of Saint Peter and Saint Paul, and how things had changed since.*

***

In June 2015 I attended an "historical re-enactment" of the ritual of the *tarantate* organized by the municipality of Galatina and by its Club UNESCO in occasion of the festival of Saint Peter and Saint Paul—a performance harshly criticized by many locals, and especially scholars of *tarantismo* and performers of *pizzica* music and dance. The street was crowded with tourists and locals, and I, squeezed between the wall of a building and a horde of spectators, saw two women with loose hair, bare feet, and dressed in white gowns, and a man arriving in a wooden cart pulled by horses. They stopped in front of the chapel of St. Paul, and, accompanied by the group of musicians and by a woman dressed in black acting as the *macara* (meaning "witch" in the local dialect), they began performing the arrival of the *tarantate* for their yearly appointment with "the Saint" at the chapel of St. Paul. Bales of hay delimited a small area just in front of the door of the chapel. The *macara* set the stage for the ritual by laying a big white cloth on the cobblestone pavement.[57]

This performance, organized in collaboration with Club UNESCO of Galatina happened in front of crowds of tourists and locals who, in an effort to record the event with their cameras and smartphones, tried to find their way through the stands of souvenirs that pack the main square of Galatina.[58] While the musicians played "traditional" *pizzica* tunes, the dancers "interpreted" the dance of liberation of the *tarantate*.[59] Indeed, the therapeutic ritual started in the front of the crowd and unfolded as a visual quotation of Mingozzi's 1961 documentary, appearing to my eyes as a form of remediation, or "visual quotation." Policewomen surveyed the area, preventing the spectators from crossing the circular border bounded by the bales of hay. After just a few minutes of enthusiastic dancing, the women, the man, and the musicians moved into the chapel, followed by cameramen. Someone closed the doors of the chapel. Nothing visible was happening in front of our eyes, the eyes of the spectators. From outside the chapel, only the repetitive, pulsing ternary sounds of the *tamburieddhri* could be heard. The spectators of a spectacle that could not be "seen"

57 The woman who was interpreting the role of the helper told me, in a personal conversation (December 2015), that she was asked by one of the "*tarantate*" to be the *macara* in the performance. When I asked her why she thought the dancer used this term, she told me she did not know. Another woman of the group claims that they use the term *macara* to refer to someone who helps, who gives strength, often by using magic.

58 "Galatina. "Festa SS. Pietro e Paolo 2014". Video Wild Italia. July 2, 2014. Video, 7:33. https://youtu.be/wwyR3JTkTos.; Galatina. "La guarigione delle tarantate." Dino Valente. June 29, 2014. Video, 18:43. https://youtu.be/RIkZ_uRcuAM

59 See, e.g., Del Giudice, "Healing the Spider's Bite," and "Folk Music Revival"; Laviosa, "Frontier Apulia and its Filmmakers," and "Tarantula Myths and Music"; Pizza, "Tarantism and the Politics of Tradition."

remained there, waiting for something to happen, and for the ritual to unfold behind the closed doors of the chapel.

All the while, in both standard Italian and in the local dialect, locals offered various narratives and interpretations of *tarantismo* to curious and sometimes anthropologically informed tourists. Many of the latter asked extemporaneous questions of their fellow-spectators, deemed to be authorities by virtue of being natives. Some of them talked about *tarantate* as a phenomenon that affected mostly women in the past and describe them as sexually repressed; others considered them simply to be persons bitten by a spider and explained the disappearance of *tarantismo* through the introduction of pesticides in agriculture. One explained that an old acquaintance of hers, who had been "bitten" by a tarantula spider, felt anxious and restless every June but did not want to go to Galatina anymore. Moreover, she claimed that because the spider that bit her was yellow with red dots on its back, she had since then been unable to tolerate the color yellow. Moreover, this old acquaintance had found herself incapable of hurting spiders and destroying spider webs. If she ever did so accidentally, she would always ask "her Saint Paul" to forgive her. Another Salentine woman joined the conversation, arguing that she had heard that tarantula spiders, far from declining in numbers, were actually starting to repopulate the Badisco area, having been reintroduced by biologists. Some cited the name of Ernesto de Martino, often unwittingly attributing to the famous Italian ethnologist their own, more or less idiosyncratic, understandings of the phenomenon. Locals and foreigners alike seemed to agree on one single point: *tarantismo* was something that belonged to the historical past of Salento, not to its present. It was, so to speak, part of its local patrimony (or heritage).

One of my friends and I had spent the previous night at the stand of an itinerant tambourine maker, helping him sell his hand-made *tamburieddhri* and CDs of *pizzica* to local musicians and tourists. I had elected this position as a further "observation point" for my research in Salento. The night had begun with a concert of local musicians and groups who played reinterpretations of the traditional *pizzica* music and had ended at 6 a.m., after dawn, with spontaneous *ronde* (circle) dances. Sometime in the middle of that night, those who were to perform the aforementioned ritual the following morning made their appearance at the festival. They had left their purses and other belongings at our stand and had initiated a couple of small *ronde* (dancing circles), all the while playing, singing, and dancing *pizzica*: one in front of the chapel of St. Paul, the other close to our stand. While these types of *ronde* are a fairly common kind of performance by Salentine standards, happening during local festivals and concerts, the same cannot be said of the one that took place in the late morning of June 29th. The locals connected to the official world of *pizzica* music in Salento received the latter with some consternation and even indignation as an irreverent "fake"; the people of the historical re-enactment had intended it as an authentic healing ritual, a ritual that somehow complied with the expectations and with the imaginaries of anthropologically informed tourists, and with the "patrimonializing" goals of the people from the Club UNESCO of Galatina.[60]

The reactions to this re-enactment were very strong among my Salentine acquaintances, both *de visu* and on Facebook and other social media. Local intellectuals and scholars of *tarantismo* strongly criticized this "charade," and some found it even offensive and disrespectful of the memory of the *tarantate*, whose dance was the result of their suffering. Some also found it disrespectful of the "Salentine identity." The whole idea of the possible existence of "contemporary

60 It is worth noting that this particular re-enactment was not too dissimilar from the *cerchio*'s rituals I attended to in the following years. Although we never met in that precise location, I participated with the Sisters in many "healing sessions" that involved *pizzica* dancing and live music.

tarantate," in fact, is not just considered impossible but even intolerable to most of the Salentinians I met outside Pagan circles. If, it goes without saying, the *tarantate* studied by de Martino and video-recorded by Mingozzi are not alive anymore and *that particular expression* of *tarantismo* cannot be found in contemporary Salento, it is also true that there is a lot of resistance in acknowledging the "right of self-determination" to those who explicitly refer, in various ways, to the phenomenon of *tarantismo* as a meaningful dimension of their lives *today*.[61] In other words, similar to what Daboo observed about modern *tarantate*, I see this as an expression of the "tension between what the 'authorities' may decide and define as being authentic, and the types of performances that occur" in contemporary Salento.[62] [63] Because de Martino's interpretation of *tarantismo* focused on the subaltern condition of the *tarantate* and their harsh socio-economic conditions, and since his interpretation is still so popular and widespread, accepting that *today* Salentine women (and men) might still feel the need to rely on these

61 See, e.g., Del Giudice, "Folk Music Revival"; Lüdtke, "Dancing towards Well-Being"; Daboo, *Ritual, Rapture and Remorse*.

62 Daboo continues claiming that "if performance is understood to be process rather than product, then the idea of 'authenticity' is itself a construct...In this way . . . it is the point where 'authenticity' itself is commoditized and marketed into a fixed object that creates the conflict between this and the proceed of change and fluidity, which is the experience of those who are engaged in the playing and dancing of the forms" (*Ritual, Rapture and Remorse*, 215–16).

63 Andrea Carlino, a historian, writes in the introduction of one of the most recent important contributions on *tarantismo*, Pizza's *Il Tarantismo Oggi*, that "while it might be possible to state with a certain peace of mind that *tarantismo* does not exist in basso Salento, it has nonetheless survived outside [*al di qua*] the discourses of anthropologists, through the recuperation of its memory—although sometimes altered, contaminated, distorted or merely simplified and banalized—that is done through the transposition of its shadows, and maybe also of its substance, in many and multiple musical, dancing-related, and festive activities that spread in this region. This is what happened to the bitter tradition of the bite of tarantula spiders in particular in the last twenty years, when these activities have been reconducted, implicitly or explicitly, both in opportune and opportunistic ways. A tradition, it must be reminded, full of individual pain and locally shared suffering." (See Pizza, *Il Tarantismo Oggi*, 14.)

rituals would be like admitting that contemporary Salento and Salentinians are as "backwards" today as they were in the 1950s.[64] Clearly, this is both false and unacceptable to the majority of Salentinians. While the latter are truly and legitimately proud of their origins, history, and culture(s)—in other words of their tangible and intangible "patrimony" or "heritage"—they have very strong opinions on the fact that *tarantate* belong to the past, and that, so to speak, they and *tarantismo* need to remain there.[65]

In contemporary Italy, as elsewhere, "patrimonialization" is not just linked to material objects but, following UNESCO's definition of intangible cultural heritage, is extended to intangible objects such as local gastronomic traditions and, in this case, *tarantismo* and *pizzica* music. As Palumbo would put it, *tarantismo* and *pizzica*, in contemporary Salento, are a form of "*merci-patrimonializzazione*," a neologism that merges the words *commercialization* and *patrimonialization*, meaning "the construction of local cultural specificities in terms of patrimonial goods."[66]

The "re-enactment" performed in collaboration with the Club UNESCO of Galatina and with its municipalities could

---

64 The concept of "backwardness" is not an analytical one that I introduce, but the one used by many of the Salentinians I spoke to.

65 The action of "making patrimony," according to Ballacchino, "can be understood as giving value to a cultural object. In order to understand intangible patrimony one needs to take into consideration the non-static nature of the same patrimonial object, and its changing nature. One needs to look at the patrimony not as neutral, but as the result of a process continuously reinvented, dynamic and relational . . . in which many social actors, often also conflicting, play a role." (Katia Ballacchino, "Per un'antropologia del patrimonio immateriale. Dalle Convenzioni Unesco alle pratiche di comunità," *Glocale* 6–7 (2013): 19.) Since "making patrimony" is a political practice, one may argue that framing *tarantismo* as something that belongs to the past is the result of certain particular political ideologies.

66 Berardino Palumbo, quoted in Pizza, *Il Tarantismo Oggi*, 106 n. 6. As Ballacchino notices, quoting the work of Fabio Dei, "definition of popular culture today cannot avoid reading the relationship between traditional folklore and cultural mass industry folklore. . . [popular culture] starts to be conceived as a sector of consumption and not of production." (Ballacchino, "Per un'antropologia del patrimonio immateriale," 21.)

be seen, at least partially, as an example of this (see chapter 5). The same could be said for *La Notte della Taranta*, and, for example, for the recent presentation of the Dior Cruise 2021 collection (by Maria Grazia Chiuri) in Lecce. Here, the models of the famous French luxury fashion house paraded in the *Piazza del Duomo* alongside *pizzica* musicians and dancers[67] The *piazza* was staged with *luminarie*—light sculptures, typical of the area—curated by Marinella Senatore and the Fratelli Parisi company from Taurisano. The *luminarie* portrayed messages in English, French, and Italian that gestured towards feminism, strength, dignity, healing, beautification, revolution, and the importance of being together. "We rise by lifting others," "We often can create revolutions without having sought them," "Be a builder of unguilt," "I'm going to make everything around me beautiful,"[68] and "A wish is revolutionary because it seeks what cannot be seen" were some of the messages that dressed the *piazza del Duomo* for the event. In this case again, *pizzica* and *tarantismo* of the past are re-interpreted in different, complex, and overlapping ways, resonating with some of the dimensions of "merci-patrimonialization." *Tarantismo* is seen as tradition and heritage, as a form of exoticism, as "glamour," and, ultimately, as a promotional feature for Dior's products.[69]

67 Christian Dior, "Dior in Puglia: the Land of Cruise 2021 inspiration," https://youtu.be/A8fvoPQ2h2s

68 The letter O of "going" is here depicted as a "female" symbol: a circle with a cross underneath.

69 Nonetheless, *tarantismo* and *pizzica* here are also celebrated in their healing potential and in their "feminist" dimensions. The collection, in fact, was prepared in collaboration with the local *Fondazione Costantine*. The latter, based in the Salento village of Casamassella, provided the fabric for the show, produced using ancient weaving techniques. "Initially a tool to promote women's autonomy and emancipation [the art of embroidery and weaving are] today a great excellence, recognized in Italy and in the world. The artisans who work [at the Costantine] produce textile products of the highest quality by weaving natural fibers with ancient wooden frames with four heddles. They use techniques dating back hundreds of years and carry out each finishing strictly by hand." Fondazione Le Costantine, "Arte della Tessitura," https://www.lecostantine.it/larte-della-tessitura/

To summarize, what is worth noting for the purposes of my research is that the commemoration of *tarantismo*—now understood not as a practice but as a discourse, as an academic interest, a historical phenomenon—indeed happens in Salento at the intersection of "folk revivals," political policies, and (touristic) market orientations.[70] In the definition of this phenomenon, though, the signifier of "*tarantismo*" is constructed and objectified on the basis of particular interpretations of this phenomenon done by particular authoritative agents. The latter seldomly substantially questioned or revised the *tarantismo* of de Martino, that is often a-critically adopted and re-instated.

***

We sit at the coffee table. I am lost in my thoughts while sipping my caffè in ghiaccio con latte di mandorla, *a local version of the ubiquitous summertime "iced coffee": an espresso "on the rocks" sweetened with almond syrup. Who am I? Where do I come from? While I ruminate on the many layers of these questions, as airy as the flaky ones of my breakfast puff-pastry treat, I hear a rattling sound coming from Fenice, on my left. I turn towards her and I see her shivering. She looks at me out of the corner of her eye while breathing slowly. I smile at her; she smiles back: something is lingering between us. Our friends are engaged in a lively conversation, so I ask Fenice, in a low voice, if she has something to tell me. She bursts into a joyful laugh and tells me: "Just one word:* fortuna*!" I look at her, a bit puzzled. She immediately adds: "An old woman of your family just told me to tell you this word:* fortuna *(fortune)!" I smile and thank her for*

70 See, for example, Berardino Palumbo, *L'Unesco e il Campanile* (Roma: Meltemi, 2003), and "Iperluogo"; Ballacchino, "Per un'antropologia del patrimonio immateriale"; Fabio Dei, "Da Gramsci All' UNESCO. Antropologia, Cultura Popolare e Beni Intangibili," *Parolechiave* 49, no. 1 (2013): 131–46; Lia Giancristofaro, "Rethinking Folklore as Economical Pattern: Overview of Sustainable, Creative and Popular Strategies in Italian Domestic Life," *Human Affairs* 25, no. 2 (2015): 173–88, https://doi.org/10.1515/humaff-2015-0016

delivering the message to me and silently add another one to the stack of questions that float in my head.

While I ask Fenice to tell me something more about this message, Fiammetta joins the conversation and adds, "I told you! It is her great-grandmother! I saw her months ago!"[71]

I smile and nod. She continues, "Look at this!" She scrolls through the photos of a cell phone and shows us the picture we had taken, about an hour before, on our way to Galatina. It depicts the five of us and a huge, bright, glowing sphere of light just behind me. "It is her! In the picture!" adds Fenice. "That shining light is your great-grandmother! She has been with us throughout our pilgrimage! She blessed us!"

I stare at the picture, looking at my image. I cannot recognize myself. I see a woman, a tired face, a melancholic smile and a ball of light behind her. I see a person who has recently become parentless, feels lost, and cannot hide it.

Who am I? Where do I come from?" Guido's questions pound in my head like the clatter of the rattles of the tamburieddhri. They are piercing through my skin, and I do not know the answers.

My head spins and my vision starts to blur, for tears are starting to fill my eyes. I blink a couple of times and I breathe, trying to concentrate on the summer sun's warmth on my shoulders.

I savor the sweet aftertaste of the first coffee of my day. Soft, sugary, and unsurprisingly sticky.

71 It was a January afternoon when Fiammetta first told me that she was seeing a woman near me. After seeing a picture, she identified this presence as that of my maternal great-grandmother, who had died in 1995.

Chapter 3

La Papessa/The High Priestess

[Keywords: Inner Wisdom, Intuition, Receiving, Active Staying]

Figure 4. Boats in Gallipoli, on the Ionian sea. Photo: Giovanna Parmigiani.

LA DANZA DI GIO
Celesti stelle si accendono
Ritmo binario incalza
Nudo il piede batte il suolo
Neri nodi scuotono
Battono il petto e la fronte
Frustano l'anima
Ne modificano lo stato
Nero diventa bianco
Celesti stelle sorridono
Al blu cobalto
Sipari di velluto
Ancora celano il non detto

GIO'S DANCE
Celestial stars light up
Binary rhythm, a rapid pace
Bare feet beat the ground
Black knots shake
They beat the chest and the forehead
They whip the soul
They change its state
Black becomes white
Celestial stars smile
At the cobalt blue
Velvety curtains
Yet again they withhold what is unsaid.

A WhatsApp message. What a strange way to share a poem: an unanticipated gift from Magenta. "It is for you," she wrote, laconically. I rejoiced, thinking about the grace and vision behind the act of circulating forms of beauty. I read her verses, and, for the first time, I look at myself with her eyes. The poem is "for me" not (only) because I am the recipient of a gift; it is "for me" because I am, together with pizzica *dancing, the protagonist.*

***

Meditadanzando is the name of the course Viola promotes for the general public. Its name is a fusion between the imperative *medita* (meditate!) and the gerund *danzando* (dancing), and it is not at all an oxymoron, according to her. The reason behind this, she claims, lies in the use of the gerund. The latter is the verbal form that refers to an action *in the moment in which it is performed*. It is the closest way to indicate the present moment, the *qui-e-ora* (here-and-now). This active stillness—the *-sti* root of the word *destino*, the *stare* of the Salento dialect, the dancing-while-meditating, or *presence*—is what, according to Viola, is at the core of the gerund—and of a particular historicity: one that is spiritually enhancing, physically grounding, and emotionally balancing.

I attended many, at least a dozen, *Meditadanzando* meetings with Viola, in many settings—in Salento and elsewhere, both indoors and outdoors. Some of these meetings were organized by Viola alone, some in collaboration with other spiritual practitioners: music-therapists, bio-dance mentors, aura-soma healers, and other "wellness" professionals. While the structure of the meeting followed a general template, the details and experiences varied according to the moments, collaborators, participants, and contexts.

The *Meditadanzando* meeting always starts with a preparation of the space made by Viola an hour before the scheduled beginning. She wants to finish preparing it before the first participants arrive so that she can be able to greet them properly. After all the participants arrive, Viola places them in a circle and formally greets them one by one. In the meantime, the Sister exploits the situation by spending a couple of words on her credentials, the *Meditadanzando* format and goals, and the possible experiences that the participants can experiment with during the meeting. Because Viola is a follower of the Umbanda religion and she works with the orixás, often the meeting is structured to facilitate connection with a particular one. I participated in events that aimed at tuning in with the energies of Iemanjá, Oxúm, Iansã, Oxóssi, and Nanã, to name just a few.

Generally, Viola introduces the characteristics of the orixás, making sure to present them in a way that does not upset the sensitivities of Catholic and Christian practitioners. She talks about energies, delves into the characteristics of those energies, and exploits the Umbanda syncretization by referring to the orixás by their name along with the name of the saints associated with them. Mostly, however, Viola presents the orixás through their material connections to natural elements. Partially, this is due to the fact that often *Meditadanzando* meetings occur outdoors, in an environment that resonates with the orixá with whom Viola has planned to work. Partially, this is because relationships with nature, she believes, are fundamental experiences for all of us, at different levels. Spiritually connecting with nature was what drew Viola to follow the Umbanda tradition. Her spirituality is "shamanic" and "Earth-based," and she finds that working with the orixás is a way to be in a relationship with nature at deeper levels—her own version of a local "poetics of dwelling.'"[1] Therefore, in her *medita-danzando* meetings, Iemanjá is presented as the sea (with all its qualities, which become the protagonists of Viola's framing of the energies); Oxúm, the unsalted waters; Iansã, the wind; Nanã, the Earth; Oxóssi, the woods. Participants are encouraged to "meet, listen to, encounter" the energies of the place and of all the elementals—that is to say, the various types of beings or spirits which live in nature.

Then, after some aura cleaning and incense smudges, Viola leads some "grounding exercises." The latter have the function of relaxing the body, of actively connecting the participants with the energies of the earth, sky, and of the elementals of the place, and of preparing them to the *pizzica* experience, which is the *forte* of the meeting. Viola very carefully chooses the *pizziche,* which she broadcasts through the computer and some loudspeakers, cherry-picking among the *pizzica* repertoire available on YouTube. They are mostly new *pizziche* or contemporary interpretations of traditional ones, performed by certain *pizzica* singers or groups. *Tremulaterra* and *Mara la Fatìa* by Antonio Castrignanò, *Verde Lumia* by *Criamu*, *Mamma la Rondinella* by Ludovico Einaudi and the Taranta Project, and *Pizzica di Torchiarolo* by Enza Pagliara, among others, are some of her go-to choices.[2] According to Viola, these are examples of "healing *pizziche,*" of a *pizzica che cura* (see chapter 5). Not all the available renderings of *pizzica,* according to her,

1 Ingold, *Perception of the Environment.*
2 See appendix for selected video links.

are performed for dancing; even less, she argues, are they appropriate for a healing, spiritual dance.

The participants of the *Meditadanzando* meeting are then encouraged to move their bodies spontaneously, following the music. Some of the ones I met already knew how to dance *pizzica,* some others did not. Knowing how to dance *pizzica* is not mandatory nor very important for Viola. The most essential part of the dance is experiencing a connection through the movement: with the music—with one's own body, mind, and soul; with nature; with one another; and, possibly, with more-than human and other-than-human persons. The dancing usually takes a good hour, and Viola accompanies the music and dancers by playing the *tammorra*—a bigger *tamburieddhru,* without rattles. She calls it *tamburo sciamanico,* shamanic drum; she uses it only in ritual occasions.

After the *pizzica* dancing, the participants are asked to lie on their mats and to follow a guided meditation. At the end of the meditation, after a few refreshments, it is time for the "final sharing," in which participants are encouraged to disclose, if they feel like it, the visions, emotions, meditations, thoughts, and considerations they experienced during the *Meditadanzando.* This is one of the most intense moments of the meetings. Sometimes it lasts a few minutes, sometimes more. Viola tries to keep it under an hour, but she always encourages every participant to stay connected, and to get in touch with her in the following days, if they wish to. The energy moved during *Meditadanzando* meetings, she claims, lasts for a few days.

Meditadanzando is only one of the ways in which my interlocutors experience *pizzica,* and it is not necessarily the most profound and intimate one. Thought of as an introduction to *pizzica* spiritual dancing for newcomers, *Meditadanzando* often attracted persons who had not lived *pizzica* in this way before. While not the main practice of the Sisters, *Meditadanzando* has nonetheless been a good point of observation for my research. I could witness people approaching *pizzica* for the first time (or for the first time in *this* way) and sharing intense experiences and personal breakthroughs. Some of them I could follow over time. Others, the ones that occurred to persons I have not had the chance to meet again, remained linked to personal narratives shared with the group at the end of the *Meditadanzando* meetings.

The type of feedback disclosed by the participants was of various natures: it could comprise visual experiences (e.g., visions, mental images, or insights related to "presences" around them), auditory stimuli (e.g., messages, words, particular emotional reactions to the sounds of *pizzica* and of the *tammorra*), and diverse sensory engagements (feeling particular energies, emotions, blockages). Most of the time, though, I noticed that, no matter what the perceptive medium was, the experiences reported could fall into one of two categories: "memories" or "desires." Examples of the former are experiences of the past, of particular childhood emotions, of visions of themselves in their childhood or in other lives, connections with "more-than-human" presences (i.e., dead relatives, other dead persons, gods or goddesses, elementals), *déjà-vu*. These were some of the possible ways to connect with one's past that I witnessed directly: often profoundly touching, emotionally charged, and somehow liberating occurrences, according to their protagonists. Examples of the "desire" dimensions of the experiences I observed are visions or oracles about the future, indications on one's life path or life mission, spiritual connections with "more-than-human" presences and places.

The gerund of *meditadanzando*, the *qui-e-ora*, memories and desires: all these gesture towards a particular historicity that imbues the spiritual experiences of the Sisters and of the protagonists of the *Meditadanzando* meetings. The more I participated in the latter, the more I realized that the transformative dimension of *pizzica*, in fact, appears to be directly linked to fostering access to a peculiar way to understand and experience time that I call "expanded present."[3]

***

I learned to dance pizzica *in a small dance studio with four other persons and our instructor, Viola. It was late September when I saw a post on Facebook that was advertising her* pizzica *course, and I immediately signed up. I tried not to overthink my decision, but, I confess, I joined the course not without some personal hesitation. Dancing was definitively something out of my comfort zone; nonetheless, I really believed that I could not study* pizzica *without trying to dance it first. As the weeks passed, I started dancing* pizzica *more and more without really putting too much thought into it. I shared my life with the lives of the Sisters, and I followed them to local festivals, I danced with them in the* ronde, *I participated in their informal gatherings, I attended* Meditadanzando *meetings, and I started to listen to* pizzica *music more often.*

By the time spring arrived, I was ready.

***

Historicities, or "forms of human awareness of being and becoming in time," are key in the "anthropology of history" subfield that emerged recently with the aim of offering an ethnographic account of the many alternatives to the historicist "linear" approach to time and history.[4] The "historicist framework" that pervades the mainstream discourses of the West and academic disciplines is commonly and mistakenly perceived as the "natural" way to understand and experience time and history–when it is, in fact, a specific

3 For a comparison on the role of temporality in spiritual practices, see Ana Mariella Bacigalupo, *Thunder Shaman* (Austin: University of Texas Press, 2016).

4 Stewart, *Dreaming and Historical Consciousness*, 223.

one, and certainly not the *only* one.[5] This recent corpus of work on historicities has produced key contributions to the analyses of historical consciousness and to the deconstruction of mainstream Western approaches to time and history. Moreover, it proves to be an important reference point also for the study of contemporary Pagan practices.[6]

Memory and expectation, a version of which is what the Sisters call desire (*desiderio*), are well-known categories for philosophy scholars. Indissolubly linked to Augustine, they are the features of his understanding of time as a "measure of the soul."[7] The Sisters and the particular historicity they follow, which I have been calling "expanded present," clearly resonate with some of the claims made by the philosopher from Hippo—not without important dissonances. Augustine, notably, claimed that within the soul past and future do not exist. Instead, in addition to the

5 On historicities and different ways to experience time and temporality, see, e.g., Stewart, *Dreaming and Historical Consciousness*, and "Historicity and Anthropology"; Hodges, "Time of the Interval," and "Reinventing 'History'?"; Palmié and Stewart, "Introduction"; Bacigalupo, *Thunder Shaman*. On the importance of "futuricity" instead, see Zeitlyn, "Haunting, Dutching, and Interference Provocations." On the "danger of homochronism" see Kevin K. Birth, "The Creation of Coevalness and the Danger of Homochronism," *Journal of the Royal Anthropological Institute* 14, no. 1 (2008): 3–20. On "history without chronology" see Tanaka, "History without Chronology." See also Phil Ford, "Diviner's Time," https://www.weirdstudies.com/66

6 Parmigiani, "Spiritual *Pizzica*."

7 Augustine's understanding of time has been the protagonist of several debates in the history of Continental philosophy. Moreover, as Italy is a Catholic country, it is not surprising that it ended up playing a role also outside academia and niche debates. While it is a legitimate matter of inquiry who, for example, is "Heidegger's Augustine" and what are its relationships with the "original" one (see, for example, Agustín C. Corti, "Heidegger, intérprete de San Agustín: El tiempo. Nuevas fuentes para la recepción heideggeriana de las Confesiones de San Agustín," *Revista de Filosofía* 32 no. 1 (2007): 143–63; and Annachiara Barizza, "Un'interpretazione fenomenologica di Agostino: Heidegger lettore del X libro delle 'Confessioni'," *Annali di Studi Religiosi* 4 (2003): 121–44), it can be relatively safely argued that the philosopher from Hippo has been a reference point for philosophers who understood time as an internal category and not mainly as a category defined by a measurable duration. In this sense, Descartes and Kant are closer to the Sisters' "expanded present" historicity than Aristotle or Newton. See also Gell, *Anthropology of Time*.

present, which is our measure of experience, we can find a "present of the past," that we call memory, and a "present of the future," that we call expectation—or, in the Sisters' jargon, desire.[8] In this perspective, the experiences of memory (present of things past) and that of desire (presence of things anticipated) coexist in the expanded present historicity that the Sisters access to by dancing *pizzica*, among other practices. Similarly to Augustine's understanding of time, this particular historicity can be considered as a "measure of the soul," but it differs from other "presents" or "here-and-now," in important ways.

The first substantial characteristic of the Sisters' historicity is that it does not comprise the arc of only one lifetime, but it spans multiple ones: whether they are considered *previous* or *parallel* lives, they are nonetheless understood and experienced as coeval. Moreover, and most importantly, the "expanded present" is not conceived by the Sisters as a "non-time," neither as an "eternal time," nor as the result of "bracketing" the past or the future times. It is not a "mythical time," out of history, either.[9] This separates the historicity of the Sisters from both old and recent references to "eternity" and contemporary "mindfulness" philosophies.

8 In his *Confessiones* XI, 20 Augustine writes that: "*Quod autem nunc liquet et claret, nec futura sunt nec praeterita, nec proprie dicitur: tempora sunt tria, praeteritum, praesens et futurum, sed fortasse proprie diceretur: tempora sunt tria, praesens de praeteritis, praesens de praesentibus, praesens de futuris. sunt enim haec in anima tria quaedam, et alibi ea non video: praesens de praeteritis memoria, praesens de praesentibus contuitus, praesens de futuris expectatio.*" "What is also clear and proved, is that neither the things of the future nor those of the past exist. Thus, it is not said properly that the times are three: past, present, and future. Maybe it could be said that the times are three [but these are]: the present of the past, the present of the present, and the present of the future. In fact, these three are in the soul, and I do not see them anywhere else. The present of the things of the past is memory, the present of the things of the present is contemplation, and the present of the things of the future is expectation." (My translation. See Augustine of Hippo, *Confessions*, trans. James Joseph O'Donnell [Oxford: Oxford University Press, 1992]).

9 On "mythical time" see, e.g., Claude Lévi-Strauss, *Tristes Tropiques*, trans. John and Doreen Weightman (New York: Atheneum, 1981 [1955]); and Bacigalupo, *Thunder Shaman*, 34.

If the history of religious thought in the West is full of references to eternity as a dimension of time, it is important to acknowledge that this concept is still of interest today and that there are contemporary "spiritual" and yet non-religious versions of it, too. The already quoted Sibaldi, for example, an Italian spiritual leader followed also by the Sisters, offers a peculiar understanding of time, elaborating on the basis of his secular interpretation of the Egyptian myths of Isis.[10] His reflection on time fosters a conceptualization of a *non-time*, or a *zona accanto al tempo* ("place on the side of time"). In his attempt to make sense of a historicity that challenges the linearity of time, he refuses a conciliation between eternity and the infinitesimal duration of the present moment by postulating the possibility of accessing a time outside time, a time that is not time anymore. The women of the *cerchio* and their expanded present historicity only superficially can appear to be in line with such an understanding of time and temporality. In fact, their time is not defined by its non-linearity but by its being *at the same time* linear, cyclical, *and* coeval. The expanded present is not conceived and experienced outside a temporality imagined as linear, but it is understood as a linearity *enriched by* a coevality. It is not an empty time; rather, it is a rich, full-textured one. This expanded present can be accessed not in a present time conceived outside or "on the side of" the here-and-now, but it is experienced within the *everyday* flow of time. The encounters of one's previous lives are at the same time acknowledged as *past* and experienced as *co-present,* and the same can be said for one's experiences of the "future." The persons that they are meant to be but are not *yet,* the ones that emerge through synchronicities, that can be accessed to through *bellezza,* and that are part of their destiny (*destino*) (see chapter 2 and below), are present in the present while not fully fulfilled in that present.

10 Igor Sibaldi, *Resuscitare: L'arte di riportare in vita ciò che credevamo perduto* (Milan: Mondadori, 2018).

Another important point can be made in reference to the notion of "eternity." As I anticipated, while "spiritual," the perspective of the Sisters is not exclusively Christian. This perspective emerges not only in the "karmic" approach to life experiences that they follow but also in their non-eschatological (but indeed teleological) understanding of time. *Eternity* is a word indissolubly linked to the latter in the history of Western thought and is therefore unfitting to describe the "expanded present" historicity. This coevality of the "expanded present" also marks a distance from popular definitions of the "here-and-now" that derive from what, among New Agers and others alike, is usually referred to nowadays as "mindfulness." The expanded present historicity, by focusing on the here-and-now, does not suggest that the linear past and present "do not exist" or that they need to be, somehow, "bracketed" in order to "live fully in the moment."[11] They are, instead, part of the texture of the expanded present in which linearity and coevality co-exist: they are part of the "dialogue" of "chronotopes" that characterizes their experience of time.[12]

11 See, for example, among many others, Eckhart Tolle, *The Power of Now: A Guide to Spiritual Enlightenment* (Vancouver, BC: Namaste Publishing, 2004), and *A New Earth: Awakening to Your Life's Purpose* (New York: Penguin, 2005); Thich Nhat Hanh, *Bells of Mindfulness* (Berkeley: Parallax Press, 2013). See also Ronald Purser, *McMindfulness: How Mindfulness Became the New Capitalist Spirituality* (London: Repeater, 2019).

12 On the notion of "chronotope" see M. M. Bakhtin, *The Dialogic Imagination* (Austin: University of Texas Press, 1981). See also, e.g., Kristina Wirtz, "The Living, the Dead, and the Immanent," *HAU: Journal of Ethnographic Theory* 6, no. 1 (2016): 346; Pellegrino, *Greek Language, Italian Landscape*. The historian Helge Jordheim has argued that the German historian Koselleck's theory of historical times has been erroneously understood as a theory of periodization. Rather, Jordheim claims, it needs to be understood as a theory of multiple temporalities, "a theory developed to *defy* periodization." ("Against Periodization: Koselleck's Theory of Multiple Temporalities," *History and Theory* 51, no. 2 (2012): 151 Emphasis in the original.) She writes that "at the core of Koselleck's work is the attempt to replace the idea of linear, homogeneous time with a more complex, heterogeneous, and multilayered notion of temporality . . .achieved by means of three dichotomies: between natural and historical, extralinguistic and intralinguistic, and diachronic and synchronic time."

So far, in order to better explain what the expanded present is, I made claims on what it is not. Another way, more explicative, to understand how the Sisters experience this particular "healing" historicity is by reading it through a lens inspired by the well-know "figural interpretation" proposed by the German philologist Erich Auerbach.[13] Scholars of literary criticism and of Dante are very familiar with the seminal work of this author who, in *Mimesis* and in *Essays on Dante*, addresses the meanings of the Latin term *figura* (figure).[14] Originally linked to the aesthetic notion of shape, or "plastic form," this term, through Augustine, becomes in the Middle Ages a synonym of "prefiguration": the removal of a concrete event from a dimension of time to an eternal one.[15]

A famous example of figural analysis is that applied by Auerbach to Cato in Dante's *Divine Comedy*: a must-read interpretation for generations of high-schoolers in Italy and for Dante scholars throughout the world.[16] The Cato who lived in the first century BCE represents a *figura futurorum* – a

---

This interpretation of Koselleck's work is important for mine for, at least, two reasons. First, it represents an important theoretical reference point to frame the "expanded present" historicity that I found in Salento, since it postulates the co-presence of linear and synchronous temporalities within a theory of modernity. Second, it offers an understanding of modernity that could allow for the coevality *different modernities*, without the need of opposing "modern" and "pre-modern." (See below, chapter 4).

13 See also Courtney Handman, "Figures of History," *HAU: Journal of Ethnographic Theory* 6, no. 1 (2016): 237–60.

14 Erich Auerbach, *Mimesis: The Representation of Reality in Western Literature* (New York: Doubleday, 1957) and *Studi su Dante* (Milan: Feltrinelli, 1967).

15 Auerbach, *Studi su Dante*, 42.

16 Dante, in his *Divina Commedia*, put as a guardian of the Purgatory the Pagan Cato. The latter, who lived in the first century BCE, was an opponent of Caesar in the civil war, and a protector of the Roman Republic. He committed suicide in the aftermath of Caesar's victory in Utica. He has been considered since an example of bravery: a person who gave his life for freedom. Dante commentators frequently pointed out how surprising it is that the Christian author of the *Commedia* gave this prominent role in the *Commedia* to a Pagan who committed suicide. Auerbach proposes to understand this through his figural analysis, which associates the Roman Cato and Dante's Cato as two

figure of the future – of the one encountered by Dante in the *Divina Commedia*. Here Cato, who committed suicide in his earthly life to affirm freedom, is the guardian of Purgatory and of the freedom that Christ granted to all human beings with his death and Resurrection. In Dante's perspective, the Cato who committed suicide in Utica and the one who guards Purgatory are two historical figures that inhabit two different times; nonetheless, they are perceived so intimately connected that their meanings in Dante's *Divina Commedia* depend on each other. Before delving into some important details of the figural analysis in order to better understand the expanded present historicity, I propose to start thinking about the aforementioned connections that the Sisters and the *Meditadanzando* attendees experienced with their memories and desires *through dancing pizzica* as "figures." These experiences, as I will show below, are understood by the Sisters as forms and pre-figurations of their *destino* (destiny, see chapter 2). While not identical to the Christian "eternity," the latter is nonetheless a time that gives meaning to the present. The spiritual experiences accessed through dancing *pizzica*, among other techniques, are *figurae* of their final destination, of their life goals, of the senses and meanings of their (multiple) incarnations.[17] *Destino* is not an abstraction in the lives of the Salentinian Pagans I met, nor is it the memory of their past lives: as it will be clearer below, they are fully *historical* conditions.[18]

There are many aspects of the *figura* that are relevant for understanding the particular historicity of the Sisters. The most important of them, for this book, are the historical

---

mutually dependent historical figures, bearers of freedom, that inhabit different historical times.

17 Clearly, a religious or spiritual framework lies at the foundations of *figurae* in the Middle Ages. A religious and spiritual one, whilst different, is at the base of the Sisters' experience of the "expanded present" historicity.

18 It could be possible to read this also in conversation with studies on the "divine double" or *daimon*. See, e.g., Charles Stang, "Reading Plato's Many Doubles." In *Our Divine Double* (Cambridge, MA and London, England: Harvard University Press, 2016).

dimensions of *figurae* and their relationship with magic. First, *figura* allows for an interpretation of two (or more) persons, events, circumstances, etc. as connected. This association is so deep that, in spite of their being different and not identical, they all contain, give meaning to, encompass, and shape the others, reciprocally.[19] These historical, although not yet fulfilled, connections between events or persons (that are not ideas or abstractions) are very important elements of the spiritual experiences of the Sisters. The past life or childhood experiences (memories) and the future ones (desires) "encountered" during *pizzica* dancing are not lived and understood as theoretical "concepts" or "abstractions" but as concrete, historical dimensions—and so are what my Pagan interlocutors call synchronicities. The historical dimension remains solidly in place even though these "encounters" are accessed through non-representational practices and in non-measurable ways.[20]

19 In the words of Auerbach: "Figural interpretation establishes a connection between two events or persons, the first of which signifies not only itself but also the second, while the second encompasses or fulfills the first. The two poles are separated in time but both, being real events or figures, are within time, within the stream of historical life. Only the understanding of the two persons or events is a spiritual act, but this spiritual act deals with concrete events whether past, present, or future, and not with concepts or abstractions; these are quite secondary, since promise and fulfillment are real historical events, which have either happened in the incarnation of the World or will happen in the second coming." (Auerbach, *Studi su Dante*, 53) Clearly, this could be also read in relation to apophenia (see footnote 117).

20 My claim on the epistemological validity of these non-rational experiences should not surprise. Many anthropologists, as a matter of fact, have argued in favor of the knowledge potential of non-representational insights. See, e.g., Bacigalupo, *Thunder Shaman*, 70–72; Michael Lambek, "The Anthropology of Religion and the Quarrel between Poetry and Philosophy," *Current Anthropology* 41, no. 3 (2000) 309–20 and *The Weight of the Past: Living with History in Mahajanga, Madagascar* (New York: Palgrave Macmillan, 2002); Stephan Palmié,"Historicist Knowledge and Its Conditions of Impossibility," in *The Social Life of Spirits*, ed. Ruy Blanes and Diana Espírito Santo (Chicago: University of Chicago Press, 2013), 218–39.; Pace, *Le religioni nell'Italia che cambia*; McCall, *Dancing Histories.* With Palmié and Stewart's words, there is an "issue that philosophical historicism banned as beyond the pale of acceptable and legitimate accounts of the past: that of historical knowledge derived not

These elements have implications that are both cognitive and emotional, intellectual and experiential. On a practical level, they transform and give shape not only to my informants' experience of temporality, but also to their ways of knowing, their experience of selfhood and of relationships, and to the ways they approach well-being. In other words, the experience of *figurae* and the "expanded present" historicity accessed through them allows for a "participatory" consciousness and experience of the world, otherwise called "magic."[21] While *figura*, in Auerbach's (mis)interpretation of magic as actions that want to produce effects, differs from "mythical thinking" or "magic," an alternative understanding of the latter, such as the one I describe in this book, could not only be compatible with figural interpretations, but could also be considered at the core of them.[22] This is what I claim about "presence magic" among

from diligent and painstaking research and reconstruction, but through revelation, mantic technique, oneiric, prophetic, or otherwise "inspired" (instead of rationally contrived) forms of knowledge production." ("Introduction," 213.) McCall, in particular, made a compelling claim, that: "clearly, positing the irrational, nonrational, or quasi-rational status of divinatory practices provides little real understanding of the forms of knowledge engaged by these processes. Rather, a positivist approach to constructing questions about divination is little more than an exercise in distancing subject and object, a bounding of both the reasoning of analysis and the reasoning of the analyzed such that any variable grounds for mutual understanding become methodologically excluded." (*Dancing Histories*, 150–51.) Moreover, an interesting point on the epistemology of dreams is made by Benjamin, who writes that "the realization of dream elements in the course of waking up is the canon of dialectics. It is paradigmatic for the thinker and . . . for the historian." (Walter Benjamin, *The Arcades Project* [Cambridge, MA: Harvard University Press, 1999], section IV 4,4.) On the Sisters and Benjamin, see below.

21 See, in particular, Susan Greenwood, *The Nature of Magic: An Anthropology of Consciousness* (New York: Berg, 2005), *Anthropology of Magic*, and *Developing Magical Consciousness* (New York: Routledge, 2019); Susan Greenwood and Erik D. Goodwyn, *Magical Consciousness* (New York: Routledge, 2016); and chapter 4.

22 Auerbach writes that "Figural prophecy implies the interpretation of one worldly event through another; the first signifies the second, the second fulfills the first. Both remain historical events; yet both, looked in this way, have something provisional and incomplete about them; they point to one another and both point to something, still to come, which will be the actual, real, and

my Pagan interlocutors. The experiences and the practices associated with the connections between *figurae* appear to be both central and necessary in their spiritual practice. The co-presence of linearity and coevality is at the very basis of the magical "participatory" experiences that I will address in more detail in chapter 4.

At a superficial level, it would be tempting to categorize both magic and *figurae* as pre-modern—and, therefore, non-scientific, non-rational and, consequently, substantially worthless or faulty. If this co-presence of linearity and coevality is evident in the figural interpretation of medieval thought developed by Auerbach, the reader could be tempted to confine them within our past, assuming that such a historicity would not be, in normal circumstances, easily considered as a product of modernity.[23] If Auerbach's description of the medieval figural system is clearly part of a *pre*-modern way of thinking and sensing, though, this does not mean that it cannot resonate with what I witnessed and experienced among the Sisters and other Pagan groups in Salento, especially if read within a Demartinian

definitive event" (*Studi su Dante*, 58) "thus history, with all its concrete force, remains forever a figure, cloaked and needful of interpretation. . . all history remains open and questionable, points to something still concealed." (*Studi su Dante*, 58.) This claim is very interesting if read in connection with the experience of synchronicities. (See chapter 4.) The framework, here, is clearly connected to Neoplatonism, but it is worth noting, in reference to the Sisters, that in both the figural analysis reading of the Middle Ages and in the experience of my interlocutors, figures point towards something that is future, but, in a way, always present (being that it is linked to eternity in the first case, and to *destino* in the second). See Auerbach, *Studi su Dante*, 59–60.

23 This appears to be Auerbach's position. He claims that: "in the modern view, the provisional event is treated as a step in an unbroken horizontal process; in the figural system the interpretation is always sought from above; events are considered not in their unbroken relations to one another, but torn apart, individually, each in relation to something other that is promised and not yet present. Whereas, in the modern view the event is always self-sufficient and secure, while the interpretation is fundamentally incomplete, in the figural interpretation the fact is subordinated to an interpretation which is fully secured to begin with: the event is enacted according to an ideal model which is a prototype situated in the future." (*Studi su Dante*, 59.)

approach, that stresses the importance of notions such as "presence," "crisis of presence," "de-historification," and "re-presentification (see chapter 4). In its contemporary Salentine version, the figural understanding I described, while deploying a historicity that postulates an eschatological perspective, is indeed informed by the multi-layered, full-textured dimension of *destino*.

The latter, in line with what is argued by sociologist Theodore Schatzki, could be teleological without being evolutionary, and oriented towards an open and indeterminate understanding of futurity.[24] The figural understanding of life-in-time is co-present with modern mainstream understandings of (uni)linear time and history. "Non-modern" or "differently modern," it is worth pointing out, are not necessarily synonyms of "pre-modern," and this is why the Salentine case could add to the complexity of regimes and experiences of modern and postmodern time and historicities in the "West."[25] As historians and scholars of esotericism have pointed out (and I will describe in more detail in chapter 4), magic and the "rejected knowledge" that it is often associated with it are not *alternatives* to modernity. As a matter of fact, they lie at the very core of it—defining, so to speak, the specificity of modernity by its claim of *not being* what it rejected—i.e., "the occult." Consequently, what we have been used to labeling (with moral connotations, too) as "pre-modern," "non-modern," or "superstitious" has always been, in fact, (to an extent that scholars have not always been ready to see and admit) an important part of modernity and, all the more so, of postmodernity.

24 See also Zeitlyn, "Haunting, Dutching, and Interference Provocations."

25 For a comparison, see on this topic, e.g., Frederique Apffel-Marglin, *Subversive Spiritualities* (New York: Oxford University Press, 2011); Jordheim, "Against Periodization" on the work of Koselleck. It is important to specify, moreover, that, often, what is usually called representations of history, historicities, and ontologies of the Global North are its mainstream discourses. There are several alternative examples within those contexts that challenge such discourses. The Sisters are one example of this.

As my ethnography with Pagan practitioners shows, these "alternative" ways to experience one's being in the world are relevant also today, and a key element to understand the complexity of the contemporary world.[26]

***

It's April in Salento. The flowers are blooming, and the fields are starting to blush with hundreds of poppies. The sun generously doles out its warmth to humans and plants, animals and rocks. I thankfully take in what I can afford to, sending blessings of gratitude. Beauty surrounds me and all feels very relieving and incredibly soothing. I took care of my ill mother in the north for a few weeks, 24/7, and I returned to Salento a few days ago for another twenty – profoundly sad and physically exhausted. Overwhelmed by the cancer of my mother, by hospitals, doctors, lab tests, medical prophylaxes, by the recent death of my beloved grandmother at the beginning of the month, by the funeral arrangements and by the uncertainty of the near future, my return to Salento feels like coming home and restoring a connection with myself. After some energy-draining, sleepless, emotionally intense and physically challenging weeks, I need this break to find some grounding, to process my sadness, to be nurtured. I need it for me, and, especially, to be able to take better care of my mom and of the situation in my birth town, where I am going to fly, shortly. I feel overwhelmed by my thoughts and worries, and I look forward to meeting Viola at the pizzica *class.*

I had a strange dream some nights ago: I was at Viola's house, which looked like a boat's deck. My mother was on it. She was younger. Wearing a light brown raincoat, she was standing with a suitcase in her hands. She was looking away, at the horizon, in the sailing direction. My sister and I were a few meters at her back. Following the Sisters' indications, I wrote the dream down in my journal, and narrated it to some of them: to Viola, first of all, one of its protagonists. Images and fragments of the dream

26 On historicities and modernities, see, e.g., Cornish, "Fashioning Magic, Fashioning History."

fluctuate in my mind, but it is mostly its emotional signature that is still lingering in me. I know *that the dream had to do with an impending farewell, from my mother: something I am really not prepared for. I gather up all the energies that I have left, and I dress up before the* pizzica *class: I put on a silk blue-green dress that I have never worn before, some long earrings, a necklace, and also some make-up. This is not at all what I would normally do before a* pizzica *class. All women dancers, Viola included, usually wear a long skirt and a shirt, and I do, too. It is easier to dance* pizzica *with such informal attire. Dressing up is definitely an unusual choice, on my part, but I feel it is the right one today. It is a special occasion, in my heart. I feel that I need to dance* pizzica, *today, in honor of my mom: as a way to connect with her, to thank her, to send her energy and love. I need it also as a way to connect with myself and with my dream, and to prepare for her departure, whenever it is meant to take place.*

I arrive at the dance school with eyes full of tears and slightly nauseated. I greet Viola and ask her if she can make sure that I dance alone during the class. She immediately understands that I need a healing of some sort. She nods and hugs me, without saying a word.

***

How do the Sisters get to experience the "expanded present" historicity? In order to try to answer to this question, to better grasp the unknown with the known, so to speak, I propose to look at the German philosopher Walter Benjamin and, in particular, at his "dialectical images." In "The Arcades Project," Benjamin distinguishes the past from "what-it-has-been" and the "present" from the "now-time" (*Jetztzeit*) by explaining the dialectical relation between the "now" and the "what-it-has-been" through the concept of "dialectical image," otherwise defined as "dialectics at a standstill." While Benjamin's definition of the latter is not unambiguous in his work,[27] dialectical images are generally understood as the matrix of both a "way to think about critical materialist historiography" and "a way to understanding a radically alternative conception of time and historical experience."[28] It is worth noting, especially after reading Auerbach and having gotten acquainted with the spirituality of the Sisters, that in Benjamin, Auerbach, and in the experience of the Salentine Pagan protagonists of this book, both the aesthetic elements and the temporal ones are interpellated to think about an alternative historicity. One that has also, notably, political implications.[29] This element is particularly evident in Benjamin's work on photography[30] and in *The Work of Art in the Age of Mechanical*

27 On historicities and modernities, see, e.g., Cornish, "Fashioning Magic, Fashioning History," in *The Cambridge Companion to Walter Benjamin,* ed. David S. Ferris (Cambridge: Cambridge University Press, 2004), 177–98; Lindroos, *Now-Time Image-Space*.

28 Pensky, "Method and Time," 178; see also Michael Taussig, "History as Sorcery," *Representations* 7 (1984): 87–109.

29 "The 'trash of history' can be revealed as 'time differential' only if removed by dominant and approved traditions of interpretations and reception." (Pensky, "Method and Time," 190.) In this disruptive action lies the political potential of dialectic images and of adopting a different historicity. See, for a comparison, Parmigiani, *Feminism, Violence and Representation in Modern Italy: "We Are Witnesses, Not Victims."* Taussig writes, on Benjamin's dialectical images: "What he advocated was a sort of surrealist technique using what he called 'dialectical images'—an obscure yet compelling notion better left to example than to exegesis; what his friend Theodor Adorno referred to as 'picture puzzles' which shock by way of their enigmatic form and thereby set thinking in motion. . . . Picture-puzzles is of course how Freud referred to the manifest content of dream imagery, and if it was to the manifest and not the latent level that Benjamin was drawn, it was because of the way such images defamiliarized the familiar and shook the sense of reality in the given order of things, redeeming the past in the present in a medley of deconstructive anarchical ploys. Unlike current modes of Deconstruction, however, the intent here was to facilitate the construction of new forms of social life from the glimpses provided of alternative futures when otherwise concealed or forgotten connections with the past were revealed by the juxtaposition of images, as in the technique of montage-a technique of great importance to Benjamin." (Taussig, "History as Sorcery," 89.)

30 Walter Benjamin, "A Short History of Photography," *Screen* 13, no. 1 (1972): 5–26.

Reproduction.[31] According to Walter Benjamin "dialectical images" emerge as "interruptions, discontinuities, repetitions" of the flow of everyday historical time. They are "images" in that they "appear" as (emotionally and intellectually charged) glimpses, intuitions, cues in the flow of historical time that challenge and disrupt it.[32] In this *sense*

31 Walter Benjamin, *The Work of Art in the Age of Mechanical Reproduction* (Lexington, KY: Prism Key Press, 2010). In Benjamin's words: "it is not that what is past casts its light on what is present, or what is present its light on what is past; rather, image is that wherein what has been comes together in a flash with the now to form a constellation . . . . For while the relationship of the present to the past is purely temporal, the relationship of what-has-been to the now is dialectical: not temporal in nature, but *figural*." (*Arcades* N2a,3, my emphasis.) Benjamin himself explains how images differ from the "essences of phenomenology": "What differentiates images from 'essences' of phenomenology is their historical index. Heidegger seeks in vain to rescue history from phenomenological abstractly through 'historicity.'" (*Arcades* N3,1.) According to Lindroos, though, "The experience of *jetztzeit* can be understood as similar to the Leibizian monad, in which the acknowledgement begins from the moments themselves as related to a subject, and are not caused by exterior events" (*Now-Time Image-Space*, 92). In this sense, to push the analogy further, images could also be understood in a Proustian way: the time of the well-known *madeleine* is a monadic time.

According to Cadava (quoted by Lindroos, *Now-Time Image-Space*, 181), "history is also to be thought of within the language of photography. . . the photographic event interrupts the present as it occurred between the present and itself, between the moment of time and itself."

The image is defined as a space in which the then and the now form a constellation. The fact that Benjamin characterizes the temporal course as dialectical but not continuous (see Lindroos, *Now-Time Image-Space*, 201) is an important remark for better understanding the expanded present historicity characterized by both linearity *and* coevality.

32 "An alternative temporality emerges, against the predominant version of continuous, chronological time, as interruptions, discontinuities, unassimilable moments, repetitions, lags of disturbances . . . in short as 'time differentials'. . . . these time differentials are contained (or expressed by) concrete historical moments or even objects that, in the "normal" context of historical time, would be dismissed as immemorable, worthless, as not candidates for meaning." (Pensky, "Method and Time," 192; see also Taussig, "History as Sorcery.")

"The New temporal moment of Now is deciphered both as the negation of the homogeneous or mechanistic conception time, and as the negation of the punctual moment of Now, which had been conceptualized in the linearly understood course of time since Aristotle's physics." (Lindroos, *Now-Time Image-Space*, 84.)

(both in the understanding of this term as "meaning" and "feeling"), the traces of signification, associations, emotions, and symbols that the Sisters and many of my interlocutors experience by dancing *pizzica* (and by engaging with other "magical" activities) could be, then, considered as "dialectical images." They generate meaning and with it a peculiar way to understand and experience time and temporality, history and futurity. If, with Lindroos, one can claim that "[t]he cariological experience of the now, in other words, is not understood as a progress but as an actualization,"[33] it is clear that in the experience of the Sisters the *figurae* take shape through the experience of "dialectical images." These though are not relegated to special events and circumstances such as *Meditadanzando* meetings or rituals, but more often than not they inhabit the everyday, ordinary lives of my interlocutors as well. Synchronicities, in fact, could be considered as "dialectical images," too, as well as the various constellations of non-linear messages or experiences that characterize the lives of the Sisters.[34]

To summarize my claims, among Salentine Pagans, synchronicities are landmarks in the path of *bellezza,* which is understood as their *destino:* their path to happiness, abundance, and fulfillment. Destiny or *destino* is conceived as both the *destination* (of their journeys on Earth) and their *fate*. It is, etymologically, the result of something that is/stays already (the "active staying" of the Indo-European root *sta-*). *Destino* and their individual *figurae futurorum* are not an idea or an abstraction for the Salentine Pagans I met. They are, *figurally*, in the Auerbachian sense, historical

33 Lindroos, *Now-Time Image-Space,* 91.

34 As I pointed out in the previous chapter, synchronicities, besides being landmarks on the path of *bellezza* and of self-realization, are "a simultaneity of the normal or ordinary state with another state or experience which is not causally derivable from it, and whose objective existence can only be verified afterwards. This definition must be borne in mind particularly when it is a question of future events. They are evidently not synchronous but are synchronistic, since they are experienced as psychic images in the present, as though the objective event already existed." (Jung, *Synchronicity*, 29.)

enactments of the lives they are meant to live—that is, of the best possible versions of their lives. Synchronicities, then, occur in the "expanded present" of this *bellezza* path as "dialectical images," as "flashes," that figurally link their present experiences and lives to the historical actualizations linked to one's *destino*. The latter, while historically distant, in a linear perspective is nonetheless accessible in the "expanded present" as a feature of its coevality. One's *destino* is, in fact, the origin of happiness: one's own and, in virtue of the "oneness" of the Universe (see chapter 2), also of everything else. Being "aligned" with *destino*, therefore, translates into being in the synchronous path of *bellezza*, which is reached also by adopting an expanded present historicity. Since the latter is explicitly employed to get in touch, experience, sense, and ultimately enact happiness, it is considered as a technique that fosters our well-being. How can we all access our *destino*, then, according to the Salentine Pagans I met? By tuning in with our *desiderio*, our desire, our infinitude. Easier said than done, it is nonetheless the reason why *tarantate* of the past (who are seen as radically affirming their dissatisfaction and discontent with what-it-is and therefore powerfully claiming their infinitude) and the *pizzica* music that supported and "healed" them are considered and honored as teachers by the Sisters, and dancing *pizzica* an apprenticeship on the path of beauty.

***

The pizzica *class starts and I am lost in the music and in my thoughts. While I whirl, jump, and pant, images of my mother and me emerge from within. They blend with the nature of Salento, that she never had the chance to visit, and with the sound of the drums. I cry and pant and jump again, over and over. Images of my dream come to my mind, and a deep sadness comes out from under my skin, blending with my sweat. My feet hit the ground with a fury that comes from a sense of impotence and helplessness, and I whirl and spin to lose track of the borders of my body, as if*

I could melt and disappear into the air around me, as if I could merge with it. I delve deep into my overwhelming emotions. I feel as if my flesh were torn apart by the pain. After this labor, then, an idea gently comes through in my mind: the liberating experience of a sudden delivery. The music stops, and I do, too, dizzy and even more nauseated. Everything spins around me, and my eyesight is blurred. I breathe deeply, and I enjoy the feeling of gradually reconnecting to my vision, to my body, to my image in the mirror. Everything looks and feels different now. The sudden and unanticipated awareness of a line of action arrived as an unexpected gift. I look at the floor: I see one of my earrings lying close to my bare feet. I pick it up, and I realize that it broke during my dance, as if neatly shorn by an invisible shear. My cell phone rings. It is my mom. The pizzica *class is still on, but I take the call: I ignore that this would have been our last, relatively lighthearted, chat.*

"Viola, I need to ask you a favor," I utter while changing clothes in the locker room at the end of the pizzica *class. "Do you remember my dream: the boat, Otranto, the sea, your wooden room? I had this feeling tonight, while I was dancing, that I have to ask you to organize a farewell for my mother here in Salento, if she dies. I will have to ask to my sister Carolina to come here and to attend the ritual, too." "Of course, I am honored," Viola replies, without asking questions.*

The dream, the pizzica, *the pain, the sudden breakthrough, the acknowledgement of an unanticipated line of action, and the emotional lightness and freedom that came with it: all new experiences for me. The dream, the broken earring, and my mother's call: random occurrences or synchronicities?*

***

Exactly two weeks later, my mom died: a sudden and unexpected worsening of her physical conditions took her away, leaving the doctors, with whom I had spoken about her situation on the phone just a couple of days before, puzzled. In spite of having rescheduled my booked flight to an earlier date, I could barely make it to the hospital and arrived just moments after her final breath. I cried and told her that I was there, that I loved her, and that I would take care of my sister. I kissed her forehead. It was still warm. I looked at her face and I saw a teardrop coming out of her eye and then running on her cheek. I kissed her again and told her that I knew she was still there, that she could listen to me.[35]

***

For most Salentinians and scholars of *tarantisimo*, *tarantate* are associated with poverty, subalternity, and to cultural and economic "backwardness" (see chapter 2). Partially due to the success of de Martino's interpretations and of the work that followed his lead, and partially due to the "modernization" agenda of Salento, the *tarantate* are acknowledged and recognized almost exclusively in association with the past of Salento. They belong to its history, and *from this perspective* they are respected, narrated, and in some cases, capitalized.[36]

While the Sisters do acknowledge and respect this interpretation of the *tarantate* of the past, this is not the way they ultimately understand, make sense of, and connect with them. The *tarantate* might have not been educated and well-off; they might have struggled, in some cases, with mental health. Nonetheless, these elements are not relevant, since they do not necessarily collide with the *tarantate* being spiritual teachers. In addition to the acknowledgement of their brave dedication to follow their *desire* and infinitude (see chapter 2), they are also recognized as spiritually illuminated: *tarantate* were (and are), for my interlocutors, "shamans."[37] The association with the spider is

35 I have to acknowledge formally that both the interlocutors that had seen my deceased grandmother, in two different occasions and unaware one of the other, had foreseen some aspects linked to the death of my mother.

36 See, e.g., Lüdtke, "Dancing towards Well-Being," 44; chapter 2, and chapter 5.

37 The story of the term "shaman" is a complicated one in the fields of religious studies, anthropology and sociology of religion. Nonetheless, this is

not secondary in the Sisters' re-narration or "invention" of the *tarantate,* nor is their connection with the "countryside." Spiders are seen as potent power animals and nature as filled with elementals that strive to communicate with humans that are open to that experience—in the *filo,* thread, of the web of interconnections that characterizes Pagan neo-animist ontologies. The "embeddedness" of the *tarantate* in the natural environment is a prerequisite for their being recipients of the "bite."

The latter, according to the Sisters, is the sign that announced an impending "initiation" into higher spiritual realms. In other words, the real or alleged tarantula bite is not interpreted only and mainly as a nuisance but as a sign of election. Not unlike "shamanic" experiences and "callings" elsewhere, the physical pain and malaise following the tarantula bite is seen as an initiatory event: something that profoundly re-structured the life of the protagonists, and that, while challenging, was a necessary step in their journey towards spiritual evolution.[38] It is the path for the coming into being as a "shaman." Different from other interpretations of *tarantismo,* "shamans" are not, in fact, those who play the *pizzica* music that heals. According to the Sisters, "shamans" are the *tarantate* themselves. This simple distinction is quite an important one—one that sets apart the Sisters' understanding of *tarantate* from other, common and less common, interpretations, including those that put "healing" as the main goal of both the *tarantate* of the past and *tarantismo* itself.[39]

---

the word the Sisters use. See, e.g., Alice Beck Kehoe, *Shamans and Religion: An Anthropological Exploration in Critical Thinking* (Prospect Heights, IL: Waveland Press, 2000); Blain, *Nine Worlds.*

38 The "bite" of the tarantula spider is understood metaphorically: nobody, among my informants, was bitten by a spider before starting their spiritual journey.

39 Placida Staro suggests that "the diffusion of *tarantismo* throughout Italy is evidence of an important organizing device in the psychological structuring of a world-view, most especially governing the relationship between humans, fauna, flora, sentient and non-sentient beings." ("Reconstructing the Sense of

The studies on *tarantismo* and *neotarantismo*, beyond those by de Martino and his followers, also concentrate on other aspects of these phenomena: those of trance, possession, and ecstasis.[40] Sociologist George Lapassade, in particular, has famously analyzed *tarantismo* in a comparative perspective, underlining trans-cultural analogies between the Salentine music and rites and other forms of trance. In tracing the geographical and historical developments of the latter, he claims that what he calls "*techno-taranta*" is a contemporary form of trance linked to *pizzica* music and *neotarantismo*. In his book *Dallo Sciamano al Raver*, he claims that trance is not a synonym of possession, nor it is another way to refer to ecstasis. These distinctions allow him to understand contemporary forms of *neotarantismo* in connection to rave parties and music as collective forms of trance that allow for particular "healing" experiences. On this same line of interpretation stands also Anna Nacci, who stresses how in her studies of *pizzica* dancers throughout Italy, her informants pointed out, almost unanimously, the "liberating" or "cathartic" experience associated with this dance.[41] The trance triggered by *pizzica*, in these perspectives, is framed as a remedy for a twenty-first-century malaise. According to Nacci, the need of "getting out of oneself" is linked to the necessity to sedate the "sense of

---

Presence: Tarantula, Arlìa, and Dance," in *Performing Ecstasies: Music, Dance, and Ritual in the Mediterranean*, ed. Luisa del Giudice and Nancy E. Van Deusen [Ottawa: Institute of Mediaeval Music, 2005], 69).

40 See, e.g., Lapassade, *Intervista sul tarantismo*, and Georges Lapassade, *Dallo sciamano al raver. Saggio sulla transe* (Milano, Apogeo edizioni, 1997); Nacci, *Neotarantismo*; Del Giudice, "Folk Music Revival"; Lüdtke, "Dancing towards Well-Being"; Andromache Karanika, "Ecstasis in Healing: Practices in Southern Italy and Greece from Antiquity to the Present," in *Performing Ecstasies: Music, Dance, and Ritual in the Mediterranean*, ed. Luisa del Giudice and Nancy E. Van Deusen (Ottawa: Institute of Mediaeval Music, 2005), 25–36.

41 According to Nacci, citing Lapassade, one can talk about catharsis when personal desires and needs are included in trance rituals (*Neotarantismo*, 27). See also Gilbert Rouget, *La musique et la transe: esquisse d'une théorie générale des relations de la musique et de la possession* (Paris: Gallimard, 1980); Pizza, "Tarantism and the Politics of Tradition," n5.

oppression" of the metropolitan areas and other current hardships, such as the dissatisfaction, the precariousness, and solitude that characterizes, according to her, the contemporary world.[42]

While the Sisters and other Pagan practitioners I met in Salento do share with these scholars of *tarantismo* the acknowledgement of a possible link between *pizzica* and trance-like or ecstatic experiences, their position on both *tarantate* and on their own *tarantarsi* (making themselves *tarantate*) differs. First of all, playing and dancing *pizzica* does not always imply an altered state of consciousness. Sometimes it is indeed a *viaticum* for gnosis and connections with non-human or more-than-human presences (as, for example, for some participants during *Meditadandazando* meetings). Other times, though, dancing *pizzica* is just something as ordinary as hanging out with friends – nonetheless, this is not to say that it is less "spiritual" or "powerful" an experience. As I will point out in more detail below, there are very ordinary ways to dance *pizzica* that are as meaningful and eventful as the ritual ones. This point is linked to another central one: a key observation not only for the Sisters of the *cerchio* but also for scholars of *neotarantismo*. *Tarantismo* and *neotarantismo* have been studied and framed mainly as linked to special occasions and events such as rites, performances, and concerts. If the latter are part of the experience and interest of the Sisters, the everyday dimension of these phenomena have an important part in their points of view, too. Even those scholars who framed *tarantismo* as a form of possession have not been concentrating on the everyday life of the *tarantate*, unlike other scholars of possession elsewhere.[43] The everyday dimension of spirituality is a central point in

42 Nacci, *Neotarantismo*, 33.

43 See, e.g., Michael Lambek, *Knowledge and Practice in Mayotte: Local Discourses of Islam, Sorcery, and Spirit Possession* (Toronto: University of Toronto Press, 1993).

the life of the Salentine Pagans I met, since for them *pizzica* is not what Lapassade or Nacci claimed about ecstasis and trance. It is not something that makes one "escape" from one's ordinary life and from oneself.[44] Rather, it is an important instrument in order to connect (or re-connect) figurally with one's own *destino*: one's "true" self. It is a way to inhabit one's current incarnation in a more profound and conscious way, not a way to "escape" from it. Similarly, while the curative aspect of *pizzica* and the interpretation of *tarantismo* as primarily an illness to be healed have been central in the framing of *tarantismo* and *neotarantismo*, the Sisters do not believe that this was or is always the best approach to make sense of the phenomenon. While they indeed value *pizzica* as a healing, balancing, grounding method that could be used as a "medicine" for particular mind-body-spirit imbalances, they do not believe healing them is the main goal of dancing *pizzica*. It is framed more like a pleasant side-effect rather than the principal objective of the dance. The Sisters and the other contemporary Pagans that I met in Salento believe that, both for the *tarantate*-shamans and in their experience, trance or ecstatic states are not primarily a form of therapy. Dancing *pizzica*, even for the *tarantate* of the past, is understood primarily as a spiritual journey. The healing is a result of the latter, and not vice versa: in other words, it is not a goal, but a medium. Such an interpretation of *pizzica*, clearly, makes the whole distinction between adorcism and exorcism less useful.[45] *Pizzica*, understood as both a dance and a music, is seen, in this perspective, primarily as a transformative practice: a sort of alchemic process that transforms "copper" into "gold," guilt and remorse into memory, fear into desire, and pain into bodily and spiritual well-being.

44 Lapassade, *Dallo sciamano*, 23, 29.

45 Lapassade distinguishes between exorcism, when the spirit who possessed a person is asked to leave that person, and "adorcism," when the spirit possession is searched and facilitated. See Lapassade, *Intervista sul tarantismo*, and *Dallo sciamano*; Nacci, *Neotarantismo*, 34; Karanika, "Ecstasis in Healing."

It does so through the expanded present historicity—*de facto* a particular way to be "present" within a peculiar way to understand "history"—by connecting the dancer with one's "true self" or "higher self." It is not in itself a "cure": it is a co-protagonist, a teacher, in a transformation journey. This is why the *tarantate* of the past are seen as spiritual teachers and also why the Sisters refer to their spiritual practice as "*tarantarsi*" (make oneself *tarantata*). The "mastery" of the *tarantate*-shamans, both contemporary and of the past, is a *self*-mastery: that of *desiderio*. The latter, together with memory, in the expanded present historicity, are understood as ways to align oneself with one's own *destino*: the figural actualization of their own happiness, and, therefore, the highest achievement of a quest for well-being.

***

I just returned to Salento. I left my hometown the day after the funeral. I asked my biological sister to come with me. She did not know much about me and my research on Salento, but not without hesitations, she agreed to come. It was the first time we traveled together in many years. I explained to her the dream, the intuition, and that the ritual that Viola and the Sisters were organizing for our mom was a way to ease her way, to celebrate her life and accompany her departure. It was a way to let her go and to do so with and through our blessings. In spite of her Catholic upbringing and her understandable skepticism, Carolina agreed and followed me to Viola's place, where we all had to meet before the ritual.

The latter was taking place in a meadow close to the Adriatic Sea, a wonderful place in a beautiful spring afternoon. Viola had asked me and the participants to dress in white and to bring our instruments. She had contacted the Piccola Orchestrina Terapeutica *(Therapeutic Little Orchestra) and had chosen the right place for the ritual with Senefera a few days before.*

She also had prepared a little altar with some offerings, a small merkaba *with some offerings for Iemanjá, and asked my sister and me to bring some white flowers, candles, and some* frise *(a local bread) and wine to share with the attendees and the musicians.*[46]

***

Viola has finished preparing the space using incense, the sound of the tammorra *and some candles. There are ten of us: the Sisters and some friends. More of them will join us later. We stand in a circle, holding hands. Viola opens the ritual with a spontaneous prayer and then the* pizzica *music begins. Differently from Meditadanzando and similarly to the "tarantate ritual" in Galatina, the music is played live. Viola, Fiammetta, and I step inside the circle and begin to dance. The music carries us away, and I feel particularly attracted to the sound of the* tammorra. *The musicians immediately pick this up and start to play a* pizzica *that follows my dance, not expecting the contrary to happen. I feel moved by the generosity of this gesture, and I continue my dance. Fiammetta comes close to me and looks straight into my eyes. She stops dancing, following my steps and movements and blessing them. She utters the words of the song Senefera is singing as if she were speaking to me.*[47] *After a few* pizziche *it is time to put the merkaba in the sea. Viola had found a breach in the cliffs that resembled a uterus and asked me to follow her through that rocky womb and to release the merkaba in the sea, and, with it, my attachment and pain and anger. All this is meant to be a symbol of rebirth – for both me and my mom.*

46 *Merkaba,* or *Merkavah,* is a Hebrew word meaning "chariot" or more generally "vehicle." In esoteric contexts it is a complex concept, but it generally can be understood and conceptualized as a "bridge" between worlds.

47 Fiammetta later told me that she received some messages for me from my mother, during that dancing ritual.

Figure 5. Altar and offerings for a ritual for the passing of Maria Grazia Nicora, Otranto. Photo: Carolina Parmigiani.

Figure 6. Offerings for a ritual for the passing of Maria Grazia Nicora. Photo: Giuseppe Memmi

***

Pizzica is not only linked to rituals for the Sisters. It can be also a very mundane activity—but certainly never profane. Spirituality permeates specific events as well as ordinary life, in the experience of my Pagan interlocutors. Similarly, the expanded present historicity that they seek is not confined to special occasions or trance-like experiences.[48] As I mentioned before, the year in Salento is counterpointed by festivals (*feste*) and food festivals (*sagre*).[49] Remnants of the celebration of the agricultural year syncretized by the Catholic Church over the centuries or of ancient devotions to patron saints, every village or town in Salento has their specific festivals. The latter can be distinguished on the basis of their publics and of the season. Some festivals are more advertised and, therefore, might be more appealing to tourists, especially during the summer. Some others have smaller and more local ambitions and attract mainly Salentinians: they occur mainly, but not exclusively, during the winter months. The Sisters tend to avoid the former and can be found almost exclusively at the latter. In spite of the different audiences and ambitions, the two typologies of festivals retain many similar elements: the food, the colored merchandise stands, and the presence of *pizzica* "live." Most of the contemporary *pizzica* groups, in fact, perform in both types of festivals, and, I would say, who-plays-where, together with the location of the festival and the particular moment of the Wheel of the Year, are the most important elements in choosing what *festa* or *sagra* the Sisters should attend. While the traditional *pizzica* inventory is limited, and an important part of the repertoire of most groups, new *pizziche* come out every year—and this is not at all a bad thing for my interlocutors. Their attachment to the place and to tradition is not philological: rather,

48 This particular element distinguishes both the experience of the Sisters and my analytical framework from those that have stressed the "ecstatic" or "trance" element in *neotarantismo*.

49 On the topic of festivals and food festivals in Northern Italy, within a Pagan perspective, see Howell, *Food, Festival, and Religion*.

since tradition is a lived condition in the expanded present historicity, what makes the difference in the types of *pizzica* is not their ancestry or vocal conventions but their "healing potential," their "touching the chords of their souls."

Issues around *pizzica* and "tradition" are controversial in Salento. Some performers are more comfortable with being "faithful" to tradition by replicating the sounds and vocals of the past. Singers like Anna Cinzia Villani, for example, spent many years collecting experiences and insights on the musical performances of elders, deemed as bearers of the "true" *pizzica*. She developed a "raw" style of performance both in the choice of the instruments and in the type of vocals she uses. The old women in the fields did not receive any vocal training, and their singing was powerful while (and, possibly, in virtue of its being) "unpolished"—both in relation to intonation and style.[50] Others, for example Emanuela Gabrieli (both as a *solo* singer performer and in her collaboration with the *Triace* group), embrace a different attitude on performing *pizzica* today. Well-trained musically and vocally, she blends old and new *pizzica* songs with a more sophisticated vocal style. She introduced contemporary instruments and acoustics by collaborating, for example, with jazz players.[51] Others, such as the group Mascarimirì, are spokespersons of what they call *tradinnovazione,* a word resulting from the fusion of the terms "tradition" (*tradizione*) and "innovation" (*innovazione*). The *pizzica* songs they play are, for the most part, their own compositions, and their sound is a blend of traditional instruments and contemporary, computer-based, interventions.[52] The political, economic, and cultural aspects linked to what is and is not *pizzica* "tradition" in contemporary Salento are not to be underestimated: like the insights I gave in chapter 2 on the *tarantate* performance in Galatina, they lie at the

50 See appendix.
51 See appendix.
52 See appendix.

core of how to understand Salento today, its being both a tourist destination and a "political laboratory."[53]

Within such a panorama, the Sisters tend not to privilege a certain or other relationship between *pizzica* and "tradition": their criteria are not musical, but spiritual and thaumaturgical. There are *pizziche* that foster spiritual connections and healing, and others that do not. There are some that are spiritually enhancing and others that are not, regardless of the composition date of the songs or of the performing styles. On certain occasions, in fact, if they cannot find *feste* or *sagre* that suit them, even live *pizzica* music in pubs or restaurants could be spiritual and healing experiences for them.

The location of the live performance is also central in the choice of a festival for the Sisters, both in relation to the actual physical place and in relation to the people that attend the festival. Smaller festivals in little, even remote, places of southern Salento are, overall, privileged locations. This is for two main, energetic, reasons. Firstly, the Southern part of Salento is considered energetically special: powerful and enhancing, it carries a "chakra balancing" quality. It is not surprising, the Sisters argue in support of this claim, that it pullulates with dolmens and menhirs. Secondly, a smaller festival means fewer tourists and smaller crowds: both elements translate to a better chance to dance undisturbed and in energetically "lighter" contexts.

Usually, in these occasions, the Sisters blend in with the crowds of dancers who, in general, occupy the space between the stage of the live *pizzica* performers and the crowd of non-dancing spectators. Not every dancer attends these festival concerts with the same spirit, and normally it is likely that an external observer would not assume that the "reasons" and intentions behind the dancing of the Sisters are other than social. *Pizzica* in contemporary Salento, not different from other contemporary styles of spontaneous

53 See Pizza, *Il Tarantismo Oggi.*

dancing, is often performed just to have fun (*presciu*, in the Salento dialect) and to meet new people. In these occasions, it is almost exclusively danced in couples: male-female or female-female, with the exception of *danza scherma*, which is quite rare and danced, almost always, by men only.[54] So it is quite frequent that during these festivals, the Sisters dance with each other and with other dancers who do not share with them a "spiritual" approach to *pizzica*: sometimes they are acquaintances, some other times they are not. These *pizziche* are "*pizziche de presciu*" (*pizziche* for fun), as the Sisters call them, but are not at all unimportant. *Presciu* is an important spiritual element in the lives of my informants: it is a relational activity that fosters self-love, the sharing of "good" energy with people, and of intimacy. It is, in itself, a "figural" experience since it enacts an emotional state of joy and bliss that is in line with the *destino*. In this sense, *presciu* might also be linked to *bellezza*, and considered as a politics of "becoming."[55] *Presciu,* as a matter of fact, is a form of imagination—understood, with Karin Andriolo, as

54 It is frequently claimed that there are three types of *pizzica*: *pizzica de core*, *pizzica tarantata* and *pizzica scherma*. The first one is the most popular today. Danced in couples, it might or might not have "flirting" purposes. The second one is the curative one and associated with the *tarantate* of the past. The third is not very common today, but it used to be danced by men carrying (or pretending to carry) knives, with the purpose of settling conflicts. Today, it is mainly danced in a few towns, including Torrepaduli (especially for the San Rocco festival on August 16), Taurisano, and Galatone. The dancers do not carry knives but mimic them with the index or middle fingers. I have witnessed it live only once, outside of festival contexts, during a winter monthly informal and unofficial "dancing party" in Matino, where I followed the Sisters. Its revival, after a few years of *quasi* disappearance, was enacted by members of the Roma community that has been living in the area since the eighteenth century.

55 On the politics of becoming see, e.g., Naisargi N. Dave, "Witness: Humans, Animals, and the Politics of Becoming," *Cultural Anthropology* 29, no. 3 (2014): 433–56; Ewa Ziarek, *An Ethics of Dissensus: Postmodernity, Feminism, and the Politics of Radical Democracy* (Stanford: Stanford University Press, 2001), and *Feminist Aesthetics and the Politics of Modernism* (New York: Columbia University Press, 2012); Awad Ibrahim, *The Rhizome of Blackness* (New York: Peter Lang, 2014); Cathie Pearce et al., "The Politics of Becoming," *Qualitative Inquiry* 18, no. 5 (2012): 418–26.

"embodied minding" (see chapter 2)—and opens up possibilities that cross the boundaries of (uni)linear time.

The third central element in the choice of the festivals is linked to their connection with the Wheel of the Year. As I anticipated in chapter 1, the latter is a central part of the spiritual lives of the Sisters. In Salento, the seasons are marked by the festivals of the saints or linked to the Catholic liturgical year. Going to festivals and dancing *pizzica* are one of the main ritual activities of the *cerchio*. Embedded in the mundanity of a concert or a *sagra*, they are occasions, for example, to honor the natural environment, the other-than-human and more-than-human presences, to reflect on their spiritual journeys, to connect with one's life-mission, to delve into the energies of the season, to receive emotional healing, to experience *presciu*, and to take care of, through dancing, other Sisters. Many times, I witnessed them exploiting these dancing contexts to send each other "light" by dancing *pizzica* together, to ask the Universe for emotional balance in the turmoil of their lives, to reflect on lines of action and new perspectives. The ordinary dimensions of these circumstances should not misguide: this spiritual *neotarantismo* is not relegated to exceptional situations, but it is very much part of the ordinary, everyday spiritual life of the Sisters.

***

After this, it is time for sharing the frise *and the wine: the sun is setting, and some other friends joined us. They hugged me while sending me light and love. More music is played, and more dancing is performed. This is a lighter, recreational* pizzica: *it fosters the warmth of friendship, the serenity of a spring evening, and the bliss and pleasantness of sharing some time together. This is the place where I want to stay, this is who I am. My* destino.

Photo credit: Giovanna Parmigiani

Chapter 4

L'Imperatrice/The Empress

[Keywords: Beauty, Nature, Nurturing, Abundance]

Figure 7. An ornament on a Salentinian *loggia* (rooftop). Photo: Giovanna Parmigiani.

It is August 1. I wake up early: I have an appointment with Viola. The fact that, elsewhere, people are celebrating Lammas crosses my mind, but since this is not a festival in Salento, I honor the sabbat with some grateful thoughts and move on with my day. I agreed to keep Viola company during some everyday chores: a line at the post office, some grocery shopping, and a stop at the ATM. We decide to meet in a small town in the south of Salento. Post office lines are shorter there and shops smaller. They are less crowded and easier to roam – even in the summer, Salento's "peak season." I get into the car and hit the (bumpy) road. I put Antonio Castrignanò on (one of Viola's favorite pizzica *singers) in her honor, and I sing along, alone, in the car. While I hum the lyrics of* "Fomenta" *(Incite!, in dialect), and move my head at the sound of tambourines, a memory comes into my mind: sweet and sour at the same time. I remember when, a couple of years before, Viola and I had danced this song at a live concert.*[1] *I was mourning and grieving, trying to pull myself together after the death of my mother. Viola invited me to dance with her that particular song, and Angelo, a friend from another Italian region who had seen us dancing several times before, decided to video-record us. He probably had sensed and understood that the* pizzica *we were dancing was a special one: emotionally healing and spiritually uplifting for both Viola and me. I vividly remember her laying her hands over me, holding space for my sorrow, while I frantically pirouetted, furiously stomping my feet with rage and despair. As often during these types of* pizziche, *as I whirled and turned, my emotions and point of view did as well.*

I honor Viola, the song, my memories, and my grief – all wise teachers. I dwell in gratitude and appreciation.

***

I arrive in the small piazza *of the village in that time of the day when shadows are darker and the sunlight brighter – drawing a masterful* chiaroscuro *on the stone floor of the main square. In*

1 Antonio Castrignanò, "Fomenta," November 8, 2015, video, 4:39, https://youtu.be/4qCTJc5_23A

most of Salento summer mornings, the air retains a bit of the cool of the night. This is a quasi-liminal space, right before the heat kicks in, burning skins and fields and yellowing shrubs. Viola is already waiting for me: dressed in greens and browns, her bright ginger curls gleam, hit by sunrays. Strong and grounded like a tree, she seems to be sprouting out directly from the ground. The light wind moves her long flowing skirt and her curls, and as I approach her I can smell her perfume: a floral essence, exuding directly from her crown.[2] "La 'ndore te menta lu ientu me 'nduce" *(lit. The wind blows towards me the smell of mint), I sing in my head – a line from* "Fomenta" *– while I smile at Viola and at the wisdom of the Salento dialect. We hug and greet. We move together toward a small café and order our coffees. It is the third one for me already. I normally reach for four* espressi, *before midday, when I am in Salento. This is both a social need – drinking coffee together is an important relational ritual – and a consequence of my constant sleep deprivation. After all, I think, the nights of Salento* are *long, long as Viola's hair.*[3] *I smile, again, with affection, at the conversation that is going on in my head, staring at my coffee. Viola looks at me, a bit puzzled:* "Cumpagna, ce sta faci? *(Mate, what are you doing?)" I blush – lost in my thoughts and in the refractions of dark browns on the surfaces of the ice cubes that emerge, like icebergs and thoughts, from the coffee in the glass in front of me. I apologize, grab my cup, and look for a free table in the room. Viola suggests looking for one in the small open area behind the café, and I follow her.*

We sip our caffè in ghiaccio *in the shade of an olive tree, and, per usual, talk about recipes and music, books and politics, and complain about Italian bureaucracy, the heat, and the crowds of tourists. We laugh and smile, sweat and hug. Do you remember that bakery close by, the one that uses good flour and the mother dough? Viola asks. Of course, I do. We went there a couple of times in the past. Viola bought some bread and* taralli *once, and*

2 I am referring to the "crown chakra," but also to the fact that in Italian, human hair and tree's crowns share the same name: *chioma*.

3 This is a twisted line from *Luna Otrantina* (see chapter 1).

the owner, Giorgio, offered us some red wine "del contadino" *(lit. of the farmer) in glasses – because "wine cannot be appreciated in plastic." He had asked his helper to bring him some glasses and local wine from his backroom and started pouring wine from the bottle he had opened for his own lunch. We then shared an improvised* aperitivo *together. The smell of baked goods coming from the bakery and that of the blooming rosemary and myrtle from the street are impressed in my mind and in my nostrils as a particularly cherished fragrance, and so is the pleasantly tannic taste of the wine in my mouth. I smile and nod, and Viola continues. "His flour is good, he uses local ancient grains –* the Senatore Cappelli.[4] *He is very* 'ngraziato,[5] *his work is precious. Do you want one of his* taralli? *Viola opens her bag and a plastic container in it. I see beautifully browned* taralli, *and I smell the oil and the fennel in these baked treats. I grab one, and she does, too.* Grazie, *I say. I take a bite – out of the* tarallo *and of the loving energy that the baker kneaded into it.*

***

We move through Viola's chores with light-heartedness and ease, surprised, once again, at how much "time flies" when we are together.[6] We walk and chat, and find ourselves just outside the village on a small dirt road. Olive trees everywhere and cicadas' songs in the background. The sun is hot, now, and the grass yellow and dry: it rattles harmoniously, when played by the wind. The dry-laid stone walls are warm and still, offering the usual sense of stability and comfort. The sounds of the village are distant, and we enjoy the oneness of the nature around us and of our – lowered – voices as a counterpoint. We keep walking and notice a small rectangular aedicule on the side of the road, a few meters ahead. Carved in a local stone, it holds a painting of a Madonna. *Neither of us would think about herself as a Catholic,*

4 The *Senatore Cappelli* is a local ancient cultivar of durum wheat.
5 Literally "having grace" meaning, well-mannered, decent.
6 In Italian *"il tempo vola."*

but we both feel "called" by that icon – sacred to some.[7] *We stop talking and look at each other. Then, with a single voice and a complicit look, we whisper, nodding: "Let's go there!" In silence, we immerse ourselves in the sounds around us, which feel louder and almost physically embracing. I can feel their echoes on my skin, reverberating across me out of a shiver. We get closer to the old, crumbling aedicule, and put our hands on it. In unison, we close our eyes.*

I start tuning in with the energy of the place. I find that my senses are heightened, and I start to feel connected with everything around me: with the wind, the sun, the heat, the stones, the trees, the cicadas. While I bask into this feeling, which came to me effortlessly, I now actively try to expand my sense of connection to include Viola, and the energy of the Madonna. *The top of my head tingles, and I feel a pressure on what my Sisters would call the crown chakra." My head starts spinning when, suddenly, a word comes to my mind:* nives *(in Latin, snow). I open my eyes in disbelief (and to relieve some of the pressure I was feeling at the top of my head). What does the word "snow" have to do with this? And. . . in Latin? Isn't it summer? Am I not in Salento, where it rarely snows?* Sancta Maria ad Nives*?* Madonna della Neve *(Our Lady of the Snow)? This sounds feasible, although I still do not know what this might have to do with Salento. While I wonder, with my wandering eyes open, I see that Viola is opening hers. Relaxed and blissfully smiling, she looks at me. She tells me that she visualized fresh water, and that she then noticed that someone had carved on top of the aedicule some tiny drainage gutters, and four small water receptacles on its angles – possibly, to collect rainwater, or to bless the four directions. I am puzzled, and second-guess myself, but I decide to share with Viola my experience, anyways. I tell her about* nives*, the snow, and she immediately joins her hands and bows at me. She associates "my" snow with the fresh waters that she had visualized. We both think*

7 On the devotion to the Virgin Mary in Salento see David Gentilcore, *From Bishop to Witch: The System of the Sacred in Early Modern Terra d'Otranto* (Manchester: Manchester University Press, 1992).

about the situation in Siberia, and the series of wildfires that are bringing it down to its knees.[8] *We decide to thank the* Madonna *and to bring her some offerings: some bread and flowers. After all, I say, it is Lammas! Viola laughs and hugs me. We start walking back towards the village, resuming our chats.*

***

*Minutes later we are in the small grocery shop of the village. The walls are crammed with piles of food, amassed with no apparent rationale – surely there is one, devised by a great-grandfather, and passed down across generations within the family that has been owning the shop for decades. A plump, joyful, and smiling lady greets us behind the bread and deli counter. Her hair is tied, and she is vigorously adjusting her apron, too loose on her waist. In dialect, she comments about the wind and the heat, and we join in, playing along her lines. We share laughs and brief moments of human connection. Switching to Italian, with a teasing voice and caricaturing the quite aseptic features of formal standard Italian, she asks, "*In cosa posso servirvi?*" (literally, in formal Italian: In what may I serve you?). We laugh, again, and choose a bread loaf among the many stacked behind her. She grabs it, and we ask if she could cut it in twelve parts. We want to leave a piece at the aedicule as an offering and share the remaining with the other Sisters and with some friends. She complies, and we warmly thank her. We add some other items to our shopping bag and move toward the cashier – here, we found the same deli lady who helped us before. "I do it all here!" she comments. We laugh.*

To our surprise, the date stamp of the receipt perfectly matches our bill: 11.08 euros, on 01/08, at 11:08. Viola understands this as a synchronicity, as a validation that we are blessed by the "universe," a confirmation of the "message" we received, an

8 In July 2019 a series of wildfires burnt millions of hectares of forests in Siberia.

endorsement that we are "in the flow,"[9] *and that we are doing the right thing. We pay, smile, and start walking.*

***

We are at the aedicule now. After a brief, spontaneous, prayer, Viola and I leave a piece of bread on the aedicule, giving thanks to the Mother, and some flowers we took on our way from the village. Now, we are ready to go home. We hug each other. Viola's eyes are sparkling. She tells me, "Ciao, cumpagna! Ne vidimu!"(*Bye, mate! See you soon!) and slowly walks towards her car—with her signature elegant gait. I smile, and I realize that I miss her so much when I am in the US.*

On my way back, I stop at Fiammetta's workplace to grab another coffee. Mostly, I want to share with her what had just happened. When I mention the word "nives," *snow, she interrupts me and immediately adds with an excited and surprised voice: "I just read an article about Our Lady of the Snow in the local newspaper this morning! Look!" She grabs the newspaper, buried under a pile of others, and gives it to me.*

I am puzzled: "What does a Madonna della Neve *has to do with Salento?" Fiammetta explains: "I did not know this, but apparently there is a legend linked to a statue of Mary in Neviano, a small town here, in Salento. The festival in honor of this particular legend and statue is held on the day of Our Lady of the Snow, four days from now: on August the 5th." I had totally ignored all this: I feel excited but mostly confused.*

Magia is Italian for "magic," and *macare* is the most common Salentine word for "witches."[10] The origin of the term "magic" is the Ancient Greek *mageia*—a word derived from Persian, the language of Greece's political enemies; *magi*, in Persia, were Zoroastrian priests. From its etymology, it

9 Being "in the flow" is another way to describe being "in the expanded present."

10 As David Gentilcore shows, in the past the local world for witches was "*magare*," a term even closer to *magia*, the Italian for "magic" (Gentilcore, *From Bishop to Witch*).

appears that magic has been a word for alterity, difference, and, arguably, distrust right from its beginnings.[11] The burden of embodying and representing alterity is something that has been characterizing the intellectual history of this word for centuries. Especially since the Enlightenment, magic became a word for a heterogeneous number of practices and beliefs: an ambiguous,[12] fuzzy,[13] and unstable[14] one. Academics, too, contributed to the association between magic and alterity: anthropology, in particular, with its colonialist origins, has been a protagonist of the "reinvention of the discourses in which Europeans dealt with the occult."[15] While the academic studies of magic undertaken by anthropologists, historians, and sociologists took different paths, I would like to stress two aspects and dimensions of magic that, in my opinion, had a particularly significative weight in the intellectual history of term. These two—linked—aspects are: the relationships between magic and "modernity" and the strenuous, long-standing attempts at distinguishing "magic" from "religion."

As many scholars have argued, differently from common understandings of magic, the latter—and the semantic field it evokes—is not something that is to be understood in opposition to modernity, its rational progress, and disenchanted

11 Bernd-Christian Otto and Michael Stausberg, *Defining Magic: A Reader* (London: Routledge, 2012), 3.

12 Magliocco, "Witchcraft as Political Resistance."

13 Otto and Stausberg, *Defining Magic*, 3.

14 Michael D. Bailey, "The Meanings of Magic," *Magic, Ritual, and Witchcraft* 1, no. 1 (2006): 2.

15 Peter Pels, "Introduction," in *Magic and Modernity*, ed. Birgit Meyer and Peter J. Pels (Stanford: Stanford University Press, 2003), 6. Historians, anthropologists, and sociologists, and, more recently, scholars of esotericism are now the protagonists of a reframing both of current studies on magic, and of the intellectual history of the term. The links between colonialism and anthropology are not evident only in the latter's origins. As the scholar Peter Pels notes, "The movement in anthropology that replaced the emphasis on pragmatic magic as a universal human trait with the intellectualist agenda of studying witchcraft as a local system of beliefs . . . was at least in part fed by the problem of controlling and modernizing colonial societies" (Pels, "Introduction," 13).

ethos. As Pels points out, magic is not only a "counterpoint" to modernity. Rather, modernity itself "produces its own forms of magic."[16] In fact, by analyzing the academic literature on magic, it appears that magic not only *"exists in* modernity," but it *"belongs to* modernity," in ways that go beyond what is commonly acknowledged.[17] One aspect among many: magic is essential to define what modernity is not, and, therefore, indirectly, modernity itself.[18]

Moreover—and central to my argument—it is worth noting that there is no one modernity, but different modernities and modernizations.[19] The "practices of inventing or reinventing magic in modernity," in fact, are manifold, as multiple are the configurations that these relationships take in different places and contexts.[20] In other words, as Pels, following Asad, claims, what appears to be more important, as an object of research, is the study of the practices and power relationships that frame, label, judge, and "imagine" magic, rather than chasing a thorough definition of magic.[21] A similar claim can be said about modernity and post-modernity, and about the visions of the persons, of the world, of history, and of knowledge that they entail—including and beyond magic. In Salento, for example, as the historian David Gentilcore has shown, modernity unfolded

16 Ibid., 3.

17 Ibid. (emphasis in original).

18 According to Peter Pels, "Magic designated a conceptual field—shared with such notions as shamanism, fetishism, witchcraft, the occult, totem, mana, and taboo—that was predominantly made to define an antithesis of modernity: a production of illusion and delusion that was thought to recede and disappear as rationalization and secularization spread throughout society. However, this image of magic as the other or the past of modernity was always balanced by less dominant arguments about magic's universality, either as hidden wisdom .... as poetic imagination ... as a wishful 'omnipotence of thought'... or as the 'institutionalization of human optimism" (Ibid., 4).

19 See also Birgit Meyer and Peter J. Pels, *Magic and Modernity* (Stanford: Stanford University Press, 2003).

20 Pels, "Introduction," 30.

21 Ibid., 16; see also Talal Asad, *Genealogies of Religion* (Baltimore: Johns Hopkins University Press, 1993).

historically in peculiar ways, and so did the normative efforts of the Catholic church to distinguish orthodox, less-orthodox, and unorthodox practices linked to healing and life-crises (including *tarantismo*).[22] Compared with much of Europe, in this part of the Italian peninsula the post-Council of Trent Counter-Reformation policies took root slowly, and some of the practices that elsewhere were considered magic have persisted, while transformed, in Salento for centuries. By analyzing the diocesan and ecclesiastic records from the area, Gentilcore was able to gather information on the various activities and practices that the mainstream Catholic church proposed, prescribed, tolerated, and proscribed in Salento.

As a matter of fact, it is interesting to note, for the sake of my argument, that the same fact that Salento—at that time called *Terra d'Otranto*—was considered the "Indies from right here" by Jesuits, and that it remained indeed the object of centuries-long missionary efforts by the Catholic church is a proof of the existence and of the persistence of a certain variability in the approach to magic, religion, personhood, healing, and forms and practices of knowing.[23] This is evident in many instances. An example of this is the non-exclusive role of the local clergy in mediating between lay people and the "orthodox" Church. These "extra-liturgical" interventions, which represented ways to approach misfortune and illness, were performed by clergymen as well by laypeople, including the "wise women" called *magare,* the ancient version of *macare*. These practices ranged from the

22 Gentilcore, *From Bishop to Witch.*

23 As David Gentilcore importantly notes, for the *Terra d'Otranto* area, "There has been the tendency to dwell in the distinction between magical and religious rituals according to the way they were supposed to work: that is, depending on whether a given act had a mechanical efficacy (considered magical) or relied on the intervention of the divine (therefore religious). However, given that so-called magical invocations often gained their efficacy through recourse to saints, and that many religious rituals and devotions were assumed to have automatic effectiveness, it is difficult to maintain this distinction." (Gentilcore, *From Bishop to Witch,* 10.)

widespread use of forms of prayer to exorcism, from the recitation of the rosary to the use of sacramental objects—such as, for example, the *breve*, a paper with the names of God or other biblical text used for protection purposes, and wax medallions called *Agnus Dei*.

Interestingly, Gentilcore points out that these spontaneous forms of religiosity, contrary to the Catholic sacraments whose efficacy is believed to be derived *not* by the power of the minister who performs them but from the sacrament itself, were not considered "*ex opere operato*" (in Latin, meaning from the work performed), but "*ex opera operantis*" (from the work of the performer). In other words, the efficacy of these *sacramentalia* was perceived as directly dependent from the power, disposition, and qualities of the person who officiated them.[24] This is an important remark, and it has many consequences: some of them ontological, linked, for example, to the way the intervention of the divine in human lives is imagined and assessed. In fact, the belief in the "*ex opere operantis*" implies a conception of personhood that differs from "orthodox" ones, attributing, for example, divine qualities to selfhood and personhood. This is especially true since, as Gentilcore points out, with the historian Gabriele de Rosa, what is usually referred to as "popular religion" does not have anything to do with class. The folk-practices that normally go under the label of "vernacular religion" have been shown to be shared—and somehow re-interpreted—transversally by both lay and clerical, literate and illiterate, rich and poor people.[25]

Another historical example that gestures towards the necessity to adopt a much more complex understanding of modernities is that, as Gentilcore notes, in the *Terra d'Otranto*, there was no witch hunt comparable to the northern European one. In this area of the region of Apulia, as in much of the Italian peninsula (with the exception of certain

24 Ibid., 95.
25 Ibid., 3.

Alpine areas), the Inquisition tended to deal with women accused of witchcraft by considering them as "*illusae*"—misguided, ill-advised, substantially foolish, rather than fearful, fierce, and, ultimately, dangerous women.[26] The framing of these women as deluded indirectly indicates that personhood and selfhood were understood as including dimensions that could be "acted upon," and were not, necessarily, considered as well-bounded, individual, and autonomous as our current understanding suggests.

These historical remarks are not meant to set aside Salento or Italy as an "exceptional" place. Rather, they seek to deconstruct our perception of modernity and of "the West" as unitary and uncomplicated. In Salento, as elsewhere, different ontologies, experiences and understandings of personhood, and epistemologies coexist—now as well as in the past. Often, they coexist within the same individuals (synchronically and diachronically), and emerge in different ways, positionally and contextually.[27]

In spite of the fact, then, that modernities are inflected differently in different contexts and within the same ones, it is worth noting that the typical modern efforts of policing, normalizing, and validating some discourses and practices over others seem to be particularly widespread for what concerns the notion and practices of magic. In fact, these power dynamics play a role in the study of magic, too. The

26 Ibid., 12–13.

27 At the level of the history of ideas and of philosophy, a similar point on the presence of different modernities can be made by referring to the work of the Italian philosopher Roberto Esposito (2010). In his book *Pensiero Vivente* (Living thought) he convincingly claimed that the Italian modern philosophical thought, which he calls "living thought," developed differently than in the rest of Europe by putting at its center the concept and experience of "life." Both the work of Gentilcore and of Esposito are examples that help in tracing the contours of a modernity, in my ethnographic field, as differing from the common ideal-type and from that of other places and traditions. (See Roberto Esposito, *Pensiero Vivente: Origine e Attualità Della Filosofia Italiana* [Turin: Einaudi, 2010].) On Inquisition and women see, as a comparison, Silvia Federici, *Caliban and the Witch* (London: Autonomedia, 2004) and *Witches, Witchhunting, and Women* (Oakland: PM Press, 2018).

attempt to distinguish, separate, discriminate, judge, and give value is evident in the academic research and, in particular, in the long-standing attempt to distinguish magic from religion. One of the tenets of historians and social scientists, for centuries, in fact, has been describing magic in contrast to religion (and *vice versa*), and the difference between the two always had—explicit or implicit—moral connotations, Christiano-centric premises, and colonialist implications.

While I consider the distinction between magic and religion, in the light of more recent scholarship, no longer tenable at the theoretical level, it is worth noting that the term magic did not disappear—neither in academia nor in popular culture.[28] One of the reasons for this is that in many contemporary forms of Paganism and witchcraft, magic is reclaimed and used as an "emic" category in order to describe specific spiritual practices—often in opposition to institutionalized religions. This, from a scholarly point of view, obviously makes the case for continuing to consider magic as a meaningful, if a heuristic, category.[29] Moreover, this explains why academics have not yet completely dismissed the term (or some of its variants). In popular culture, however, magic and its semantic field enjoy an ever-growing success. As the recent blooming scholarship on Esotericism shows, this could be partly described by Partridge's notion of "occulture"[30] (see below). As

28 As Asprem and Granholm point out, "Even though many scholars stress the scholarly artificiality [of] categorically distinguishing between religion and magic the need to maintain such distinctions live strong" (Egil Asprem and Kennet Granholm, eds., *Contemporary Esotericism* [London: Routledge, 2013], 9).

29 Ibid., 11.

30 In recent years, "post-secularism" became a widely adopted framework in order to understand the role of religion in the contemporary world. Post-secularism does not imply a "return to religion," but "rather, an awareness of the continued relevance of religion in secular societies, as well as changing perceptions of what actually counts as religion, what functions it may have and where it can be located" (Asprem and Granholm, *Contemporary Esotericism*, 309). Bringing forward a problematization between the "secular" and the "religious," this notion has the advantage of favoring more complex

Magliocco warns us, though, it is important to keep in mind that even though Pagans today reclaim the words "witch" and "magic," it "... is not to say that they share a same understanding of what magic is and means."[31]

Much has been written on the history of magic in anthropology and in the social sciences to the point that one could recognize today a sort of "canon" in the approach to this topic.[32] While articulated differently, there are two main

---

understandings of the study of religions today, including esotericism and contemporary Paganism. Partridge's notion of "occulture" and the role of magic within it need to be understood within such a framework—less linked to a hypothetical re-enchantment of the West, and more to a different paradigm to understand modernity *tout court.* According to Partridge (e.g., *Re-Enchantment of the West: Vol. 1* and *Vol.* 2, and "Occulture is Ordinary," in *Contemporary Esotericism*, ed. Asprem and Granholm, 113–33), occulture "refers to the environment within which, and the social processes by which particular meanings relating, typically, to spiritual, esoteric, paranormal and conspirational ideas emerge, are disseminated, and become influential in societies and in the lives of individuals. Central to these processes is popular culture." ("Occulture is Ordinary," 116; see also below and Parmigiani "Magic and Politics").

31 Magliocco, *Witching Culture*, 101. While Alister Crowley's definition of magic(k) as " the science and art of causing change to occur in conformity with will" is widespread among contemporary Pagans, it is by no means the only one circulating. Moreover, even when accepted, it is not universally understood in the same way. It is worth noting, though, as a general observation, that magic implies often both a change in one's attitude, and a change in the outside world (see, e.g., Harvey, *Contemporary Paganism*; Magliocco, *Witching Culture*, 101–102).

32 Pels, "Introduction," 12–14. For a *status quaestionis* on the study of magic, see, e.g., Meyer and Pels, *Magic and Modernity*; Kennet Granholm "The Secular, the Post-Secular and the Esoteric in the Public Sphere," in Asprem and Granholm, eds., *Contemporary Esotericism*, 309–29; Otto and Stausberg, *Defining Magic*; Hanegraaff, *Esotericism and the Academy*. On magic and historicities, see Cornish, "Fashioning Magic, Fashioning History." The works, for example, of Frazer, Evans-Pritchard, Lévy-Bruhl, Malinowski, Mauss and Hubert, Durkheim and, more recently, of Comaroff and Comaroff, Taussig, Tambiah, Greenwood, and Magliocco have become part of a scholarly narrative that helps students and scholars of religion to contextualize some of the uses and understandings of words like "magic" and of some of its perceived semantic field. The latter includes cognate terms such as "witchcraft," "spirit possession," and "shamanism." Not surprisingly, then, recent additions to the anthropological and ethnographic study of the history of these terms have been written "in dialogue with" (sometimes quite literally, see Greenwood, *Anthropology of Magic*) some of the founders of the discipline and with their main

ways to understand magic in the anthropological tradition: magic as a "way of knowing," and magic as a psychological, self-centered, tool. Clearly, both dimensions could be and are present at the same time, as more recent attempts to understand magic in the legacy of Lévy-Bruhl have been showing. Their focus on "participation," in this respect, is particularly meaningful.[33] Anthropologist Stanley Jeyaraja

---

arguments. See James George Frazer, *The Golden Bough: A Study in Comparative Religion* (Edinburgh: Canongate, 2004 [1890]); E. E. Evans-Pritchard, *Witchcraft, Oracles and Magic among the Azande* (Oxford: Clarendon Press, 1937); Lucien Lévy-Bruhl, *La Mentalité Primitive* (Paris: Librairie *Félix Alcan, 1922);* Bronislaw Malinowski and Robert Redfield, *Magic, Science and Religion, and Other Essays* (Boston: Beacon Press, 1948); Marcel Mauss, Henri Hubert, and Robert Hertz, *Saints, Heroes, Myths, and Rites*, ed. Alexander Riley, Sarah Daynes, and Cyril Isnart (New York: Routledge, 2016); Émile Durkheim, *The Elementary Forms of Religious Life* (Oxford: Oxford University Press, 2001 [1912]); Jean Comaroff and John L. Comaroff, "Occult Economies and the Violence of Abstraction: Notes from the South African Postcolony," *American Ethnologist* 26, no. 2 (1999): 279–303; Michael David Bailey, *Magic: the Basics* (London ; New York: Routledge, Taylor & Francis Group., 2018); Michael Taussig, *Mimesis and Alterity: A Particular History of the Senses* (New York: Routledge, 1993), and *The Magic of the State* (New York: Routledge, 1997); Stanley Tambiah, *Magic, Science, Religion, and the Scope of Rationality* (Cambridge: Cambridge University Press, 1990); Greenwood, *Anthropology of Magic*; and Magliocco, *Witching Culture*.

As Peter Pels points out, it is important to recognize that "the conceptual slippage from magic to other notions (the occult or even the irrational) is itself constitutive of modern discourses on magic, whether they involve the demarcation of philosophy, the fantasies of popular culture, or the playfulness of modernist literature. The attempt to define magic runs into the same kinds of problem that Talad Asad identified in relation to the definition of *religion*: the attempt to produce a definition not only has to confront the problem that its constituent elements are the product of a specific history but that any general definition of magic—or witchcraft, or fetishism, or shamanism—is itself the product of a history of Christian discipline and Occidental science. Following Asad, I maintain that it is more important to study the practices and power relationships in which those things that we tend to call magic . . . are caught up." (Pels, "Introduction," 16).

33 In the words of the anthropologist Stanley Jeyaraja Tambiah, "participation, according to Lévy-Bruhl, signified the association between persons and things in primitive thought to the point of identity and consubstantiality." (*Magic, Science, Religion*, 86.) Moreover, he claims that "participation can be represented as occurring when persons, groups, animals, places, and natural phenomena are in a relationship of contiguity, and translate that relationship into one of existential immediacy and contact and shared affinities." (*Magic, Science,*

Tambiah, for example, influenced by the philosopher J. L. Austin, stresses the illocutionary and (what the philosopher Stanley Cavell would define as) perlocutionary aspects of magic by showing how magic "does things with words."[34] Anthropologist Susan Greenwood, on the other hand, argues in favor of magic as a non-scientific, nonetheless epistemologically sound, aspect of human consciousness based on a "participatory" experience of the world. While neglected by Western modernity, she claims, magic is a universal form of knowledge, and as well-attested in the West as elsewhere.[35] Finally, anthropologist and folklorist Sabina Magliocco, while likewise situating herself in the Lévy-Bruhlian legacy, underlines the artistic aspect inherent to magic and sees in the achieving altered or alternated states of consciousness through "participation" the goal of magic among contemporary Pagans.[36] One of the important achievements of these works, that I second in my analyses, is that magic is a perfectly legitimate way to inhabit the world—both epistemologically and ethically. Magic is a way of knowing, and not an example of faulty thinking;

Religion, 107.) Peter Pels, in particular, in reference to the work of Tambiah, noticed that "it is significant that one of the few recent overviews . . .of the anthropology of magic and religion in relation to science and rationality concludes with a critical view of rationality, rather than of magic and religion." (Pels, "Introduction," 14.)

34 The philosopher Cavell notably defines the illocutionary and perlocutionary statements as follows: the former refers to what is done with words and the latter to what is done by words (see Stanley Cavell and Russell B. Goodman, *Contending with Stanley Cavell* [Oxford: Oxford University Press, 2005]; Michael Lambek, ed., *Ordinary Ethics* [New York: Fordham University Press, 2010]; Parmigiani, "Spiritual *Pizzica*").

35 Magliocco claims that Greenwood "has further characterized the participatory orientation as involving the senses, creating emotional connections to the world, using holistic language, expressing itself through metaphor, narrative, and ritual, seeing the world as 'inspirited,' or animated by spiritual forces, and making use of alternate states of consciousness." (Sabina Magliocco, "Beyond Belief: Context, Rationality and Participatory Consciousness," *Western Folklore* 71, no. 1 [2012]: 11.)

36 See Magliocco, *Witching Culture*, "Beyond Belief," and "Witchcraft as Political Resistance."

magic is ethically responsible, and not the result of selfish psychological manipulations.

In spite of the differences between the aforementioned approaches, what all these frameworks have in common—arguably, necessarily[37]—is a framing of magic within a modern way of understanding the categories of space and time: a (uni)linear one. The primacy of the issues about "knowing," "will," "efficacy," "psychological fulfillment," "laws," "causes and effects," and, more in general, the "logic of magic" in describing and thinking about such phenomena that characterizes the history of the scholarship around this topic follows a modernist framework and, implicitly, a linear understanding of time. Such a framework shares with modern thought the need to rationalize, order, enumerate the irrational along a vision of time that is, substantially, linear. This is not to say that some of this work, especially the one developed in the legacy of Lévy-Bruhl on "participation," is incorrect or unhelpful to understand magic as an embodied practice among contemporary Pagans, or elsewhere.[38] Rather, the recognition that magic is traditionally described by a set of laws that govern the interconnectedness of the universe (the macrocosm and the microcosm),

37 Since the academic disciplines are the result of the evolution of modernity and its scientific and rational reasoning, this is, to a certain extent, unavoidable. Given the interconnectedness between modernity and magic, one is inclined to think that this need for causal explanation of magic might be, in itself, a feature of this connection.

38 Magliocco argues that "a set of techniques for training the imagination by attuning to the elements, phases of the moon, cycle of the seasons, and emotional connections between inanimate objects" (*Witching Culture*, 100) "prepares Pagans to experience the world from a more participatory standpoint" ("Beyond Belief," 18). Moreover, these are comparable to an art form, since "like art, the goal of magic is to bring about a set of emotional, affective responses that cause a change in consciousness—that allows participants to switch to a more participatory view of the world" ("Beyond Belief," 18). The "ultimate goal" of magic, for Magliocco, is attaining participation through altered or alternate states of consciousness ("Beyond Belief," 18). The latter, besides "implying an ordinary consciousness that differs from these said states" (*Witching Culture*,160), are understood as part of the human experience of participation.

and that are mastered by the will of some through various techniques,[39] is an important element not only to describe and understand the phenomenon but also to shed some light on the implicit categories that shape the gaze of those who study said phenomenon. In other words, much of past and contemporary understanding of magic has to do with the role of "purpose," "causality," "knowledge," and "will" in the description of magic; all these terms, I argue, are intertwined with the adoption of a linear understanding of time—typical of modern hegemonic discourses, the same ones that traditionally shape academic research. What if, instead, as scholars or practitioners, we adopted a coeval understanding of time in the study of magic? Would this "presence-magic" show us something else about magic?[40] Would descriptive terms such as "purpose," "causality," and "will" take other, additional meanings and connotations? What if magic could be understood and described, instead, *also* through other filters? While this book offers a novel perspective on the study of magic, my contribution to the literature on this topic needs to be understood as a way to complement the current scholarship, rather than an attempt at overriding it. After all, the experience of coevality and linearity (and cyclicity) of time coexists in the experience of many human beings, and the complexity of the experience of magic cannot be reduced and flattened into a uni-dimensional approach.

What is "presence magic" then?

***

It's August 5 – Our Lady of the Snow. Fiammetta and I decided to do a "pilgrimage" to Neviano, a village in Salento, on the

39 See, e.g., Magliocco, *Witching Culture*, 97–121.

40 It is worth noting, in this context, that, in her article "Beyond Belief," Magliocco quotes Steven Posch, a Minnesota Pagan high priest that claims that "Paganism is not about belief. It is about being" ("Beyond Belief," 18).

*occasion of their festival of the "*Matonna te la nie*" (dialect).*[41] *As the legend goes, some merchants from Gallipoli, a Salentinian city on the Ionian coast, in a period of the past that has not been ascertained, coming back from a market, had to face a bad storm. They took shelter in a cave close to the village that it is now called Neviano. Since the storm was rumbling with thunder and did not seem to stop, the merchants decided to pray to an image of the Madonna that they had been carrying among their merchandise. They placed it on a stone, in the cave, and started praying. The prayers, according to the legend, gave way to sleep. When the men woke up, they noticed that the storm had ended and that some sun rays were illuminating the image of the Virgin Mary. Grateful to the* Madonna *for her help, the merchants wanted to resume their journey but, to their bewilderment, the image of the* Madonna *was stuck into the stone and could not be removed – a clear sign that She wanted to stay there.*[42] *Therefore, they decided to build a church in that same place, around Mary's image that, since then, has been venerated by Neviano citizens and pilgrims – now including both Fiammetta and me.*

***

*I am at the gas station close to the highway, waiting for Fiammetta. To save money, fuel, and time, we usually meet here when we want to share a car ride. There is a big parking lot and, most importantly, a free one. Fiammetta arrives, parks her car, and jumps into mine. She smells of flowers and clean laundry: her eyes sparkle, and she hugs me – both with her arms, and with her voice: "*Ciaoooooo Sisterrrrrrr.*" She brought some cookies she had just baked with whole wheat flour and almonds, some Calabrian anisette-flavored licorice candies she had bought at a*

41 On the tradition of pilgrimage devotion in Salento see Gentilcore, *From Bishop to Witch*.

42 This is a trope in the narratives about icons of the *Madonna* in Salento. See Gentilcore, *From Bishop to Witch*.

stand at a local fair (my favorite), and her drum. She places the latter on the back seat, close to mine.[43]

***

After a coffee on the go, only my second, we head for Neviano. The countryside is beautiful, and while I tell Fiammetta that I've never been to Neviano before and that I had to look on Google Maps to find its geographic position, she mentions how strange it is that many Salentinians do not know their territory well. I smile, feeling honored to having been indirectly included in this community by Fiammetta. She tells me that she had been to Neviano just once or twice before and starts naming people that she knows that are, directly or indirectly, connected to this village. I know some of them and, I have to admit, knowing that someone among my acquaintances has walked the streets of this unknown village does make it more familiar. After a twenty-minute ride and a chat, we arrive in Neviano. As the street sign with the name of the village greets us, we start looking for the Madonna della Neve. *The village is on a small hill while the church we are looking for is at its bottom. We arrive at the* Madonna della Neve *church, but it is closed. Only a man, possibly the keeper, is around. He is power-washing the area outside the church in preparation for the festival that is taking place in the evening. Fiammetta and I approach the man, and she asks him if we can visit the church and play the drums. He says that he can open the church, which at that moment of the day is closed to the public, for us, but that we cannot play the drums in the church. We thank him, heartfully, understanding the situation. In spite of the fact that drums and tambourines are frequent in Salento, they are not generally used for devotional purposes. Fiammetta and I enter in the church, and the man closes the door after us. The energy is very dense in the empty church. A statue of the* Madonna *and one of the Archangel Michael, taken down from their usual places, lie in the middle of the church, surrounded by scattered white cloth and wooden*

43 Actually, I had left mine in the US, and Fiammetta had lent me one of hers for the summer.

bars. They – the Madonna *and St. Michael – need to be prepared for their yearly stroll in the village on the occasion of the* festa. *Fiammetta and I find a seat on a bench and we close our eyes. I immediately start to "journey," without any effort or preparation: I start to visualize in my head a path, some presences, and to receive some "messages." While immersed in this meditation, I start humming a song that I cannot recognize. The sound of my own voice breaks the silence of the church, and acts like a soothing lullaby to my discomfort – the one of the types that, quieted during the day and when in company of others, hits when I am alone with myself. I have been holding in my heart some concern, for some time now: about my academic future, about the place I should call home, about the purpose of my life journey. The emotional heaviness of these have been at the center of my attention, occupying most of my thoughts and energies during my "free time." While I sing to myself an unknown, yet not unfamiliar, song with my eyes closed, I feel the clearing of an emotional fog, and I start perceiving and experiencing myself differently: powerful, conscious, unbroken. This is the Giovanna that I am, I think. Only not yet. Then some images, in rapid succession, emerge in my mind – like photographs, or "dialectical images." An eight-pointed star, a forest, an eye. I feel some presences around me that I recognize as what I had learned to call "my guides": I feel connected, united, complete. I experience a sense of wholeness, of meaning, of full potential. My troubling concerns are still there, but they seem less meaningful from this empowered position and place of wholeness.*

This is what I need to focus on – the feeling, the awareness, my unbroken unity – not my contingent circumstances. In this experience of myself as unexpectedly whole, unbroken, and complete, I find solace, clarity, and meaning. I open my eyes, surprised and slightly light-headed. I am still singing. I hum the last notes, and I give thanks in my mind and heart, for this breakthrough. I look around. Fiammetta is not there anymore. I hear, now, the sound of her drum coming from the outside. Holding to the emotional feeling I just experienced, stretching it in the attempt of not allowing it to fade, I wait for her to finish. I reframe the questions I hold in my heart with new words – uttered from this empowered experience of myself. They also look and feel transformed.

***

I meet Fiammetta outside. We return to our car, thanking the Mother and the keeper. We want to visit the village and its main church, devoted to the Archangel Michael: Fiammetta claims it has an image of the saint, to whom she is very devoted.[44] *I drive in loops, trying to find a parking spot in a village that I do not know and partially closed to the traffic in preparation for the festival. As an aftertaste to the feeling I just experienced, images of my childhood start coming to my mind, triggered by some of the elements that I see around me. They are not memories, since what I recall is not something that I actually experienced – at least in this life, my Sisters would say. A new story of me unfolds in my mind, with new images, new words, new feelings. This is odd, but I strongly feel the presence of my grandmother near me. It is as if a toddler me were there with me, also, looking with my same eyes, feeling with my same skin, at the sound of my same heartbeats. We are accompanied by my and her grandmother. It is as if I were experiencing two levels of reality – it is true, after all, that real and existent are not always synonyms.*[45]

This, I realize, is not at odds with but a consequence of the sense of unity that I had experienced in the church, minutes before. At one level of awareness, I am in Neviano as an adult; at another, I am in Neviano as a kid. I never experienced something similar, and I keep blinking to make sure I am awake. I think I might need another coffee, and I pay attention to the street signs – but these

44 The devotion to St. Michael is quite widespread in Salento and Apulia. In the Gargano area of Apulia there is the oldest European pilgrimage site dedicated to the Archangel Michael: Monte Sant'Angelo. A town with eleventh-century Norman origins, Monte Sant'Angelo's main attraction is the thirteenth-century sanctuary, a popular pilgrimage site for those who were traveling to Jerusalem. It was visited also by St. Francis of Assisi.

45 See Jason Ānanda Josephson-Storm. 2021. *Metamodernism : the Future of Theory*. Chicago: The University of Chicago Press.

ordinary thoughts do not override my split awareness, as much as the latter does not interfere with my driving and parking-hunting skills. I park the car and start walking with Fiammetta, in silence. This double layer of experience absorbs all my attention now: I feel surprised and perplexed – even a bit scared, at moments – but intensely engaged in it. I look at the houses around me, at the shop signs, at the panorama, and I discover a sort of familiarity with a place that I had never visited before. I feel the presence of my grandmother, and I experience some very precise emotions that I can trace back to particular contexts, smells, feelings that inhabit the parts of my childhood that I had shared with her. I had been used, in the past years, to follow the cues of my emotions, when they appeared to be overwhelming, or unknown. By associating, in a chain of memories, feelings (and not only events or ideas), I had learned to look a bit more deeply and to better understand sentiments that appeared so foreign, or odd, at first. Similarly, now, in this experience equally unknown and foreign, I follow the emotional traces that this place is triggering in me, and I am surprised at the fact that I start to look at my life differently, getting several insights, seemingly out of nowhere. I feel some emotional tensions dissolve and heal in unanticipated ways. After all, I had not asked for this to happen to me, nor had I even thought that something like this was possible. I try to explain this to Fiammetta, who tells me that she is feeling the presence of my grandma, too, and she explains to me that she thinks I am receiving a "download." I look at her, not disguising some surprise for her choice of words; I am not quite sure of what she actually means by this term. She explains that the guides, or spirits, as she calls them, but also particular moons or astrological situations – like a stellium, *for example – sometimes transmit some knowledge to us in ways that are not primarily understandable in a cognitive way but in an emotional, bodily, synesthetic one. Differently than rituals, special works, or initiations, this "magic" appears not to be confined to exceptional circumstances and not to be initiated by our own active agency. "If it happens," she said, "it means that you are open." This openness is a form of "active staying," of being in the "expanded present." This openness is "presence" – it's "presence magic."*

***

"Presence" is a term indissolubly linked with the work of the ethnologist Ernesto de Martino. Presence, is also, with the "expanded presence" historicity, at the core of the Sisters' experience and understanding of magic. From a conversation between these two "presences," "presence magic" emerges. To understand the latter, it is essential to understand what "presence," "crisis of presence," "de-historification," and "re-presentification" mean in the work of the Neapolitan ethnographer, since they are key notions for comprehending the connections between "presence magic," a coeval historicity, and well-being in the experience of the Sisters.

One of the main critiques that ethnologist Ernesto de Martino had against theories on magic was their ahistoricism. In particular, he thought that the "participatory" aspect of magic described by the French anthropologist Lucien Lévy-Bruhl was responsible for a specific "violence": that of "thinking ahistorically about the givenness of presence."[46] According to de Martino, in fact, the French scholar took for granted in his analyses of "primitive thought" that the unitary experience of the individual

46 de Martino, *Il Mondo Magico*, 213. This was the result of ethnocentrism and colonialism. De Martino writes that: "This violence depends on the assumption of a world that is set or already secured as the only one possible, of a presence not at risk as the only reality, of a givenness that is considered the only form of reality that presence can experience. It is precisely these assumptions that needs to become a problem, if we want to radically go beyond the polemical instances that limit our historiographic horizon and that keeps us from "understanding" the magical world" (ibid., my translation).

The relationship de Martino and existentialism is complex. If, on the one hand, de Martino seems to identify presence and *Dasein*, on the other, he rejects the idea of the "nothing." See e.g., Ernesto de Martino, *La Fine del Mondo: Contributo All'analisi Delle Apocalissi Culturali*, ed. Clara Gallini (Turin: Einaudi, 1977).

(presence) is a "given" – an experience common to all. As a consequence, Lévy-Bruhl, according to the Italian scholar, addressed the differences between rational and participatory thought just as a matter of representation.[47] The problem with the theories of the French ethnologist was that he did not acknowledge that our "presence in the world" is not secured at birth once and for all but is reached (and re-reached) through historical and cultural circumstances.[48] In fact, what we call "magic" could be considered, for de

47 de Martino, *Il Mondo Magico*.

48 History and culture are tied up together in de Martino, and it could be argued that history, to a certain extent, is synonymous with "world." According to Ernesto de Martino, historicist ethnology implies that Spirit manifests in history – both human and non-human forms, I would add. The idea of the existence of a relationship between Spirit and history is a popular one in the Italian philosophical context of the first half of the twentieth century, strongly influenced by the Italian idealism of Benedetto Croce. The relationship between the Italian ethnologist and Croce, his mentor, was a complex one. If, on the one hand, de Martino consistently, in his career, attempted to insert his ethnographic discourse in a Crocian understanding of history, on the other hand, as Gallini points out, the distance between the two is evident (see de Martino, *La Fine del Mondo*). If not in the language used, certainly they departed at a theoretical level. De Martino's understanding of magic (as a category) is central in this rift, as is his understanding of the "metahistorical." While, for Croce, this refers to what is outside the historical becoming, for de Martino "metahistorical" refers to the process of de-historification (as an important moment in the process of the "rescue of presence" and re-historification) (de Martino, *La Fine del Mondo*).

While de Martino employs the word "world" (*mondo*, etymologically meaning both "universe" and "something ornated" and, therefore, "clean") in order to describe the planes of existence in history, it is worth noting that his notion of de-historification is not a synonym of what Greenwood would call "the otherworldly" (see Greenwood, *Anthropology of Magic*). In fact, the process of dehistorification could be better understood, with Gallini, as putting together de Martino's two "souls": that of the "transcendentalization of the historical," and of the "historification of the transcendental" (de Martino, *La Fine del Mondo*, xxxvi).

Interestingly, the idea of world is linked to that of historicities, as de Martino shows in *La Fine del Mondo*. In particular, according to Gallini, "the historical variation of the category of time is part of the concept of *mondo*: the historical time is a cornerstone of a structure that needs to be analyzed in a historical and cultural setting" (*La Fine del Mondo*, xvi, my translation). Clearly, I would add, this needs to be applied not only *vis-à-vis* an essentializing idea of "cultures," but in the analyses of the complexities and multifaceted aspects of post-modern

Martino, as a cultural form to establish presence in history and to cope with the angst that derives from the possibility of "not-being" in a cultural world: the so-called "crisis of presence."[49] Importantly, as it emerges from his notes, published posthumously,[50] this crisis is not only the result of a personal struggle; rather, it is an everlasting psychic structure that plays out in specific historical conditions and situations.[51]

According to de Martino and his commentators, what makes possible our being-in-the world (i.e., the "redemption" —*riscatto*—of the crisis of presence) in cultural forms, historically determined, is what is usually referred to as the "transcendence ethos."[52] This ethos implies the presence of culturally recognized structures and practices that allow for a process of "de-historification," prior to the following re-historification or re-presentification.

De-historification is not a synonym of ahistoricity. It is not a denial of the contingencies of being in history but the choice of temporarily "be[ing] in history as if you were not in it."[53] By culturally acknowledging the possibility

---

societies, including the one I am studying in Salento—where multiple historicities are experienced simultaneously.

In *La Fine del Mondo,* de Martino's use of the Latin *mundus* (in Italian, *mondo*) refers to the Roman yearly festival called "*mundus patet*"—a celebration of the end and of the re-birth of the world.

49 *Crisi della presenza.* See, e.g., de Martino, *Il Mondo Magico*, 73; Vittorio Lanternari, "Ernesto De Martino fra storicismo e ontologismo," *Studi Storici* 19, no. 1 (1978): 187–200.

50 See de Martino, *La Fine del Mondo.*

51 See also Lanternari, "Ernesto De Martino," 193. This understanding of presence as a psychological structure generalizes some claims that de Martino had made in *Il Mondo Magico, La Terra del Rimorso,* and *Morte e Pianto Rituale nel Mondo Antico.* For a contemporary de Martinian reading of Paganism and politics, see Magliocco, "Witchcraft as Political Resistance."

52 *Ethos del trascendimento,* see Gallini's comments in: de Martino, *La Fine del Mondo*, xix. Gallini edited de Martino's *La Fine del Mondo.*

53 See Bronzini, 256. As Signorelli would put it, "de-historification" is to "put [something or someone] outside of history" (*porre fuori dalla storia*). See Amalia Signorelli, "La destorificazione del negativo in Ernesto de Martino," *L'analisi e la classe,* January 8, 2017, http://ferdinandodubla.blogspot.com/2017/01/la-destorificazione-del-negativo-in.html

of the crisis of presence and of the need to overcome it through culturally shared practices that "suspend" the anguish of the crisis from its historical manifestations, de-historification allows for a re-integration of presence and for its redemption—its re-achievement. A notable example of this, already addressed in this book, is *tarantismo*. In *La Terra del Rimorso*, de Martino explicitly applies this to the *tarantate* of the past, whose malaise was understood as a manifestation of a "lack of presence" triggered by their subaltern existences. The musical-therapeutic rituals and the yearly appointment in Galatina at the chapel of Saint Paul, then, were considered culturally determined forms of de-historification that allowed for a redemption of presence.[54]

The crisis and redemption of presence framework is a useful filter to understand how my interlocutors think about and experience magic today. In this respect, de Martino's understanding of magic as not something primarily oriented towards knowing the world or transform it, "but to secure a world in which being-here is made present,"[55] seems particularly telling in order to describe presence magic among the contemporary Pagans with whom I am working. In fact, it could be argued that the function of adopting an expanded present historicity stems precisely from the necessity to handle presence, its crisis and de-historization, and its re-presentification. In this sense, the expanded present historicity *is* magic: it is a way to secure and re-establish presence in the world, that, through one's "active staying" allows one to be "in history as if you were not in it." This is particularly true in the context of Salentine

54 It is worth noting that there is a link, as I will point out in the next chapter, between de-historification, presentification, and healing. The healing rituals of *tarantismo* worked until they stopped being acknowledged as a culturally appropriate way to heal the *tarantate*. With the hegemonic spread of biomedicine and with the pathologizing of those cultural manifestations, *tarantismo*, as both an illness and a cure, disappeared.

55 *"In realtà il problema del magismo non è di 'conoscere' il mondo o di 'modificarlo,' ma piuttosto di garantire un mondo in cui l'esserci si rende presente"* (de Martino, *Il Mondo Magico*, 118–19 [my translation]).

Pagans, whose understanding of "presence," in their "presence magic," deeply resonates with the process of re-presentification described by de Martino.

In the aforementioned vignettes, as well as elsewhere in the book, I described some of the practices that Salentine Pagans—and, in particular, the Sisters of the *cerchio*—use in order to experience the expanded present historicity and with it to safeguard presence. Dancing *pizzica,* as I pointed out before, is one of the main ways to achieve this goal—both in ritual and everyday settings. *Pizzica* is central for presence magic not only because of the (well-researched) trance-like qualities of the music but also because of the connections that the very notion of presence has with *tarantismo* and with the *tarantate* of the past. In addition to this (central) practice, there are other ones that the Salentinian Pagans share with other Pagan groups: moon rituals, various forms of divination, neo-shamanic journeys, and meditations, among others. Many of those, if analyzed individually, could be understood through some of the common theories of magic: the "participatory" experience, the "contact with the otherworldly," the "altered state of consciousness" that rituals—even unstructured, *impromptu* ones as the one I described above—can trigger. Nonetheless, both at a closer look and by embracing an expanded presence perspective, my ethnographic findings could highlight aspects of magic currently undetected that could complement current studies on this topic.

First of all, differently from much of the current literature on the subject, it appears that magic is something quite ordinary in Salento, among my Pagan interlocutors. While, as I pointed out before, rituals and special events do have a place in contemporary Pagan spirituality, it is the everyday aspect of magic that is particularly relevant in my ethnographic fieldwork. This ordinary magic is not so only because of its ordinary setting. It is so because of the expanded present: this historicity itself redefines the same boundaries between "ordinary" and "extraordinary," "magic" and "mundane," "sacred" and "profane," "altered" and "non-altered" states of consciousness that we scholars use in order to describe magic. In a coeval experience and understanding of time, such binarisms cease to exist and cease to be particularly illuminating ways to describe the world heuristically.

The dimension of the "ordinary life" has gained importance in anthropology in the past twenty years, shifting the attention of researchers from the "exceptional" events of rituals and performances to the everyday conditions of life.[56] In particular, anthropologist Michael Lambek has argued in favor of the study of spirit possession in Madagascar beyond religious celebrations and in its more ordinary implications. This gaze-shift allowed for the emergence of new dimensions to understand such a complex phenomenon. Conversely, anthropological works on magic have been concentrating, even in the recent past, primarily on special events, rituals, and practices. Authors such as anthropologists Susan Greenwood and Tanya Luhrmann, for example, tried to gesture towards the presence of magic in everyday life, but their analyses did not result in describing or theorizing the everyday *as* magic. Rather, they made an important contribution in describing magic in ordinary settings.[57] The "everyday" aspect of magic I am addressing

56 See, e.g., the works of authors such as Veena Das (*Life and Words: Violence and the Descent into the Ordinary* [Berkeley: University of California Press, 2007]) and Michael Lambek (e.g., *Ordinary Ethics*).

57 Greenwood, for example, addresses the "ordinary" aspect of magic in her *Anthropology of Magic*. The ethnographic evidence she presents in support of her argument, though, is a Tarot reading that she and a friend performed at a fair. In that context, while the setting could be considered ordinary, the act of reading Tarot cards could still, arguably, be seen as the result of a ritual (of divination) and of an explicit agentive effort. Similarly, Luhrmann describes some examples of "non-special" events, but, here again, the practices she mentions are more a description of how magic happened also outside usual rituals, rather than a proof of the interconnectedness between magic and everyday life. Both of them did not push their argument far enough to the point of showing how ordinary life *is* magical. See Luhrmann, *Persuasions of the Witch's Craft*.

in this book and that I found in Salento is more radically ordinary: it is not so only in its settings, but, especially, in its erasing the same distinction between everyday and extraordinary.[58] "Presence magic" is radically ordinary, especially, because it is not associated with any particular ritual or agentive effort. Everyday magic, in fact, does not imply a particular consciousness or will, nor does it see witches as specific agents of this magic—at least, not in the ways we are used to thinking about will, agency, and intention in relation to magical practices. As Fiammetta explains through her notion of "download," sometimes magic "happens" without one actively "asking" for it to do so. A similar point could be made, for example, about the "discovery" of the aedicule of the *Madonna* by Viola and me and the consequent expanded awareness that resulted, or about the numeral synchronicity in our grocery store receipt. These experiences (and many more) that the Sisters recognize as "magic" are not always the result of one's will, magic laws, ritual practice, or active agency.[59] They are not always the outcome of knowledge seeking, or the deliberate effects of some intentions or attempts to transform the world. Rather, they are understood and experienced as landmarks of an "active staying" in the presence magic of the expanded present of the *qui-e-ora* (see chapters 1 and 3).[60]

On divination see Diana Espírito Santo, "Divination," in *Cambridge Encyclopedia of Anthropology*, ed. Felix Stein and Joel Robbins (Cambridge: Cambridge Universty Press, 2019).

58 On magic and the "everyday" see Hanegraaff, *New Age Religion*.

59 On the one hand, I agree with Magliocco that "Neo-Pagans are reclaiming a Western tradition in which trance, healing, and possession are important parts of spirituality. They provide a context that normalizes and explains such experiences when they occur spontaneously, and teach practitioners specific techniques for achieving and controlling them" (*Witching Culture*, 165). Nonetheless, I see this as only part of what characterizes the experience of magic among Salentinian Pagans. In line with Magliocco, though, I do find the way they approach and understand magic as fundamentally oppositional (see also Pike, *Earthly Bodies, Magical Selves*, 104–06).

60 On the relationship between action and passion, and the "balancing" of agency in understanding social life see e.g., Lambek, *Ordinary Ethics*.

Linked to the very notion of "expanded present" is another feature that is central to the experience of magic of the Pagans with whom I am working and that the adoption of a coeval historicity as a framework to think about magic can highlight. This can be summarized in the statement that destiny (*destino*) is not a synonym of future.[61] As I pointed out in chapter 2, *destino* is believed to be what defines the "purpose" of a person. Contrary to (uni)linear perceptions of time (and Newtonian physics), *destino* is not the last stop of a journey, a goal that is going to be achieved after a given amount of time. *Destino* is not experienced as something that is *not* in the present: rather, it is the very essence of the present. An example of this could be my own experience of myself as unbroken, healed (or "made whole") in the church of *Madonna della Neve* in Neviano and, later, while I was driving through the village. Clearly, from Fiammetta's comments and from the collection of the life histories of many interlocutors, it is evident that this is an experience that the Pagans with whom I work in Salento are familiar with. Similarly to Auerbach's *figura*, this embodied experience of the "destiny version" of myself accessed through "presence magic" started to redefine and add meanings and layers to my experience of my present self. The latter did not shape the former more than how the former shaped the latter. My present self, in fact, somehow shifted in order to match with my destiny self, during my meditation, bringing, so to speak (if we wanted to adopt a linear way of thinking) the future into the present. Like in a suspension of the linearity of history, it worked as a healing de-historification, as a re-presentification through the "presence magic" of the expanded present: one that

61 The traditional attributes of magic of homeopathy, sympathy, and contagion could be better understood beyond its traditional spatial metaphors, and as the effect of synchronies. If understood within a coeval understanding of time, the analogical aspect of magic becomes a metonymic one.

happened through my stepping into my own *bellezza*.[62] This aspect of "presence magic" is unique, and it departs from current understandings of magic that tend to describe its internal logic within a linear historicity. Magic, in the linear time, is a set of laws of cause and effect in which the past shapes the present, and the present shapes the future. In a coeval historicity the "laws" of magic follow a different configuration, one in which every dimension of time affects and is affected by the others. This is particularly evident in "presence magic."

***

It is 2020, and Italy, plagued by Covid-19, is in lockdown. The quarantine started around February 21, 2020 in the northern part of the country and gradually spread to all of the peninsula. I am in the US, where I live, practicing "social distancing." I have been following the official reports from newspapers and other media and the unofficial ones through my Italian contacts: via

62 While "presence magic" sheds light on some specific understudied dimensions of magic, it can also contribute, theoretically, to at least three critical aspects around the study of magic. First, with its de Martinian stress on the importance of history, it allows one to go beyond a certain perennialism and atemporality that characterizes some current understandings of magic (see e.g., Asprem and Granholm, *Contemporary Esotericism*, 13–14). As Gallini importantly points out, "When myth and history are equated, they lead to Nazism." (de Martino, *La Fine del Mondo*, xlviii.)

Secondly, the adoption of an understanding of magic in reference to presence and the expanded present historicity offers a "third way" *vis-à-vis* the main understandings of magic. The latter, in fact, is currently either seen through a rationalist and modernist lens, or through what Pels calls the "revival of Romantic celebration of separate, alternative, or visionary realities" of magic, that "continues to this day in what can be called a post-modern form" ("Introduction," 14). Focusing on history could better frame also the present and possible relationships between magic and politics (see, e.g., Magliocco, "Witchcraft as Political Resistance" and Egil Asprem, "The Magical Theory of Politics," *Nova Religio* 23, no. 4 [2020]: 15–42; Parmigiani, "Magic and Politics").

Thirdly, if, as Pels ("Introduction," 31) claims, "the modern study of magic is largely a study of human subjectivity," presence magic, by validating another historicity among the range of human relationship with time, could illuminate some ways to conceive personhood beyond individuality.

social media, WhatsApp messages, and Zoom calls. I have been in touch with my Pagan interlocutors and friends daily, and I have been sharing with them thoughts, feelings, prayers, Tarot readings, casual conversations, and hopes and visions for the future. Facebook is one of the ways in which we keep in touch, and this is why I tend to check it at least daily – multiple times. I open my Facebook, and I find this post by Clara:

> Some time ago, as well, I distanced myself for a while from the social [media], since I found contributing to the diffusion of the points of view of physicians, lawyers, and other figures that I admire and trust unproductive. In the meantime, the Guides informed us, "from heavens above," that, in this moment, every human being has already chosen in which "side they stand." Therefore, each one of us will continue to follow what resonates more with them.
>
> Humanity, in this historical moment, is therefore divided in two macro parts. It appears that this separation will be long-lasting.
>
> We have several means of communication committed to divulge news: official and unofficial, from the system and of counter-information, scare-mongering and trust-infusing. By now, we have it all.
>
> At the "political" level there are dominant voices and, in the meantime, alternative and dissident voices emerged.
>
> Each one [of us] can join thoughts and actions according to what they feel their own.
>
> Besides informing all of us (those who want to listen to them, obviously), the Guides, for what pertains to my experience, exhort me to let . . . it go . . . because the Flux is in a great energetic movement within these two, 'opposite, ways.'
>
> When they [the Guides] talk to us, it is wise to listen. They never insist, because they totally respect our free will. I learned how to fully trust their messages. Therefore, for now, I will sparingly use my notice board for two reasons.
>
> One: each one of us is useful, but not indispensable.
>
> Two: because I Want/Need to take care [of myself] by hanging out with those with whom I resonate the most, possibly in everyday life, in person.

In this long Facebook post there is all the suffering, composure, and faith of Clara. I know her well, and I immediately connect with the "subtext" of this message (not evident, maybe, at first sight) when I first see it appear on my Facebook newsfeed. I have spoken with Clara a few times in the previous weeks as well, and her post does not come as a surprise to me. She is facing, as many, her own struggles during the lockdown: the contradictory news, the fear for the future, the lack of human interaction. While some of these dimensions are contingent, some are not, and the unprecedented circumstances of the spread of Covid-19 is only exacerbating some old issues. Clara is no exception, and, as it appears "between the lines" of this composed message, isolation and the consequent need to find a "community of sense"[63] *are her challenges, right now. The tension between visibility and the need of recognition is a long-standing topic of many conversations between Clara and me, and this is why her voluntary isolation from Facebook (especially in this particular context) and her wishes to connect in person, with like-minded, like-sensing (and less judgmental) persons, sound like a cry to me.*

I pick up my cell phone and, without mentioning this post, I send Clara a picture of her that I took two years ago, typing a few emoticon hearts as a comment. She looks beautiful in this image: in nature, her eyes closed, she is immersed in her thoughts—prayers, in fact. I distinctively remember the moment in which I took that picture, and I am sure she does, too. We were doing a meditation in the woods, just Clara and me, and we had just shared some spiritual insights and details of our personal histories that I had found very illuminating. I am very grateful to her, for that moment we shared. I send the picture without mentioning the post: I want to make her feel that she is seen, appreciated and, above all, recognized.

It is April 17, 2020. Italy is in total lockdown due to the COVID pandemic. People are confined to their homes; radios, TVs, and the Internet share around the clock dire news about daily victims

63 See Beth Hinderliter et al., eds., *Communities of Sense: Rethinking Aesthetics and Politics* (Durham, NC: Duke University Press, 2009); Parmigiani, "Spiritual *Pizzica*."

and the numbers of those infected. Bergamo and other cities are particularly hit by the new virus, and people are required to stay at home, with the hope of curbing the spread of the disease. The hospitals are overwhelmed, and many are struggling to adapt to the personal and economic consequences of COVID-19. A video of a pizzica dancer goes viral on Facebook and YouTube. Originally posted on Facebook by filmmaker Sara Dimastrogiovanni, the post is captioned with the words: "We are resisting ♥."[64] *The dancer, in a black, flowing dress, is videorecorded while dancing alone, stomping her feet, and whirling in an uncanny, empty Piazza Sant'Oronzo – the main piazza of the city of Lecce. The woman dances at the music of Taranta, written and recorded by the local pizzica group, Canzoniere Grecanico Salentino. These are the words of the song:*

> *I hold anguish in my chest/ that is consuming me/ and never stops/ The earth is shaking under my feet/ my falling down/ never stops/ What I eat/is tasteless/there's no more light for me/ and no colors/ People knew how you could cure yourself /if your illness was called taranta / And now that times have changed/who can feel/my pain?/ Who can bring me the healing water?/ To whom I should ask for the grace/ of being healed?/ I don't know if it is taranta what got me/but it does not leave me/ and makes me crazy/ If it is taranta do not abandon me/If you dance alone you cannot/ you cannot heal /If it is taranta let it dance/if it is sadness/ let it out.*[65]

64 "17/04/2020 Pizzica Salentina (Taranta) @ Lecce, Piazza Sant'Oronzo (Southern-Italy)." CareonVR. 2020, video, 2:59, https://youtu.be/FDzPQuTRnVk

65 *Io tegnu nu tormentu intra lu piettu/ Io tegnu nu tormentu intra lu piettu/Ca me consuma e nu/Ca me consuma e nu/Ca me consuma e nu se ferma mai/Me tremula la terra sutta li peti/Me tremula la terra sutta li peti/Nu c'e' mai fine pe/Nu c'e' mai fine pe/Nu c'e' mai fine pe /lu miu cadire/Quiddhu ca mangiu nu tene sapore/Quiddhu ca mangiu nu tene sapore/Pe mie nu c'é chiui luce/Pe mie nu c'é chiui luce/Pe mie nu c'é chiui luce ne culore/La gente sapia comu t'i curare/La gente sapia comu t'i curare/ Ci lu tou male se/Ci lu tou male se/Ci lu tou male se/chiama taranta/E osce ca li tempi hannu cangiati/E osce ca li tempi hannu cangiati/Ci è ca po sentire/Ci è ca po sentire/ Ci è ca po sentire lu miu dulore/E ci me porta l'acqua pe sanare/E ci me porta l'acqua pe sanare/A ci chiedu la grazia/A ci chiedu la grazia/A ci chiedu la grazia pe guarire/Nu sacciu ci è taranta ca me tene/Nu sacciu ci è taranta ca me tene/Ma nu me lassa e me/ Ma nu me lassa e me/Ma nu me lassa e me face mpaccire/Ci è taranta nu me abbandunare/Ci è taranta nu me abbandunare/Ci balli sulu nu/Ci balli sulu nu/Ci balli sulu nu*

This video was extensively shared during the COVID-19 pandemic – within and beyond Salento, in Italy and internationally – and commented by many viewers in various languages and from different countries, all somehow "connected" through the lockdown experience. Coen M., for example, writes in a comment to the video on YouTube: "Here from the Netherlands. May this angel dance for us all in these trying times" (my emphasis).[66]

What is "crisis of presence," today? If it is fairly easy to understand how the notion of crisis of presence could have explained phenomena such as *tarantismo* in the past, it might not be as clear what could trigger it today, particularly among my interlocutors. Magliocco, who also relies on the notion of crisis of presence as an analytical tool in some of her readings of contemporary Paganism,[67] makes a similar point when she writes about de Martino and contemporary Pagans.[68]

A possible answer to this question, I argue, is buried in a footnote of *Il Mondo Magico,* where de Martino makes an important claim – one that he will further develop in *La Fine del Mondo*. He states that "also in our civilization there are 'marginal' situations. . . . The possible reproduction of the

---

te puei curare/Ci è taranta lassala ballare/Ci è taranta lassala ballare/Ci è malencunia/Ci è malencunia/Ci è malencunia cacciala fore.

66 See Giovanna Parmigiani, "'If You Dance Alone, You Cannot be Healed.' See also Laura Tempest Zakroff, "A Witch's Dance of Healing," May 11, 2020, https://www.patheos.com/blogs/tempest/2020/05/a-witchs-dance-of-healing.html

67 See Magliocco, "Beyond Belief," and "Witchcraft as Political Resistance."

68 Magliocco writes that "It is unclear what he [Ernesto de Martino] would make of groups of modern Pagans who intentionally use magic to re-enchant the world, reclaim agency, and construct authenticity" ("Beyond Belief," 14). Moreover, she adds that "We have seen how those who grew up with a worldview that allowed for the existence of a spiritual realm can re-connect with a participatory view of the world at a moment of crisis, a numinous moment at which they perceive themselves to be vulnerable, lacking in agency, or engaged in a high-stake enterprise. . . . . But now we must address a different problem: What of Modern Pagans, people who for the most part have grown up within a dominant system that rejects the existence of a spiritual realm, but who are engaged in re-enchantment of the world?" ("Beyond Belief," 17.)

magic reality also for the educated Western individual indicates how a determined and secured presence is a historical good and, therefore, revocable under certain conditions."[69] Crisis of presence, especially in *La Fine del Mondo,* appears to be not only the result of psychological hardships but an anthropological condition—that unfolds in different ways, according to particular cultural, existential, and situational contexts.[70] Specifically, according to *La Fine del Mondo,* crisis of presence appears to be affecting *Western individuals,* and, especially, its middle class. In this sense, the viral video of the pizzica dancer during the Covid-19 lockdown appears to be an example and a vivid reminder of this, for many of us.[71] This claim is also valid within the neo-animist ontology

69 de Martino, *Il Mondo Magico,* 129 n. 89, my translation.

70 It is worth noting that, as in Lévy-Bruhl (see Tambiah, *Magic, Science, Religion*), magic in de Martino is not primarily an individual practice, issue, or disposition. "The magical world" is a cultural one and, therefore, it implies a communitarian dimension. This, I argue, is why the connections between presence magic and politics are particularly strong. See Parmigiani, "Magic and Politics."

71 As I argue elsewhere ("If You Dance Alone) the case of COVID-19 could be read in relation to de Martino's notion of "cultural apocalypses." In the words of de Martino, translated by Ilaria Vanni, Cultural apocalypses, in their general connotation, are manifestations of cultural life that involve, in the context of a given culture and historical moment, the theme of the end of the current world, regardless of the way in which this end is actually lived or represented. In this more general connotation the theme is not necessarily linked with religious life as traditionally understood, but it can surface—such as in the case of the diverse modern and contemporary apocalypses of the bourgeois society— in the secular sphere of the arts, literature, philosophy, customs: it does not necessarily entail the end of the worldly character of human existence, but it can also take on the social and political traits of the end of a certain historical world and the coming of a better one, such as in marxist apocalypses: it is not necessarily explicit in the consciousness of the historical actors involved in these apocalypses, but it can become more or less explicitly manifest in the actors' Stimmung, in their behaviour, in the direction and affective tone of their thoughts; and finally a cultural apocalypse does notrefer necessarily to collective movements, to overall tendencies of an epoch or of a society, but it can concern in a particular way a singular historical actor, who within the frame of certain environmental circumstances, opens up or renews a particular cultural sensibility to the end of the world. (de Martino quoted and translated by Ilaria Vanni "'Oggetti Spaesati', Unhomely Belongings Objects, Migrations and Cultural Apocalypses," *Cultural Studies Review* 19, no. 2 (2013), 162–63).

that characterizes Salentine Pagans (see chapter 5), and in the context of my fieldwork where presence magic appears to be closely linked to an aspect that is at the basis of a political and existential struggle that is widespread among my Salentinian interlocutors—as Clara's Facebook post testifies. This struggle could be framed within the issue, popular in both studies on contemporary Paganism and of Esotericism, of the relationship between "marginality" and "mainstream." In Pagan studies, this issue often takes the form of oppositionality.[72] For example, as I pointed out above, the widespread adoption of the category of magic among contemporary Pagans is, to a certain extent, the result of a tendency to craft their identities *vis-à-vis* an understanding of Christianity as oppressive. In the field of esotericism, the issues around marginality and mainstream are even more multifaceted, given the explicit and ubiquitous ties between this body of knowledge and matters of secrecy. As pointed out above, esotericism(s) could be considered, first of all, as a "rejected knowledge"—one that is not "discovered," but "produced" by certain (modern) hegemonic regimes of knowledge and epistemologies. This rejection implies, often, a stigmatization. Within such an understanding of the field, the notion of *cultic milieu* seems to be central—both as a way to understand the past and the present configurations of Esotericism. Originally coined by Campbell in the 1970s, this term refers to a counterculture that holds oppositional beliefs and knowledge.[73] While oppositional, *cultic milieus* are in a dialectical relationship with mainstream practices and beliefs. In the context of Esotericism, the idea of *cultic milieu* encounters that of the "occult," i.e., what is hidden. Here, where the dialectic

72 See e.g., Magliocco, *Witching Culture*; Pike, *Earthly Bodies, Magical Selves*; Salomonsen, *Enchanted Feminism*.

73 Campbell, "The Cult, the Cultic Milieu and Secularization."

between marginality and mainstream meets issues around secrecy, different modalities of being in the world emerge.[74]

If notions such as stigmatized knowledge and *cultic milieu* well describe some of the issues between marginality and mainstream that characterize esotericism (which includes contemporary Paganisms), it is worth mentioning that recently the relationship between hegemony and subalternity in this field started to play out differently. I am here gesturing towards the aforementioned notion of occulture. "Very briefly, occulture includes those often *hidden, rejected* and *oppositional* beliefs and practices associated with esotericism, theosophy, mysticism, New Age, Paganism, and a range of other subcultural beliefs and practices, many of which are identified by Campbell as belonging to the cultic/mystical milieu."[75] This corpus of ideas, practices, symbols, and beliefs are available, today, more than in the past and, in particular, they can be found in popular culture.[76] Occulture, therefore, is ordinary, and neither "hidden" nor "extraordinary."

As I have elsewhere argued, in relation to conspiracy-believing in contemporary Paganism, though, the widespread presence and visibility in popular culture of the "occult" is not, *per se*, a sign of its "normalization."[77] By referring to the work of the French political philosopher Jacques Rancière, I have shown how visibility, such as that of esotericism in occulture, neither necessarily re-balances

74 On secrecy and the occult, see, e.g. Diego Maria Malara,"Sympathy for the Devil: Secrecy, Magic and Transgression Among Ethiopian Orthodox Debtera." *Ethnos* 87 no. 3 (2022): 444–462. https://doi.org/10.1080/00141844.2019.1707255; Susannah Crockford, "What Do Jade Eggs Tell Us About the Category "Esotericism"?" in Asprem and Strube, eds., *New Approaches to the Study of Esotericism*, 200–16; Lilith Mahmud, " 'The World Is a Forest of Symbols': Italian Freemasonry and the Practice of Discretion." *American Ethnologist* 39, no. 2 (2012: 425–38, https://doi.org/10.1111/j.1548-1425.2012.01373.x and "In the Name of Transparency: Gender, Terrorism, and Masonic Conspiracies in Italy," *Anthropological Quarterly* vol. 85 no. 4 (2012): 1177–120.

75 Partridge, *Re-Enchantment of the West: Vol. 1*, 68, emphasis in original.

76 Ibid., 84–85.

77 Parmigiani, "Magic and Politics."

power structures nor automatically grants political and social recognition. This, at least, seems to be the case for the Italian Pagans with whom I am working, whose struggle over presence (and the subsequent adoption of presence magic), is not only a consequence of personal struggles, but also of power structures and structural inequalities. Differently from other esoteric, New Age, or Pagan groups, the Salentinian Pagans *do* care for community-belonging, and they strive to make their voices, epistemologies, and knowledge heard, validated, and approved by mainstream society. They want to be authoritative, and to make their voices heard in society at large. For them, presence in history then takes the shape of being socially relevant, recognized, and validated. Unlike other spiritual groups, they do not choose marginality as a way to enact a counterculture of resistance; rather, they *find themselves* marginalized—while desiring to be acknowledged and recognized in their ways to inhabit the world. Therefore, their "invention of tradition" *vis-à-vis tarantismo* (see chapter s1 and 2), their adoption of a non-hegemonic, coeval historicity and their practice of presence magic are understood and experienced as ways to secure their presence. The crisis of presence for them is the threat of not being relevant, seen, and recognized.

In line with de Martino's perspective on history, it could be argued that the hegemonic marginalization or even the erasure and pathologizing (see e.g., de Martino on schizophrenia) of historicities other than the linear one could be framed as an act of "violence"—to use the terms of the critique of Lévy-Bruhl by de Martino. Similarly, by engaging with more recent literature on the political dimensions of time and temporality, it could be also argued that this phenomenon is the result of a form of "chronochracy."[78] The

78 Chronocracy, according to the anthropologists Elisabeth Kirtsoglou and Bob Simpson, refers to "the ways in which governance is shot through with the power to shape the temporalities in which people live out their everyday lives" (*Time of Anthropology*, 3).

erasure of alternative historicities is an erasure of alternative possibilities of being—that are at the core of how my Salentinian interlocutors experience "*tarantarsi*" and their being in the world, today. Their suffering, the "threat" to their presence, takes the form of a marginalization of their ways to inhabit time and the world, of a pathologization of their participatory forms of knowledge, and of the delegitimation of *their tarantismo* as a contemporary healing practice. The rescue of presence, of recognition, of "appearance," to use Rancière's terminology, is central in their (political) re-invention of the tradition of *tarantismo* and of the role of *pizzica* dance and music as contemporary ways to rescue their presence. This, as I will address in the next chapter, is particularly true in relation to healing and well-being.

Chapter 5

La Temperanza/Temperance

[Keywords: balance, health, purpose]

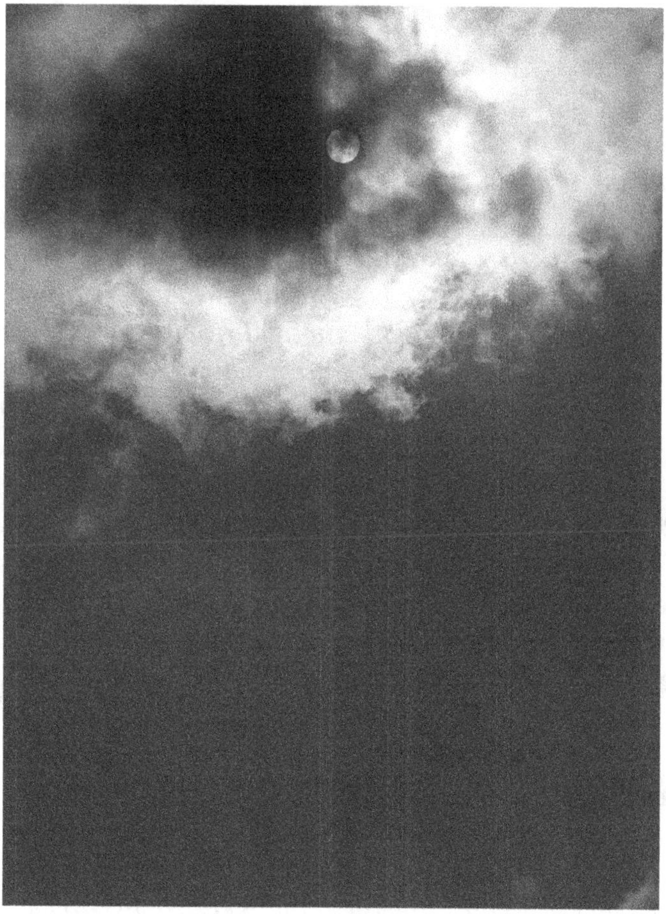

Figure 8. The Salento sun, hidden behind some clouds. Photo: Giovanna Parmigiani.

The air smells of salvia officinalis and incense. The white, circular room of the trullo is filled with hundreds of crystals and with the sound of drums. It is a hot and humid mid-July Sunday afternoon in northern Salento. Pictures of Sai Baba lie next to stuffed animals and statues of different sizes. A banner with Sanskrit characters, with their transliteration, is hanging from the door, silently reciting Om Mani Padme Hum in the minds of those who rest their eyes on it. Bare footed, we sit on the colored pillows that cover the stone benches contouring the perimeter of the room. There are only two chairs: one is for Fenice, and the other, empty, is intended for the person who "will need to work." The atmosphere is dense, but the energy is bubbly like sparkling water: enthusiastic and somewhat unnatural, uncanny. Fenice is dressed in her "work clothes": a white T-shirt and a long, light-blue skirt. It is the same attire she wears during her curanderías, and, apparently, it carries all the powerful and healing energies of those rituals. She is a strong, beautiful woman in her seventies. Her long, gray hair falls symmetrically on her shoulders. Her olive complexion stands out against the white walls of the circular room; her bright, dark, captivating eyes sparkle in excitement. Focused on my senses, I sit quietly and wonder if I will indeed be able to follow the works and to participate actively in them. Observers-only are not welcome here.

There are fifteen of us. In addition to Fenice – the woman that the others call "sciamana" (female shaman) – I know only one of them: Fiammetta. She is one of my Sisters and a regular at Fenice's meetings. She seems to know the majority of the people gathered in the trullo. She briefly introduces me to the others before we all enter into the circular room. We share our names and shake hands. Most of the other participants seem to know what a "family constellation" is, but Fenice starts the meeting by spending a few words on the "rules" that govern these types of works. She warns us that not everybody will be able to "work directly" on their issues, but she reassures us that "the field" (il campo) will take care, directly or indirectly, of the needs of every participant. Some of us, she adds, will be asked to "embody some *energies." We'll be able to decide freely whether or not to fulfill these requests. Moreover, what happens during the work is confidential, and nobody can talk about the constellation's content and happenings for the two weeks following the ritual. The field, she claims, will continue to be active for 14 days, and talking – even between us – about the details of the ritual would just weaken its power and efficacy.*

Lorenzo volunteers to be the first. He takes a seat on the "working chair." He then, prompted by Fenice, gives voice to the question he wants to ask to the field: he wants to better understand the relationship with his father. I feel anxious and insecure, like an unprepared student before an exam, and I find myself hoping not to be chosen. It is my first time at a family constellation, and I feel ill-equipped for it. Fenice asks Lorenzo to choose who will embody whom: his father, his mother, and himself, to start with. Luckily, Lorenzo does not ask me to embody any of the protagonists, and I feel grateful to be able to witness the process "from the outside." The persons who accepted the invitation to work with Lorenzo step into the middle of the circle and start to move around. Then they begin to share their feelings and to verbalize their thoughts. If this is a theatrical performance, I think, it seems quite convincing. If the participants are actors who play particular characters, they seem to know their script pretty well. "I certainly do not have any libretto to follow, nor performing abilities," I ruminate in silence.

With guidance from Fenice, the director, the impromptu play starts to unfold in a particular way and spatial display, and Lorenzo is asked to witness the dynamics of his life from an external point of view.[1] *Both Fenice and Lorenzo ask questions to the actors, who seem to answer appropriately. After a while, Fenice summons other, dead, relatives of Lorenzo – his ancestors. They are all there, sharing the room with us, apparently.*

1 As Konkolÿ Thege et al. point out, "Family constellation therapy was developed in Germany in the early '90s integrating elements of – among others – psychodrama, family sculptures, contextual therapy, and certain South-African aboriginal traditions." *The Effectiveness of Family Constellation Therapy*," 410.

The participants at the center of the room are giving them voice and words.

After this moving act, Lorenzo steps into the circle to "perform himself." Fenice wants Lorenzo to understand some of the burdens that linger in his lineage and that, she claims, are affecting his life. She therefore asks questions to the spirits of Lorenzo's ancestors, impersonated by some of the participants of the constellation. The latter unfolds with a fair amount of emotional intensity, with Lorenzo's dead grandfather performed by Simone, another participant at his first family constellation. He gives voice to a confession of a secret that Lorenzo's ancestor had kept to himself during his lifetime. A secret that had affected him, his relationships, and the life of his family. This, according to Fenice, was impacting Lorenzo's life as well, and had a role in his difficult relationship with his father and in the latter's troubled relationship with his own father.

This constellation ends with an intervention from Fenice. She wants to fix some communication problems among the members of Lorenzo's family and asks him to repeat some statements, perform some forgiving rituals, and state some empowering affirmations. At the end of all this, Lorenzo bursts into tears, and I feel emotional too, moved by the cathartic experience.

I am surely affected by Lorenzo's story, but I cannot help thinking about my own. I am still processing the grief linked not only to the recent deaths of my mother and grandmother, but also to that of my father. It has been almost seven years now. It was summer when he passed away, during the night of San Lorenzo: he died under a sky illuminated by a cascade of falling stars.[2] *I wish I could talk to him or that he could talk to me: it could certainly heal some old wounds, as has just happened for Lorenzo. I look at the latter, while he tries to regain his composure, and I wish I were him. Glimpses of memories of the time preceding my parents'*

2 Around the night of St. Lorenzo, on August 10th, the Earth's orbit crosses that of the Perseids, making visible a shower of falling stars. This night is often celebrated in Italy by spending time outdoors and making wishes for every fallen star spotted.

death cross my mind as the shooting stars traversed the firmament on that San Lorenzo night. His dying hands. My mothers' tears. Lugano – the Swiss city where my paternal family comes from and in which reside some of my most fragrant and noxious childhood memories. "I always tend to associate memories to smells," I think, pausing the stream of memories for a second.

I love-hate Lugano, a place of family and of alterity, of belonging and exclusion, of welcome and rejection. I always thought that being born in Italy across the border with Switzerland had shaped me in several ways. Since my father was a frontaliere *– a person who routinely crosses the border for work purposes – I joined him once a week in his trips to Lugano. During our weekly car drives across the border I could always measure the existential dimension embedded in the physical traversing of frontiers. In spite of the continuity in weather, natural landscape, and language and dialect across the two state lines, the differences in status, prestige, economic situation, and living have always been striking. As a child, I spent my days in a multilingual school and my weekends crossing frontiers. Maybe unsurprisingly, "being one who crosses borders," became, pretty soon, an identity marker for me and provided an existential perspective. "I think this is why I eventually became an anthropologist," I think, taking an additional break from what now is a flood of images and feelings. I go back to wandering between memories of my childhood and of my family, trying to tie my current life and the one of the young Giovanna into a single, unitary, narrative.*

In my search for unity, for wholeness, my mind finally rests on the last time I was in Lugano. I was accompanying my mother to the oncologist that had assisted her several times, for several years, for several cancers. I clearly remembered him writing with an expensive fountain pen on a white piece of paper the word GUARITA! *– HEALED! – underlining it twice with a swift movement of his hand. I also remember the mixture of joy and worry in my mother's eyes while she was looking at that word. Less than six months later, she died. She might have been healed, but, clearly, she had not been cured. Another inclusion-exclusion* *memory of Lugano, another unattained promise. I am angry at that city. I do not know if I will ever forgive it.*

***

While the notion of well-being has been used extensively in disciplines such as psychology and economics, only in recent years has anthropology focused on it as an explicit object of analysis.[3] Notably, scholars such as Mathews and Izquierdo and Ferraro and Barletti address the uses and abuses of the term and set the stage for a more thorough understanding and description of what well-being means, within and without its specific cultural inflections.[4] Comprising the three dimensions of *healing, happiness,* and *prosperity,* well-being encompasses both objective and subjective (including culturally specific) experiences.

Studies of well-being fueled important debates among medical anthropologists, religionists, psychological anthropologists, humanists, and applied anthropologists, and raised ethical and epistemological questions of who should define well-being, what we understand with this particular term, and around researchers' positionalities. While these

3 See, e.g., Ian Steedman, John R. Atherton, and Elaine Graham, eds., *The Practices of Happiness* (London: Routledge, 2010); Iza Kavedžija: *Values of Happiness: Toward an Anthropology of Purpose in Life* (Chicago: HAU Books, 2016).

4 According to Gordon Mathews and Carolina Izquierdo, "Well-being is an optimal state for an individual, community, society, and the world as a whole. It is conceived of, expressed, and experienced in different ways by different individuals and within the cultural contexts of different societies: different societies may have distinctly different culturally shaped visions of well-being. Nonetheless, well-being bears a degree of commonality due to our common humanity and interrelatedness over space and time. Well-being is experienced by individuals—its essential locus lies within individual subjectivity—but it may be considered and compared interpersonally and interculturally, since all individuals live within particular worlds of others, and all societies live in a common world at large." (Gordon Mathews and Carolina Izquierdo, *Pursuits of Happiness: Well-Being in Anthropological Perspective* [New York: Berghahn Books, 2009], 50.) See also Emilia Ferraro and Juan Pablo Sarmiento Barletti, "Placing Wellbeing," *Anthropology in Action* 23, no. 3 (2016): 1–5.

works criticize and show the flaws of an indiscriminate and unquestioned application of Western-based assumptions on what well-being is, they do not limit their work to the *pars destruens*. On the contrary: while affirming that the contents of the term appear multifaceted and culturally relative, they do not argue against "soft" forms of comparativism. In their *pars construens*, informed by the ethnographic methods of anthropology, they try to complement, rather than dismiss, health and prosperity as analytical and measurable tools. In doing so, they introduce and disarticulate concepts such as "happiness" or ideas around "living a good, fulfilling life," to enrich the complexity of the terms and to stimulate different forms of social and political intervention. In this spirit, I read the work of those who, through their ethnographic accounts, argue in favor of the importance of place-making and relationships in their thinking about well-being.[5]

If space and place, then, have been researched as cross-cultural dimensions fostering "well-being," another dimension—time, which is a crucial part of human experience—is absent from anthropological perspectives on well-being. Is the way we think about, experience, and make sense(s) of time, history, and temporality relevant for well-being? On the basis of the ethnographic data and research that I am providing in this book, I argue that there is a connection between well-being, the "expanded present" historicity, and the "presence magic" that I have been describing so far. My claim, though, differs from those of scholars who understand the importance of time only in reference to "time-spans" of happiness.[6] Instead, based on the ethnographic evidence I gathered, it considers how a non-linear

5 On well-being and place, see, e.g., Emilia Ferraro and Juan Pablo Sarmiento Barletti, "Placing Wellbeing"; Jonathan Miles-Watson, "Teachings of Tara: Sacred Place and Human Wellbeing in the Shimla Hills," *Anthropology in Action* 23, no. 3 (2016): 30–42.

6 Joel Robbins, "On Happiness, Values, and Time," *HAU Journal of Ethnographic Theory* 5, no. 3 (2015): 215–33.

historicity can be experienced to foster well-being and happiness.

What does "healing" mean in the context of Salentine Paganism? How do the "expanded present" and "presence magic" impact subjective and objective experiences of happiness, prosperity, and healing – i.e., well-being? What is their role in the pursuit of *bellezza*? Healing – as the anthropologist Sarah Pike and the scholar of Western Esotericism Wouter Hanegraaff, among others, have shown – is at the very core of New Age and many contemporary Pagan practices – surely, of "global Pagan" ones.[7] As one of Pike's informants, Lisa, put it: "The act of healing – be it spiritual healing, emotional healing, the healing of one's own self-esteem, as well as the healing of the physical body – is at the root of all magical disciplines."[8] Although not every practitioner under the "Pagan tent" practices magic, many of my Pagan interlocutors do, and they do share Lisa's approach. For them, *pizzica* (also in its connections with the experience of the *tarantate* of the past) is a practice that, first of all, *cura* – it heals.

Cura – cure – is the Italian word that my Pagan interlocutors associate with their practices, and with dancing *pizzica* in particular. Their *pizzica* is a "*pizzica che cura*" – *pizzica* that cures. And the dimension of curing and caring is overwhelmingly present as a *leit motiv* of many of their practices. From dancing *pizzica* to family constellations, from *curanderías* to the use of Aura-Soma pomanders and bottles, from Reiki practices to Magnified Healing, from shamanic journeys to the use of crystals, the majority of their ritual and spiritual practices entail some sort of healing process. Interestingly, they do not use the verb *guarire* – to heal; the term normally used in biomedical contexts to refer to the absence or remission of disease – to talk about both their experiences and the pursuit of well-being. Etymologically

7 See Pike, *New Age and Neopagan Religions*; Hanegraaff, *New Age Religion*.
8 Pike, *New Age and Neopagan Religions*, 91–2.

linked to the action of guarding and preserving, *guarire* is only one dimension of healing, of "making whole."[9] *Curare*, instead, is much more aligned with the restoration of "wholeness," or unity with the divine, according to my interlocutors, as it encompasses both the meanings of healing *and* caring. *Curare*, etymologically, is linked to the word *cura*. From the root *Ku, Kau, Kav*, meaning to observe, *curare* refers to the action of looking after, to give attention. While both the actions of *guarire* and *curare* are rooted in a practice of observation, it is clear that the performances and meanings of "seeing" are understood very differently in the two cases.

To better grasp the variances in the relationship between seeing and health, according to my interlocutors, I propose to look at how they refer to the Japanese art of *Kintsugi*.[10] Both a philosophy and a practice, *Kintsugi* is the Japanese art of mending broken pottery with a golden paste. Its objective is not concealing imperfections, but to celebrate them by adding value and beauty to a once-damaged and often useless and valueless ceramic. Often mentioned and applauded by my interlocutors, *Kintsugi* entails an understanding of health/wholeness as both a condition and a process that need to be celebrated and appreciated—and not as a worthiness constantly threatened by internal or external factors. *Cura* is this, for the Salentine Pagans: an action of care and healing that adds importance and value, not through an idea of mending or fixing, but through one of embellishing and transforming. It is the result of a gaze that sees beauty—in Italian, *bellezza*—in the process of

9 On New Age and the importance of healing in New Age and contemporary Pagan spiritualities, see, e.g., Pike, *New Age and Neopagan Religions*; Hanegraaff, *New Age Religion*, and "The New Age Movement"; James R. Lewis, "Approaches to the Study of the New Age Movement," in *Perspectives on the New Age*, ed. James R. Lewis and J. Gordon Melton (New York: State University of New York Press, 1992), 1–12.

10 On a world-anthropologies" approach, see footnote 137.

becoming, and a celebration of the process of filling the gaps of what separates us from the best version of ourselves.[11]

If my interlocutors' conscious word choice of *curare* is not completely alien to what stems from debates in medical anthropology on the different dimensions of healing, curing, and caring,[12] I argue that this verbal choice is also a result of their particular ontology and that it speaks to a peculiar way to understand both personhood and one's place in the world.

What is the relationship between this "healing/*curare*" and alternative historicities—and with the "expanded present," in particular? I was having a conversation on the phone with one of my interlocutors once. We were talking about a spiritual work—*lavoro*—that we had done—*fatto*—a few days before. I remember she used a particularly useful story as a metaphor to explain to me the efficacy of that work—one that can be easily and purposely transferred also to "presence magic" and the "expanded present" historicity.

"Imagine you are very much in love with a person with whom you are in a romantic relationship," she said. "They are your best friend and lover, and you want to spend your life with them. Now, imagine that, as it sometimes happens, this relationship comes to an end—and not by your choice. They decide to break up and you feel broken and in pain." She briefly paused, and then continued, "Now imagine that, a couple of days after the end of your relationship,

11 Interestingly, these "gaps" are also those celebrated in the summer solstice, the period of the year when the *tarantate* were healed in Galatina. See, for a comparison, also the notion of *bellezza* in chapter 2.

12 On "caring," "curing," and "healing" see, among many others, Donald W. Winnicott, *Home is Where We Start From* (New York: Norton, 1986); Cristiana Giordano, "Political Therapeutics: Dialogues and Frictions Around Care and Cure," *Medical Anthropology* 37, no. 1 (2018): 32–44; Daboo, *Ritual, Rapture and Remorse*; Waldram, "Efficacy of Traditional Medicine"; Linda L. Barnes and Susan Starr Sered, *Religion and Healing in America* (Oxford: Oxford University Press, 2004; Joseph D. Calabrese, *A Different Medicine* (Oxford: Oxford University Press, 2013).

you find a picture of the two of you together—happy, smiling, and hugging each other. That particular picture that was taken in a moment of joy as a memento of your happiness is now a thorn in your heart, right? It feels incredibly painful. It measures the distance between what you had and now have not, of who you were and now you are not." After another brief pause, she continued, "Time passes, and now, two years later, you find yourself in another moment of your life. You changed cities and jobs, perhaps, and you are in another relationship. You feel content and look at the future with positivity and hope. You find the same old picture. What do you do, now? How do you feel? You probably look at it and smile! You look at a younger version of yourself with compassion and tenderness. And, in what feels like a hug to your former self, you are able to see and feel all the emotions that were attached to that photo (the bliss, the anger, the sorrow, the love, the sadness, the passion, etc.) as different layers, without "wearing" any particular one of them. You only feel compassionate and loving. And, kindhearted, you look at your image and that of your previous partner and see a part of you that taught you lessons and that does not hurt anymore. This," my friend concludes, "is what happens during rituals. They allow us to make the 'two years jump' of the story I just told you, but in the space of a couple of hours. Rituals do not erase memories, they just help infuse them with different and more empowering emotional flavors."

This is a good metaphor to understand how "presence magic" and tuning in with the "expanded present" can work as a cure, a particular healing gaze, that favors one's well-being: by allowing us to access different dimensions of time *coevally*, it encourages to look at our lives, pains, and challenges with a different look—that of *bellezza*, that of *cura*.

Lorenzo's constellation is now over, and we are taking a five-minute break before continuing with someone else. I think about what I have just seen, and trying to understand the unknown with the known, I wonder about Aristotle and the cathartic potential of tragedies. I am puzzled, though, by a few elements: Lorenzo did not seem to know personally the men and women who impersonated the protagonists of his life, nor did they seem to know him. Nonetheless, they all felt so comfortable in playing impromptu the role of strangers: Lorenzo's relatives. Certainly, I would not have been able to do it; I would actually have been scared to mess things up. What a responsibility! Given the sensitive issues at stake and the emotional reactions of Lorenzo, I would have feared to hurt, mislead, or fail him. "Clearly, family constellations are not for me," I think. And I try to soothe my anxiety by repeating to myself that, in the unfortunate case I would be asked to impersonate a character, I would be free to decline the request.

***

It is time to resume our work. Fenice calls Luca and asks him to sit next to her. Luca is a tall, good-looking man in his forties with a tanned complexion and bright blue eyes. A bit shy, he slightly blushes when called by Fenice. While I observe the situation, I start feeling a slight pain in my right eye. "Strange," I think, "I have never experienced a similar discomfort." Luca wants to work on his relationship with his mother. Fenice asks him to choose from among the participants "his mom and himself." In spite of my hopes, I still fear that I will be chosen. I tend to resist this thought by rationalizing. People here know that I am new and inexperienced; who would ever choose ME to work on such delicate questions? I, certainly, would not. Moreover – I repeat to myself as a mantra – in the worst-case scenario, I could refuse to step into the constellation arena.

My eye pain is starting to bother me, but I try to concentrate on something else. I feel a surging discomfort, my mind wanders. I cannot focus long enough on any thought to be able to step out of my sense of uneasiness. After a short walk around the room,

Luca stops right in front of me and reaches his hand out, asking, "Vuoi essere me?" *Do you want to be me? "Yes," I immediately answer, while holding his hand and walking towards the middle of the room – slightly anxious, quite surprised, and very disappointed at myself for my unanticipated choice to follow him. It is as if my body decided to ignore my head: I feel a bit irritated and wonder why I chose to participate in the performance. While Luca resumes his walk around the room with the intent of choosing his "mother," I feel my heart pounding and my hands sweating. My right eye is still in pain, and my discomfort is growing. Another woman joins me at the center of the room. Fenice asks Luca to position us. He moves me in front of the other woman and goes back to his chair.*

While I mull over my choice to participate in the constellation, I look at the woman performing as Luca's mom. I can't stand her gaze. I feel I need space and to stay away from her. Her presence is overwhelming and limiting my movements. The more I move away from her, the more she follows me, demanding that I look at her, see her, follow her. She accuses me of fleeing, of not caring, of being a coward. I feel I lack air, both physically and metaphorically. I can't breathe – I need oxygen, space, and to be left alone. I need my space – I cannot think, live, or move with her around. I feel she wants to connect with me, but I do not want to. I feel her needs, but I cannot fulfill them: I feel immobilized and inept, unable to respond to her demands. I let myself down for this, but I cannot help it, I feel trapped and the only thing I want to do is to tell her "Lasciami stare!" *– Let. Me. Be!"*

I am surprised to actually hear those words, thrown at her like a brick against a window. My mouth shouts at her, with rage and a sense of foolishness; with pride and fear of the consequences. I feel mad at her, at me, at the situation. I cannot sense a way out. I want to yell and cry.

I look around me, slightly embarrassed, but with a sense of relief. I see Luca nodding his head while sharing some words with Fenice. I realize that I am in the middle of the room and that everybody is looking at me: "The constellation is probably about to begin," I think, trying to focus. Even so, my only preoccupation remains staying away from that woman, and I only partially follow the conversation between Fenice and Luca, and I care even less about the work.

Fenice asks Fiammetta to join us in the middle of the room: it is only then that I understand, a bit surprised, if not shocked, that the constellation had already started, and that I was actually already *performing Luca. Maybe – a thought crosses my mind – what I feel is what* he *feels. This thought soon disappears, as Fiammetta enters the circle. I feel comforted by her presence, and my distress momentarily recedes. Fenice does not tell who my Sister is impersonating. She only asks us to react to her energy. I feel relieved by the presence of Fiammetta (or whoever she is, at that point), and I find myself following her. Fiammetta: my coveted liberation from the presence of the other woman. I ask Fiammetta to stand between me and Luca's mother, to shield me from that woman. My Sister does not seem to be as disturbed by the presence of Luca's mom as I am, but she looks at her sternly, eye to eye. Luca's mother asks her to move away: she is not really interested in her presence and keeps chasing me. Overwhelmed and anxious, with my eye still sore, I turn towards Fenice and ask her to make that woman – Luca's mother – stop. It is a desperate call, for my part. I want this to end. Fenice, acknowledging my discomfort, then asks me and Fiammetta to step to the side and Luca to step in, together with other characters. Fiammetta, Fenice now reveals, is Luca's soul, his "higher self." "Is that why I felt so reassured by her presence in the circle?" I wonder.*

***

Luca's constellation unfolds in front of my eyes, now those of a spectator. The eye pain is slowly fading, as is my discomfort and my sensation of lack of air.

When the constellation is over, Luca comes towards me with tears in his eyes and hugs me while uttering a heartfelt thanks. I hug him as if he were a dear friend, with a heart full of love. I feel an uncanny, deep connection with him, a stranger. We hold each other for a while, then I put my hands on his cheeks and, looking at him directly in his eyes, I wish him all the best, and I return to my chair. As soon as I sit, the eye pain disappears completely.

***

Fenice asks us if we have any comments or anything to share with the group before moving on to the next constellation, and I tell about my right eye pain, how it started just before being chosen by Luca, and how it stopped as soon as I returned to my seat. Immediately, Luca replies – nonchalant, as if I had just told him something unexceptional – "Oh, I have a problem with my right eye. I've been having an issue with it for many years. No surprise that you felt that pain: you were me!" Fenice smiles and nods. I feel a bit confused, and I wonder, mindful of the anthropological literature I read on spirit possession, is this what it really means to be "possessed?"

***

The sociologist Paul Heelas and the scholar of Western esotericism Wouter Hanegraaff, among others, have claimed that the heterogeneous spiritualities that are normally labeled (not unproblematically) as "New Age" are, *per antonomasia*, "spiritualities of the self."[13] Therefore, it is

13 See, e.g., Paul Heelas, *The New Age Movement: The Celebration of the Self and the Sacralization of Modernity* (Oxford: Blackwell, 1996); Hanegraaff, *New Age Religion*; Lau, *New Age Capitalism*; Purser, *McMindfulness*; Jennifer Rindfleish, "Consuming the Self: New Age Spirituality as 'Social Product' in Consumer Society," *Consumption Markets & Culture* 8, no. 4 (2005): 343–60; Muir, "The Good of New Age Goods." My argument here is more aligned with the position of Michael Houseman and Marie Mazzella di Bosco, "Dances of Self-Development as a Resource for Participatory Democracy," in *Ritual and Democracy: Protests, Publics and Performances*, ed. Sarah Pike, Jone Salomonsen, and Paul François Tremlett (Sheffield: Equinox, 2020), 115–38. Houseman and di Bosco, following, e.g., Aupers and Houtman, "Beyond the Spiritual Supermarket," go beyond simplistic understandings of "alternative spiritualities" as "spiritual supermarkets." It is worth noting that, in his more recent work, Paul Heelas's vocabulary changed from centering on the "self" to "inner-self" and "spiritualities of life." See Paul Heelas, *Spiritualities of Life: New Age Romanticism and Consumptive Capitalism* (Malden, MA: Blackwell Pub, 2008).

generally inferred that this ethics of the self is paired with epistemological and radical individualism[14] and that it blends well with market economy and with neoliberal technologies of the self.[15] In *Ripples of the Universe*, for example, anthropologist Susannah Crockford analyzes contemporary New Age spirituality in Sedona, Arizona, and makes important claims on the possible relationships between New Age spiritualities and neoliberalism today—claims that go beyond "sociological critiques of spirituality that it is a consumerist commodification of religion" (52). She argues that

> Neoliberalism is often used vaguely as a buzzword; however, it can be used with more precision as a series of policies implemented by national and local governments first in North America and Western Europe and then imposed globally, through which the social safety net was cut and the market was allowed to dictate the terms of exchange. There is a similarity of form with spirituality, in which four defining characteristics stand out: financialization, privatization, deregulation, and individual responsibility.[16]

In conversation with the work of anthropologist David Graeber, Crockford maintains that

> Spirituality is the complement to neoliberalism; the spiritual side of its pure capitalism. The financialization of everything in economic life has been accompanied by the spiritualization of everything in religious life. The immateriality of money takes on spiritual significance when money is seen as energy. Making money becomes manifesting abundance, and earning a wage can be imagined as consonant with spiritual development. The morality of exchange comes into question because how you make your money is part of how you develop spiritually." [17]

14 See, e.g., Palmisano and Pannofino, *Contemporary Spiritualities*.

15 With Michel Foucault, by the expression "technologies of the self," I refer to all those practices and techniques used by individuals to fashion and transform themselves.

16 Crockford, *Ripples of the Universe*, 27.

17 Crockford, *Ripples of the Universe*, 28.

While I find these claims quite compelling, I also recognize them as very locally-specific – i.e., useful descriptors of how the New Age spiritual discourses are received and enacted in the (particular) North American context and, possibly, due to the global prevalence of Anglocentrism, in "global" Paganisms and New Age spiritualities. In these contexts, as a matter of fact, the "self" seems to be still understood within anthropocentric Cartesian assumptions – that reinstate the primacy of the mind over the body. While I am not denying, here, the validity of such a framework to understand some developments of New Age and alternative spiritualities, both in reference to the late 1990s and early 2000s and to their present developments[18] – e.g., on Instagram,

18 Also Crockford's important remarks on the consequences of New Age discourses vis-à-vis social class, inequalities, race, and cultural appropriation in the US seem to be equally grounded in a peculiar context and in the specific ways in which "difference" is understood and perceived in the UK and North America. In this respect, and in reference to the non-Anglophone context of this book, Crockford's central claim that "there is an imperialism to universalism" could be complemented and better understood in dialogue with other European critical and philosophical traditions – for example, with the thought of feminist philosopher (of difference) Rosi Braidotti and her decades-long work on (post-anthropocentric) "nomadic subjects" and with its focus on "becoming." The project on nomadic subjects stems from Braidotti's engagement with feminist studies, post-structuralist philosophies, post-colonial studies, anti-racist philosophies, critical theory, and social theory and aims at engaging three set of interlinked problems: cultural, political, and ethical. From Braidotti's point of view, within the latter, in particular, "The emphasis falls on a cognitive brand of empathy, or intense affinity: it is the capacity for compassion, which combines the power of understanding with the force to endure in sympathy with a people, all of humanity, the planet and civilization as a whole. It is in an extra-personal and a trans-personal capacity, which should be driven away from any universalism and grounded instead in the radical immanence of a sense of belonging to and being accountable for a community, a people, and a territory." Rosi Braidotti, "Posthuman, All Too Human. Towards a New Process Ontology." *Theory, Culture & Society* 23 nos. 7–8 (2006): 205. "Territory," in Braidotti's work as well as among my Salentine interlocutors, explicitly refers to our planet Earth, it is non-anthropocentric, and includes other-than-human beings. See also, e.g., Rosi Braidotti, "We" Are in This Together, But We Are Not One and the Same." Journal of Bioethical Inquiry 17 no 4(2020): 465–69; George Maciunas Foundation, *European Alternatives: On /nnomadism Interview with Rosi Braidotti.*

TikTok, and other social media—my ethnographic data allow also for the emergence of some different features.[19]

On the one hand, I agree with previous works that suggest an interpretation of New Age and contemporary Pagan spiritualities as "spiritualities of the self," entailing a "sacralization of the self." This is an undeniable element, and well-argued in the relevant academic and non-academic literatures. In particular, I agree with Crockford and Asprem, who argue that we should take in consideration, when studying the global spread of New Age Spirituality, the "cultural baggage" that comes with it—especially the political, ideological, and economic projects linked with the "sacralization of individuality."[20] On the other hand, though, I would like to encourage a less deterministic approach, stressing how different contexts react to this "baggage" differently, with, sometimes, unexpected outcomes. If we problematize what we generally understand by "self," for example, when looking at New Age and alternative spiritualities spaces, we could draw some alternative conclusions. In other words, the experience of the self that I found on the field expressed through "presence magic" does not unproblematically translate to the unitary, individualistic, autonomous, well-bounded self that much of the anthropological and sociological literature around New Age and contemporary Paganisms, especially in Anglophone contexts, has taken for granted. A result of the Cartesian legacy, which focuses on the predominance of rationality in defining who a human being is, this body

19 On contemporary Paganism and social media, see, e.g., Ross Downing, "Hashtag Heathens: Contemporary Germanic Pagan Feminine Visuals on Instagram," *The Pomegranate: The International Journal of Pagan Studies* 21, no. 2 (2020): 186–209; Áine Warren, "The Morrigan as a 'Dark Goddess': A Goddess Re-Imagined Through Therapeutic Self-Narration of Women on Social Media," *The Pomegranate: The International Journal of Pagan Studies* 21, no. 2 (2019) 237–55; Charlotte Rodgers, "High Glamour: Magical Clothing and Talismanic Fashion," *The Pomegranate: The International Journal of Pagan Studies* 21, no. 2 (2020): 172–85; and the "WitchTok" thread on TikTok.

20 Susannah Crockford and Egil Asprem, "Ethnographies of the Esoteric."

of scholarship has uncritically attributed to the "West" an idea of an individualist and unitary agentive subject[21], ontologically distinct from others and from objects. Even if one decides to keep, for heuristic reasons, the terminology of "West" (versus "the Rest")—something I am not inclined to do for a number of reasons, including its inadequate descriptive function in the contemporary world—such a limited understanding of personhood raises many questions. Among other problems, the uncritical adoption of the Cartesian self as a "default" option to understand European experiences of self conceals a certain variability of experiences of personhood within the "West." It replicates the long-standing marginalization of Southern and Eastern-European cultures within Europe. It neglects the presence of different ontologies both in the "West" and in individuals. And it denies a positional and contextual variability of experience of the self. Consequently, to avoid replicating such problems, I propose to reframe the question of the relationship between New Age and Pagan spiritualities and selfhood. In order to do so, I believe that both the literature on spirit possession and the one on "neo-animism" could be better starting points to assess and conceptualize contemporary New Age and Pagan selves and personhoods—in and beyond the Salentine context I am studying. This could lead to a more complex description of the topic, with important implications for the understanding of contemporary forms of magic and their connections with well-being and neoliberalism.

21 In particular, as Rosi Braidotti has shown, this Cartesian "human subject" is "not at all a neutral category. It is rather a normative category that indexes access to privileges and entitlements. . . . Humanity is a quality that is distributed according to a hierarchical scale centered on a humanistic idea of Man as the measure of all things. This dominant idea is based on a simple assumption of superiority by a subject that is masculine, white, Eurocentric, practicing compulsory heterosexuality and reproduction, able-bodied, urbanized, speaking a standard language. This subject is the Man of reason that feminists, anti-racists, black, indigenous postcolonial and ecological activists have been criticizing for decades." Braidotti, "'We' Are in This Together," 2.

In anthropology, "individual," "self," and "person" are not synonyms. While definitions of the latter especially vary, it is generally acknowledged that "individuality" (to be distinguished from "individualism") pertains to the biological level and refers to being a member of humanity. "Selfhood" belongs to the psychological level and is defined as the locus of experience. "Personhood" is linked to socio-cultural dimensions and is primarily defined by relationality and agentivity.[22] If within a Cartesian legacy, perceived as the "norm," the notions of individual, self, and person are considered as completely overlapping, a conspicuous anthropological literature has shown that this is not the case, in other socio-cultural contexts.[23] In other

22 On the notion of personhood see, e.g., Grace Gredys Harris, "Concepts of Individual, Self, and Person in Description and Analysis," *American Anthropologist* 91, no. 3 (1989): 599–612; Michael Lambek, "The Continuous and Discontinuous Person: Two Dimensions of Ethical Life," *Journal of the Royal Anthropological Institute* 19, no. 4 (2013): 837–58; Katie Glaskin, "Death and the Person: Reflections on Mortuary Rituals, Transformation and Ontology in an Aboriginal Society," *Paideuma* 52 (2006): 107–26, and "Anatomies of Relatedness: Considering Personhood in Aboriginal Australia," *American Anthropologist* 114, no. 2 (2012): 297–308; Ian Keen, "Ancestors, Magic, and Exchange in Yolngu Doctrines: Extensions of the Person in Time and Space," *Journal of the Royal Anthropological Institute* 12, no. 3 (2006): 515–30; Maria Pandolfi, "The Expanded Body and the Fragmented Body: Inside and Beyond Narrative," *Surfaces* 2 (1992).

23 As Thomas Csordas points out, "Self is neither substance nor entity, but an indeterminate capacity to engage or become oriented in the world, characterized by effort and reflexivity." (See Thomas J. Csordas, *The Sacred Self: A Cultural Phenomenology of Charismatic Healing* [Berkeley: University of California Press, 1997], 5.) On conceptions of personhood in anthropology relevant to my argument see, e.g., Marilyn Strathern, *The Gender of the Gift* (Berkeley: University of California Press, 1988) on individuality; Elizabeth Pérez, *Religion in the Kitchen* (New York: New York University Press, 2016), on "distributed personhood"; and Lambek, "Continuous and Discontinuous Person." Moreover, as Harvey notes, "Both Moderns and Indigenous people can be either individuals or individuals (or both at different times or in different relations) in lived reality, but their 'cultures'—the sedimentation of locally commonplace or widely shared acts, inspirations and aspirations—shape people in particular directions" ("Bear Feasts," 199). For the notion of personhood in relation to different types of modernities, see Gentilcore, *From Bishop to Witch*; and chapter 4. On multiple subjectivities and ethnography, see, e.g., Fadeke N. Castor, "Subjectivity:

geographical areas and cultural instances, the intersections between individual, self, and personhood appear to be much more complex—including, sometimes, objects, lands, other human, more-than-human, and other-than-human persons. This, for example, happens in what has been described as "distributed personhood," an ontological approach in which personhood appears to be distributed outside one's body, for example in objects.[24]

One of the circumstances in which mainstream Cartesian understandings of personhood and experiences of selfhood are challenged is linked to the phenomenon known as spirit possession. In her study of Candomblé, medical anthropologist Rebecca Seligman investigates spirit possession as a way to promote healing. Interestingly, for the sake of my argument, this healing, she argues, is the result of a *change in the sense of the self*,[25] and the ability to shape one's self and well-being through the interaction of meaning and embodied experience is not a rare faculty of particularly gifted human beings.[26] Rather, it is "a function of the nature of selves," in which religious beliefs play a central role.[27] On

Offerings from African Diasporic Religious Ethnography," *Fieldwork in Religion* 17 no 1(2022): 72–83.

24 See, e.g., Pérez, *Religion in the Kitchen.* See also, as a comparison, Diana Espírito Santo, "Assemblage Making, Materiality, and Self in Cuban Palo Monte" in *Social Analysis* 62 no. 3 (2018): 67–87 and "The Ontogeny of Dolls: Materiality, Affect, and Self in Afro-Cuban Espiritismo." In *Material Religion* 15, n.o 3 2019): 269–92.

25 Specifically, Seligman writes that "becoming a medium is associated for many with a fundamental change in the sense of the self—both in terms of who these individuals understand and experience themselves to be and how they project themselves into the social world." (See Rebecca Seligman, *Possessing Spirits and Healing Selves: Embodiment and Transformation in an Afro-Brazilian Religion* [New York: Palgrave Macmillan, 2014], 9).

26 Ibid., 10.

27 Ibid. Rebecca Seligman notes further, "religious beliefs serve as cultural resources mobilized in the process of reshaping cognitive self-representation and self-narratives" (Ibid., 13). This is in line with previous observation on "presence" and "participation." As I pointed out in chapter 4, according to de Martino, Lévi-Bruhl's limitation was not in postulating participation, but the assumption that experiencing the individual "unity"—otherwise called

the basis of this research on spirit possession in Candomblé, I suggest that similar conclusions could be drawn for "presence magic," its "expanded present" historicity, and for the participatory experience they facilitate.[28]

In the case of the family constellations I described above, "presence magic" was active in the bodily performances of the "actors" and in the affective resonances, and the "expanded present" historicity was allowing for the copresence of humans and ancestors. Quite literally, Lorenzo and Luca could see, in front of their eyes, the unfolding of their own lives, across time and space, in the present of the ritual. Their selves were not perceived as confined to one body, but, at least during the family constellation rituals, they were shared among different bodies and objects. For example, Fiammetta and I "were" Luca, for a short time, and his perception of his self, albeit briefly, went beyond the confines of his physical body, not aligning with the Cartesian notions of individuality, selfhood, and personhood that characterize other, more ordinary, interactions. Nor did mine: the pain in my eye, the sense of oppression, the anger I was feeling while "being" Luca seemed to exceed the boundaries of my individual self, that, during his constellation, felt partially inhabited by another person. While I am not sure what to make of this experience, personally, it is clear that, for my interlocutors, it should be understood as gesturing toward a wider and more inclusive experience

---

"presence"—was a "given," and not historically determined and accessed through particular cultural devices, including magic (de Martino, *Il Mondo Magico*, 207, 213). On the healing dimension of non-Cartesian experiences of the self, see, e.g., Itzhak, "Making Selves and Meeting Others in Neo-Shamanic Healing;" Calabrese, *A Different Medicine*.

28 According to Magliocco, contemporary Pagans are reclaiming a "tradition in which trance, healing and possession are important parts of spirituality. They provide a context that normalizes and explains such experiences when they occur spontaneously, and teach practitioners specific techniques for achieving and controlling them" (*Witching Culture*, 165). I argue that this allows for the emergence of different experiences of the self.

of selfhood.[29] Moreover, in line with previously mentioned understanding of magic in the legacy of Lévy-Bruhl, it represented a form of "participatory consciousness" or "presence." "We are all one," my interlocutors claim, and "we can use this connection to heal (*curare*) one another" — human and non-human persons alike. Interestingly, as Luca's family constellation shows, our ancestors (as well as unrelated deceased persons) can be healed.[30] The importance of the principles of the unity of the cosmos and of relatedness are fundamental tenets of New Age and contemporary Pagan spiritualities, as many scholars pointed out.[31] Nonetheless, in the case of contemporary Paganism in particular, this ontological stance is often associated with another one: neo-animism.

***

The Facebook announcement indicates the cemetery of Supersano as the meeting place for the trip. Viola and Roberta, a friend of my Sister, have organized a "hiking in nature with meditation" event, to start the new year off on the right foot. It is mid-morning on a beautiful early January day. I spent the fall in the field and I am only now starting to piece together many of my ethnographic observations and experiences. The weather is quite nice, especially here, in the southern part of Salento – to me, used to New England and northern Italy, it feels more like spring than winter.

29 For a psychological and anthropological perspective on these types of phenomena, see, e.g., Tanya M. Luhrmann, *How God becomes real.* (Princeton, NJ: Princeton University Press, 2020).

30 See, e.g., Antonella Screti, *La Storia di Rahida e la Chiesetta* (Neviano: Musicaos Editore, 2015). In this small book, the Salentine author narrates the story of Rahida, a more-than-human presence that Screti and some friends energetically "detected" in the areas around a small Salentine church and,subsequently "freed."

31 In her 2004 monograph, for example, Sarah Pike describes well the historical and philosophical foundations of healing, illness, and cure among members of the New Age and contemporary Pagan spiritualities, pointing out the importance of the notion of the interconnectedness of the cosmos and of its role in understanding and experiencing healing. (See Pike, *New Age and Neopagan Religions.*)

I drive to the meeting place – not without the usual connection hiccups with the car's navigation system, due to the bad cellular reception – wondering why Viola and Roberta chose a cemetery as a meeting place. Maybe because of the free and easy parking? "I guess I will discover it soon," I tell myself while parking the car. I get out of my vehicle and walk toward a group of strangers who appear to be particularly excited, given the loud voices and laughter that I can distinctly hear from a distance.

I smile and ask them if they are here for the same reason, and they answer "Yes!" almost with one voice. "Bene!" *(good!) I reply, while my gaze floats around to assess the situation and the context – a habit that I learned over the years from my Salentine interlocutors, who appear to be always overly concerned with their surroundings. What was once a foreign habit has become more like a* habitus, *now.*[32] *While I look around, I notice that Viola is also there. She is talking with a woman that I think might be Roberta, a few meters away from us. I see Viola, and my heart smiles along with my lips. I beam not only because she is the only person I know, but also because I am looking forward to spending some time with her.*

The hiking starts a few meters away from the parking lot, at the foot of a magnificent church that Viola explains is dedicated to the Madonna di Celimanna.[33] *"We will start our journey, both physical and symbolic, from one sanctuary dedicated to the Mother," my Sister continues, "and we'll end it at another sanctuary of the Mother, that of the* Madonna della Serra."[34] *While we start our trip and walk slightly uphill, I quietly follow Viola*

32 For Pierre Bourdieu, *habitus* is the physical embodiment of cultural dispositions, habits, and values. (See Pierre Bourdieu, *Outline of a Theory of Practice* [Cambridge: Cambridge University Press, 1977].)

33 Celimanna comes from the Latin "*coeli manna,*" meaning manna from heaven, one of the titles of the Virgin Mary in Catholic devotional piety. The original crypt is Medieval, with frescoes from the thirteenth century and inscriptions in both Greek and Latin. Adjacent to it, there is now a sanctuary that is believed to have been built in the mid-eighteenth century as an act of devotion by a Roman prince, miraculously healed with the intercession of the Madonna.

34 The *serre* or *murge salentine* are the only hilly areas of Salento, otherwise quite a flat land. With a height of under two hundred meters, they provide a stunning view of the surrounding area.

and listen to her explanations. Her description of the program is punctuated by her gesturing towards particular plants and trees and intermingled with sparse spiritual comments and remarks.

After a couple of hours of hiking, we arrive in a big olive grove. The silvery colors of the leaves and the sound of the wind between the branches make the atmosphere quite festive, clashing a bit with the silence of the serra. *The church of the* Madonna della Serra, *located a few hundred meters away, watches over us. We follow Viola through the olive grove, and we take advantage of a break for drinking some water and having some small talk. We had been silent for most of the hike, and it feels good to get to know the other participants a bit. After five minutes or so, Viola calls us and asks us to find a spot in a circle that she has just finished preparing with both care and alacrity. In the middle of the circle, arranged in a circular pattern, lie some cards depicting geometrical images associated with foreign words – the names of the orixàs. After a few remarks, in which she briefly introduces us to her orixàs, Viola starts explaining in more detail the spiritual work that we are about to start. "The meditation will begin with a simple yet crucial gesture: choosing one of the cards that are in the middle of the circle and sharing it with the group," Viola says. "Please pick the card and drawing that you are drawn to – or called by—and not the one you like the most," she warns. "There is a big difference between these two criteria of selection." She explains that we need to tune in with our intuition and not to pick our card "with our heads." "Then, after some grounding exercises, we will find a spot in the grove – under a tree, on a rock, or on the grass – " she continues, "and with our card in hand, we will ask permission to get in touch with the orixà we chose (or were chosen by)." Every orixà is associated with a natural element and will "speak to us" through that element, Viola clarifies. "There are lessons for us that Nature is happy to reveal. We only need to listen.[35] After the meditation," Viola concludes, "we will rejoin the circle and share our experiences."*

35 Viola uses the expression *stare in ascolto,* literally, "staying in listening." This is another form of "active staying," as explained in chapter 1.

I look at the drawings in front of me, and my eyes keep landing on the same card: a lilac one with the name "Nanã" written on it. I show it to Viola with some hesitation. Viola smiles at me and says: "Nanã, the old Mother, she who governs life and death. The earth, the fertile dirt, the mud. She is syncretized as St. Anne." Then, standing up, she slowly starts stomping her feet, in a movement that reminds me of a basic pizzica *step – only in slow motion. "This is her mudra," she adds, "her movement."*

***

I chose an olive tree as my meditation partner. Its trunk is an upside-down braid that expands towards the sky. Back-to-back, I can feel its knots and bulges between my shoulders. I smell the perfume of the dirt under me and I observe the frantic movement of an ant, desperately trying to find her way around a stick that lies on the ground. I close my eyes and, obedient, I call on the Goddess Nanã, asking permission to listen to her teachings, if I am worthy of them. While invited to this pantheon by an Umbanda practitioner, I still feel a bit weird about contacting divinities in general, and foreign ones in particular. The fact that Nanã is associated with St. Anne and with the dirt helps a bit. I remember quite well meditating on the figure of St. Anne as a kid, during my Catholic Sunday school, and I am definitely very familiar with the dirt that covers my hand – cold and moist. Anxiety and awe merge together with feelings of incompetence and foolishness. I am clearly out of my comfort zone, here in terms of location, practices – and, I should add, of cultural boundaries. Nonetheless, I decide to go on with the meditation, apologizing, if only with words, to Nanã – as if I know her – for interfering with her world.

I close my eyes and wait for something to happen. The wind rustles in the pauses of an uncanny silence that, like a melody, fills my ears. My mind goes on and off, reaching and then abandoning a meditative state, cautiously mapping an unfamiliar interior terrain. Alternating between concentration and self-consciousness, I suddenly watch an image appearing in my mind: a placental sac, under the earth. I can see myself – my grown-up self—in it. To my surprise, I am not scared by this unexpected vision, nor do I feel cold or agitated. On the contrary, I feel warm, safe, and protected. I bask in this feeling of comfort. It is so deeply impacting me that even the scattered and self-analyzing thoughts around the psychological, unconscious meanings of this association between Nanã, *an underground womb, my own dying mother, and myself could not take away from that profoundly soothing experience. My heart is grateful, and I feel connected with the earth and, weirdly, with* Nanã. *In fact, as blasphemous as it sounds to me, I feel I* am one with *Nanã, in that moment. In addition to the overwhelming sense of safety, I perceive all her simple and intense wisdom as being part of me.*

***

We are now back in the circle. Still flabbergasted and slightly dizzy by my first "participatory" experience, I sit quietly, fidgeting with the Nanã *card, still in my hands. I eavesdrop on all the feedback from the other participants, but I cannot avoid concentrating mainly on my own experience. "I definitely went out of my comfort zone, today," I think. "But, somehow, I found dimensions of myself, in that uncharted territory, that I did not know existed. Wow, I am really liking this!" I reflect. While I know I still need to come to terms with much of what I just experienced, there, in the middle of the grove, accompanied by the sound of the wind and of the olive leaves, I feel a sudden epiphany. I decide, in my heart, that it is time for me to allow myself to go against all the warnings I received during my anthropological training. I decide that it is time for me to ignore all the advice I received in my academic education. "It is time for me to 'go native'"—I tell myself. "And this is a gooooood thing."*

Following Ernesto de Martino, I have so far argued that "presence magic" is a (cultural) way to establish presence vis-à-vis the possibility of "not-being." Linked to *bellezza* and *desiderio*, it opens up possibilities of being that, figurally, transcend (uni)linear historicities. Furthermore, I claimed that "presence magic" is obtained through what Susan Greenwood, in the legacy of Lévy-Bruhl, called "participatory consciousness"—one that goes beyond the categories of ordinary and extraordinary and, in its being grounded in an "expanded present" historicity, has healing potentials. Moreover, I showed that "presence magic" implies an experience and understanding of the self that differs from mainstream Western modern ones, in its being expanded and unbounded. I will now turn to another dimension of "presence magic"—one that is a direct consequence of all the above and, in particular, of this multifaceted self: its connection with relational ontologies.

In an article titled "Being Known by a Birch Tree," writer Priscilla Stuckey explores the implications of considering humans "not but one extension of Earth's many-faceted ability to know."[36] By recalling a personal experience of knowing and being known by a birch tree planted in the yard of her parents' house when she was born, she investigates the epistemological implications of neo-animist ontologies.[37] In line with works of authors such as the scholar of religion Graham Harvey, the anthropologist Nurit Bird-David, and the philosopher David Abram, she defines new (or neo) animism as a vision of the world that, "departing from Edward Tylor's definition of animism as belief in souls or spirits, uses the prism of relationship for understanding interconnectedness with beings of all sorts, including human and other-than-human."[38] In other words, neo-animists

36 Priscilla Stuckey, "Being Known by a Birch Tree: Animist Refigurings of Western Epistemology," *Journal for the Study of Religion, Nature and Culture* 4, no. 3 (2010): 182.

37 It is important to note that the choice of using the term "animism," even if behind the adjective "new" or "neo," is not a neutral one. Given the colonialist implications of Tylor's use of "animism," it might be argued that opting for an alternative terminology could be beneficial to both scholars and those who adhere to various relational and non-anthropocentric worldviews.

38 Stuckey, "Being Known by a Birch Tree," 188. As Harvey points out, neo-animism is inspired by Irving Hallowell's early-twentieth-century research among the Anishinaabeg in southern central Canada (see Alfred

such as the Salentine Pagans and New Age practitioners with whom I have been working, see and experience the world as intrinsically relational and populated by different persons: some of them human, and some of them more-than-human or other-than-human. The relational ontology that they embrace has not only epistemological consequences—i.e., in relation to their "ways of knowing," including the ones generated by their "participatory" experiences and by "presence magic." This neo-animist framework also impacts the ways in which Pagans experience and understand individuality, selfhood, and personhood. Notably, as Stuckey observes, within such a framework, as a matter of fact, there is no pre-relational self: the world is continuously made and remade in the interactions that we have with it, in the *fili*—webs—of relationship that connect human, non-human, and more-than-human persons.[39] This is a central point for better understanding the relationship between the expanded present historicity, "presence magic," and well-being.

Irving Hallowell, "Ojibwa Ontology, Behavior, and World View," in *Culture in History: Essays in Honor of Paul Radin*, ed. Stanley Diamond [New York: Columbia University Press, 1960], 19–52) rather than by Edward Tylor's theorizing about religion ("Bear Feasts," 198). Therefore, animists are people who think that the world is full of persons, human and not, and that experience life as relational.

39 Stuckey writes that: "In an animist world made up of persons, the world itself is continually coming into being, because to say that knowledge is constructed through relationships is tantamount to saying that the self as well comes into being through relationship." (Stuckey, "Being Known by a Birch Tree," 192.) Relational ontologies imply relational epistemologies, and neo-animism—as both a theory and a practice—postulates that relationality comes before the acknowledgement of personhood. Interestingly and importantly, Stuckey points out that neo-animism is not a form of panpsychism—it is not that matter is permeated by mind. In fact, "animism does not depend on the ontological claim that all of the world is alive" (Ibid., 189). In order to support her claim, Stuckey quotes the feminist physicist Karen Barad, who distinguishes "interacting" from "intra-acting." While the former assumes that there are separate individual agencies that precede their interaction, "the notion of intra-action recognizes that distinct agencies do not precede, but rather emerge through, their intra-actions" (Ibid., 196).

In the ethnographic vignette I just presented, for example, I described the first time I perceived a *communicative* relationship between me and Nanã—the earth. It was the first time in which I experienced the earth as a person and that I communicated with her. This type of experience is not only common among my Pagan interlocutors, but encouraged by them as a way to cultivate well-being—one that happens through a reconfiguration of the boundaries of one's self. In such a neo-animist perspective, personal relationships with the natural environment and the elements can be conceived of as instruments of well-being. They are a *cura*, an action of seeing and being seen that transforms and makes whole—the gold lining that ennobles and transforms broken pottery.

Is this neo-animist ontology something that belongs only to Salentine Pagans? Is it something that can be taught? In the article "Bear Feasts in a Land without Wild Bears: Experiments in Creating Animist Rituals," scholar of neo-animism Graham Harvey points out that "the 'turn' to an animism of relationship with other-than-human persons (trees, stones, hedgehogs and horses as much as deities and ancestors) and of relationship within larger-than-human place-communities is a more recent trend within Paganism."[40] Nonetheless, this type of attitude toward

40 Harvey, "Bear Feasts," 208. Specifically, Graham Harvey writes that "While the term 'animism' has been used for some time among Pagans, until recently, its dominant meaning was a Tylorian 'belief in spirits.' That is, it was used alongside or in contrast with claims to be theistic, polytheistic, atheistic or to identify with other kinds of theological position. The 'new animism' (mediated by books, talks or blogs) has altered the reference of the term. Many Pagans now use it to refer to efforts to renew respectful relationships with the larger-than-human world. It is part of a larger and ongoing evolution of vocabulary in which, for example, the representation of Paganism as a 'nature religion' has bumped up against the understanding that humans and their cultures are as much a part of 'nature' as other beings and their lifeways. David Abram's terms 'more-than-human world' and 'larger-than-human world' (Abram 1996) have gained currency" ("Bear Feasts," 209). (See also David Abram, *The Spell of the Sensuous: Perception and Language in a More-than-Human World* [New York: Pantheon Books, 1996].)

the world is something I encountered in Salento, in different forms, both within and beyond Pagan and New Age communities.

This is evident, for example, in an unexpected context: a 2014 short film, promoted by the diocese of Ugento-Santa Maria di Leuca,[41] directed by Antonio Scarcella and Michele Rizzo, with the help of Laura Campanile. Titled "*Xylella: il 'cancro' degli ulivi*" (*Xylella*: the "cancer" of olive trees), this short film is constructed around the celebration of a Catholic funeral, complete with priest, procession, and *prefiche*.[42] The viewer is dragged into this local drama only to discover at the end of the video that the deceased mourned by the local community is, in fact, an olive tree. Significantly, the protagonists of this film are mainly elders. If, on the one hand, they metaphorically represent Salento's traditions and the Salentine way of life, on the other hand, this cinematographic choice clearly suggests a commonality between beloved seniors, ancestors, and olive trees. The latter appear to belong, as a matter of fact, to the local community of elders: the deceased tree is, narratively, one of them.

Shot in the municipality of Tiggiano, this short film is meant to sensitize the population to the spread of *Xylella fastidiosa*, a disease that has been affecting Salento's olive trees since 2013. The responses of both authorities and

41 "Xyella: il 'cancro"'degli ulivi," dir. Antonio Scarcella and Michele Rizzo, Lucio Ciardo, November 18, 2014, video, 4:26, https://youtu.be/wvPZU06Lh40; *La Repubblica*, "Salento, Diocesi promuove processione e funerali per la peste degli ulivi," November 22, 2014, video, 3:39, https://video.repubblica.it/edizione/bari/salento-diocesi-promuove-processione-e-funerali-per-la-peste-degli-ulivi/184239/183089; "Xylella: la Diocesi fa il funerale agli ulivi," Il Gallo, November 23, 2014, https://www.ilgallo.it/attualita/xylella-la-diocesi-fa-il-funerale-agli-ulivi/

42 *Prefiche* (*le chiangimuerti*, in the Salento dialect) are women who performed ritual lamentations/weeping during funerals, in this area (and others, both in Southern Italy and in Greece). This practice lasted in Salento until the 1980s. See Ernesto de Martino, *Morte e pianto rituale: Dal lamento funebre antico al pianto di Maria* (Milano: Feltrinelli, 1975 [1958]); and Parmigiani, "Spiritual *Pizzica*."

Salentinians to the desiccation and death of olive trees have been quite controversial. In particular, in order to curb the diffusion of the bacterium considered responsible of the disease, the regional government, the national one, and the European Union have been implementing drastic policies, including the eradication and felling of hundreds of *healthy* olive trees. These measures have been strongly opposed by a large percentage of the inhabitants of Salento.

As this example suggests, Salento's hundreds-of-years-old olive trees, UNESCO's World Heritage Site nominees, are more than a geographical feature of this land: they are considered not only presences, but *persons*—and, especially, kin—by both Pagans and non-Pagans. In support of this claim, it is worth mentioning that this same neo-animist framework, albeit unaware, has been present also, more recently, *vis-à-vis* another threat: the construction of the TAP (Trans-Adriatric Pipeline). This project, harshly opposed by many Salentinians, transports natural gas from Azerbaijan to Western Europe, through Greece, Albania, and Salento—severely impacting one of the most beautiful beaches of Southern Italy (San Foca, in the Salento municipality of Melendugno) and requiring the felling and eradication of olive trees. In this latter case as well, the discourses around the stewardship and protection of olive trees have been inflected through neo-animist language and imaginaries. While it is probable that most of the non-Pagan, neo-animist Salentinians who consider and treat olive trees as persons are not aware of scholarly and spiritual debates around neo-animism, it is nonetheless clear that relational ontologies and epistemologies are present and active in Salento among Pagans, Catholics, and non-Pagans.

***

It's June. Days are longer, and the sun warmer. It's hot and humid—even inside the trullo. *The sound of the drums is fast and steady. The air is moist and the shamanic drum's goat skin, softer than usual, is producing deep, swollen sounds when hit by Fenice's drumstick. We lie on the floor of the circular room of the* trullo*, on our yoga mats. I am there with Fiammetta and eight other participants: we are going to embark on a "shamanic journey," my first one. I already sense the uncanny presences of two energetic signatures that I know very well: my paternal grandfather and his sister. I try to ignore them and to concentrate on my breath. I follow the visualization prompts: I visualize a tree. I choose to climb on it, and I start to poke into the sky as if I were knocking at a door. I open that sky door, with the curiosity, urgency, and vehemence of a kid opening a gift box, and I find myself in a meadow. I look around, but the proportions seem off—it is as if the outdoor environment was projected onto a vaulted ceiling. I recognize the perimeters of a small room behind the appearance of an outdoor environment, and I feel called from my left. I turn around, and I see my grandpa: I have only a few memories of him, who died when I was only three. I reach him and stand before him. I look my grandfather Alfredo in his eyes, and I wonder why everybody has kept telling me, since I were a little girl, that my eyes were like his. Our eyes do not look the same—his are grey and cold. Mine are greenish and warm. I look at him, but while he seems to reciprocate, I notice that his gaze is lost behind me. With the voice of my heart, I say hello. I sense peace and affection, but I also have an impression of limitation. He asks me to follow him, and I do so. We leave the vaulted room and enter a long, rectangular room of what seems like a palace, with old furniture on our left, many windows, and tapestries on the wall on our right. The floor is decorated with geometrically shaped tiles. The room is bright and warmed by a slightly golden light. I feel good, at peace, but a bit worried about such an uncanny encounter. It is the first time I have such an experience.*

My heart pounds fast, and I lose my concentration. I open my eyes and see the comforting presence of Fenice and her drum. I close my eyes and resume my journey.

My grandpa is silent. He walks in front of me. I follow him. We leave the long, rectangular room behind, and we are now at the center of a circular room. We stop right in the middle of the room, at the center of the circle, where the tiled floor is outlining a red, eight-point star. I look at my grandfather and ask him if there is something I should know. He tries to sooth my anxiety and says that no, this is not a premonitory vision. His reassurance clashes with his emotionless face. At this point, his sister appears from behind him. He does not turn around and keeps looking at a vanishing point behind my eyes. I greet her, and I ask her what is wrong with her brother, who seems to behave a bit strangely. She replies, "He can look, but he cannot see. You can both look and see." I feel puzzled by this cryptic answer, but I decide to follow her lead and enter into another small room in front of us, which is a study. A big, wooden desk lies at the center of the room, in front of two windows. There are many books, both on the table and around the room. I know my aunt is there, but I feel drawn to the windows. I get closer to them, and I look at the view. We are up high—I can see a serene landscape with gentle hills and ponds. I turn around and my aunt shows me two tarot cards: an ace of swords and a ten of pentacles. Following her prompts, I look at the desk and open a notebook. I stare at an empty, light yellow, lined page. My vision is blurred, but I see a word appearing slowly on the page: "clairvoyance." I feel a bit scared and very puzzled. I look for my aunt. I want to ask her some explanation. She is behind me and, with a sense of serenity and knowing, she puts a feather in my hand and gently suggests that I need to write. She tells me it is time to go back. All these conversations happened without me nor them uttering a word. The communication appears to be telepathic and together with her explicit insights, I receive many others, in what appears to me to be a chain of "aha" moments. Before I leave the room, she asks me one more thing, to draw the plan of the parts of the palace I visited, as soon as I come back from my journey. I thank her and say goodbye.

The sound of the drums is getting faster, a clear sign that is time to go back. I run through the circular room to the rectangular one. I peek at the vaulted meadow-room on my left before climbing down the tree and taking a seat on its roots. An eagle is flying above me, and I feel illuminated and grateful.

***

We are now slowly regaining our senses and transitioning out of the meditation. I open my eyes and see the trullo *and the face of Fenice. I sit on the yoga mat and start writing down my journey. Following my aunt's instruction, I draw the plan of the castle and I show it to Fenice. "AN OLD KEY!" she exclaims, laughing.*

As I explained above, it is my claim that neo-animist understandings of personhood and contemporary Pagan ideas of the self affect both the pursuit of well-being and its understandings, in the Salento context. In both cases, the "expanded present" historicity plays an important role—both as "presence magic" and as a particular ontology—a way to understand one's place and journey in the world—inspired by the belief in the unity of the cosmos, the experiences of interconnectedness, and neo-animist relationalities. This implies not only that accessing, in the "expanded present," different dimensions of oneself in a perspective of becoming promotes well-being, but also that the pursuit of well-being itself cannot be understood as an individual practice. Rather, and against the grain of much contemporary understanding of New Age and contemporary Paganisms, healing is a communitarian enterprise: one in which one's well-being is deeply linked to the well-being of what is around them—and *vice versa*. In other words, it can be argued that, by taking a closer look at contemporary New Age and Pagan practices in Southern Europe, a much more nuanced understanding of the relationship between these spiritualities and Neoliberalism could emerge[43].

In a 2012 article, anthropologist Katie Glaskin addresses the tensions between autonomy and relatedness among the Pintupi people in the northwest Kimberley region of

43 See Parmigiani, "If You Dance Alone."

Western Australia.[44] In dialogue with previous literature focusing on personhood,[45] she develops an understanding of the latter as an "ontology of embodied relatedness" that comprises more-than-human persons. Interestingly, inspired by the work of Eduardo Viveiros de Castro, Glaskin makes two claims that are particularly significant for the Salentine context that I am researching.[46] First, she argues that magic is "linked to cultural conceptions of the person that extends them spatially and temporally."[47] Among Salentine Pagans, this is particularly true in the practices of "presence magic," where "spatial extensions" go beyond the immediate environment and intergenerational relationships associated to an exclusively linear perception of time.

Second, Glaskin equates the problem of magic to the one of kinship, in an "embodied relationality" perspective. Therefore, the anthropologist claims with Eduardo Viveiros de Castro, that, if "all gift exchange is an exchange of persons," gift economy becomes "virtually indistinguishable from the notion of animism. . . [in which] things and people assume the social form of persons."[48] The explicit connection between animist ontologies, its understanding of personhood and selfhood, and challenges to market and capitalist economy is not a minor element in discussing contemporary religion. It becomes particularly important when addressing Paganisms and New Age spiritualities—often accused to exploit market and neoliberal economies to accumulate money and resources in exchange for spiritual services. The connection between neo-animism, relational

44 Glaskin, "Anatomies of Relatedness."

45 See, e.g., Keen, "Ancestors, Magic, and Exchange."

46 See Eduardo Viveiros de Castro, "The Gift and the Given: Three Nano-Essays on Kinshipand Magic," in *Kinship and Beyond: The Genealogical Model Reconsidered*, ed. Sandra Bamford and James Leach (New York: Berghahn Books, 2009), 237–68.

47 Glaskin, "Anatomies of Relatedness," 299; see also Keen, "Ancestors, Magic, and Exchange."

48 Glaskin, "Anatomies of Relatedness," 304–5, quoting the anthropologist Viveiros de Castro.

ontologies and epistemologies, well-being, and economy is evident also in the Salentine context. Here, very explicitly, these connections can be seen as challenging neoliberal understandings of selfhood and personhood, as well as favoring the pursuit, realization, and definition of well-being. As I showed in chapter 2, *tarantismo* and *tarantate* are objects of dynamics of "merci-patrimonialization" in contemporary Salento. In other words, the suffering bodies of *tarantate* women of Salento's past, firmly located in the "traditional past" of Salento (within a linear understanding of time), have become a source of income and of economic revenue. On the one hand, and to a certain extent, this is also valid for what pertains to the "merci-patrimonialization" of *pizzica,* sold *to specific audiences such as tourists* (see chapter 2 and below) as a "cure." Here, the "paid" performances of *tarantismo* rituals, among other examples, can be read in line with neoliberalist ideas and with market economy. On the other hand, though, it is also true that the connections between *pizzica* and "presence magic" and market economy and capitalism, today, are much more complicated than what can appear at first sight. It is my claim that "spiritual *pizzica*" and its "expanded present" historicity could represent, *at the same time,* re-inscriptions of and challenges to neoliberal understandings of the self and of personhood—redefining, de facto, the criteria used to understand well-being and prosperity.

In an articulated analysis of Buryat shamanism, anthropologist Manduhai Buyandelger concludes that "Shamanism uses the freedoms and anxieties of Capitalism to generate its own economy, which produces not material profits, but individual memories and communal histories," i.e., a cultural production of the past.[49] While "mutually constitutive" and not "mutually exclusive,"[50] Shamanism's

49 Manduhai Buyandelger, *Tragic Spirits* (Chicago: University of Chicago Press, 2013), 9.

50 Ibid., 12.

economy is different from that of capitalism, activating "different life-worlds and temporalities beyond the secular history of Capitalism."[51] While the Mongolian and Southern European contexts are very different and not necessarily comparable, it is worth noting how, in both Salento and among the Buryats, historicities that differ from the mainstream linear one can generate different types of economies and economical subjects. Or, to use philosopher Roberto Esposito's terminology, they can generate different "communities" (from the Latin *communitas*, where *cum*, means "with, together" and "*munus*" means "gift") of reciprocal obligations.

In the context of Salentine Pagans, this is true not only in reference to the "gift economies" that structure relationships among human persons and between the latter and more-than-human and other-than-human persons, it is also evident in the conception of healing, happiness, and prosperity (i.e., of "well-being") as fundamentally *communal* enterprises. These historicities challenge interpretations of the "neoliberal self" as responsible for its own well-being and for the well-being of economy, such as in Wendy Brown's notion of "responsibilization," as I will show below.[52]

Gift economy, in anthropology, as described by Marcel Mauss, is a mode of exchange based on the obligations of giving, receiving, and returning. Still present in many societies today alongside market and capitalist economies and barter, gift economy has "reciprocity" and "the spirit of the gift" as two of its main tenets.[53] These two notions are, in

51 Ibid., 15.

52 As Wendy Brown notes, "Responsibilization discursively and ethically converts the worker, student, poor person, parent, or consumer into one whose moral duty is to pursue savvy self-investment and entrepreneurial strategies of self-care" ("Sacrificial Citizenship: Neoliberalism, Human Capital, and Austerity Politics," *Constellations* 23, no. 1 [2016]: 9.

53 For a discussion on the evolution of studies on gift economy and of the notion of reciprocity, in particular, in economic anthropology, see, e.g., Xunxian

fact, connected. With "spirit of the gift," Mauss refers to the fact that with the gift, "one gives away what is in reality a part of one's nature and substance." Consequently, he claims that receiving "something is to receive a part of someone's spiritual essence."[54] This excess of meaning and value present in the gift is what justifies reciprocity—a key notion, albeit quite debated, in economic anthropology.[55] In the context of Salento, gift economy is ubiquitous in social interactions, having the "classic" function of creating, strengthening, and maintaining social connections and one's prestige *vis-à-vis* local communities. In fact, as a northerner who spent several months in Salento, I can testify personally that the practice of gift-giving and the social expectations around this practice are directly proportional to the perception of one's belonging to particular Salentine societies and communities, and to the level of "cultural intimacy" reached.[56] This is why the "merci-patrimonializing aspects of "spiritual *pizzica*" are often active in services catered towards tourists—i.e., towards

---

Yang, "The Gift and Gift Economy," in *A Handbook of Economic Anthropology*, ed. James G. Carrier (Cheltenham, UK: Edward Elgar Publishing, 2005), 246–61.

It is worth noting that the term "gift economy" has been recently used by Charles Eisenstein, the author of a book, very popular in New Age circles, titled *Sacred Economics*. His use of the term "gift economy," however, does not completely match the meaning of the same term in anthropology. See Charles Eisenstein, *Sacred Economics* (Berkeley: North Atlantic Books, 2011).

54 Marcel Mauss, *The Gift: Forms and Functions of Exchange in Archaic Societies*, trans. Ian Cunnison (New York: Norton, 1967 [1925]), 10.

55 See Annette B. Weiner, *Inalienable Possessions: The Paradox of Keeping-While-Giving* (Berkeley: University of California Press, 1992).

56 According to the anthropologist Michael Herzfeld, "Cultural intimacy is not . . . the simple idea of acquaintance with a culture, although the term has sometimes been used in that generic sense. To the contrary, it is that part of a cultural identity that insiders do not want outsiders to get to know, yet that those same insiders recognize as providing them with a comfort zone of guiltily nonnormative carryings-on. These may include anything from recognizable patterns of sexual naughtiness to bribery and bureaucratic mismanagement of many kinds." (Michael Herzfeld, "The European Crisis and Cultural Intimacy," *Studies in Ethnicity and Nationalism* 13, no. 3 [2013]: 491. See also Michael Herzfeld, *Cultural Intimacy: Social Poetics in the Nation-State* (New York: Routledge, 2005).

persons with whom those who offer spiritual services do not have a well-established personal connection.[57] In the specific context of Salentine and Pagan communities, though, gift exchange could be considered as the main framework to understand economic interactions—both among humans, and in connection with other-than-human and more-than-human persons.[58] This is valid in spite of what can appear at first sight, and is directly dependent on the relational and animist ontologies that inform Pagan understandings of selfhood and personhood—as pointed out before, with the words of the anthropologist Eduardo Viveiros de Castro.

Beyond interactions with tourists and foreigners, apparently, there are two main ways in which Pagans in Salento approach economic exchanges around the spiritual dimensions of *pizzica* and contemporary Pagan rituals promoting well-being, according to my observations. Both depend on the level of connection between the persons involved. One, at least at first sight, looks like a regular monetary transaction in exchange of services, and the other one is more explicitly in line with the "gifting, receiving, and returning" typical of "gift exchange."[59] This second often takes the shape of an exchange of favors; at other times, instead, it could include money or material objects as well. For example, while a gift economy framework is prevalent within closer relationships—for example, in exchanges among the

57 It is my understanding that the desire to connect at a spiritual level with *certain* foreigners (especially if they share with my interlocutors similar worldviews) allows for the presence of a dimension of gift exchange in certain economic interactions with strangers, in spite of the lack of personal connections. If this happens in some cases, it does not happen in others. The criteria used to assess who will and who will not be considered within a gift economy perspective does not seem to follow other rationale than the personal idiosyncrasies of the Sisters and other Pagan friends.

58 In relation to more-than-human and other-than-human persons, the gift takes the shape of offerings.

59 It is worth noting that I occasionally would also observe the use of barter. Given the peculiar Pagan understandings of personhood, bartering included a dimension of "gift economy" in it.

Sisters—depending on the context, monetary transactions are not, necessarily, out of the picture. If we Sisters know that another Sister is going through a period of financial duress, for example, we tend to favor a monetary exchange in trade for our participation in well-being practices organized by her or the group. While involving money, these are practices of care whose value exceeds the monetary one.

As a newcomer in Salento, I gradually transitioned from purely monetary transactions (of the ones involving tourists) to an explicit gift economy, in my economic exchanges with the Sisters and other Pagans. Nonetheless, while the modalities of economic transaction changed, contextually, I noticed that the framework used to explain and understand them did not: exchanges are always described in terms of energy—or, as Marcel Mauss would put it, of the "spirit of the gift"—among Salentine Pagans. In accordance with their animist ontology, a person who offers a service is believed to offer not *only* a specific service, but *also*, with it, a part of themselves. If the "service-exchange" aspect of the transaction could be taken care of, especially among persons who are not very close, by paying money in trade for spiritual work, this type of transaction does not take care of the dimensions of reciprocity linked to the "spirit of the gift" present in all "services-exchanges." The latter aspect of the exchange needs to be acknowledged and taken care of, independently, *always* within a gift economy perspective.

The reciprocity generated by the "spirit of the gift" is often not immediately returned, and could take the shape, for example, of an exchange of favors beyond and in addition to the monetary transaction—a material gift such as homegrown vegetables or a home-cooked meal, an acknowledgement of prestige and authority, publicity, or the request of other services.

In sum, my ethnographic analyses show that, contrary to many contemporary understandings of Pagan and, especially, New Age practices and practitioners, Southern

Italian Pagans and New Agers do not *only* participate in a market-oriented neoliberal economy. Precisely due to their neo-animist and relational ontologies and understandings of personhood and selfhood, they tend to frame their economic transactions also (and primarily) in terms of "gift economy."[60] It is especially important to note that adhering to a "gifting, receiving, and returning" economic framework does not have only economic repercussions. It also contributes to the redefinition of "prosperity" and "well-being." By linking gift exchange to an ethic and a practice of care (*cura*) – which, notably, following the Italian understanding of the word *curare*, implies also a dimension of cure – the Salentine Pagans with whom I worked solidly grounded personal well-being in communitarian practices.

As I explained above, one of the main characteristics of neo-animist and Pagan relational understandings of the self is that personhood is not confined to the individual. Evident in "presence magic" as well as in the "expanded present" historicity and in gift economy, such a redefinition of the self, I showed, fosters well-being and healing in many ways. In addition to the aforementioned dimensions of *cura*, there is another important healing protagonist worth mentioning, similarly emerging from the Pagan ontologies described above: what both Fenice and other interlocutors usually refer to as "*il campo*" (the field). A better analysis of what is referred to as "the field" in the Salento context I studied can shed some additional light not only on the practices and understandings of well-being among Southern Italian Pagans, but also on how their ways of experiencing well-being directly challenge neoliberal technologies of the self.

60 It is worth mentioning that the Salentine gift-giving dynamics that I have so far described could well fit Weiner's understanding of reciprocity as stemming from "the desire to keep something back from the pressures of give and take" (Weiner, *Inalienable Possessions*, 43); see also Yan, "Gift and Gift Economy"), in what is generally referred to as the principle of "keeping-while-giving."

Campo, according to my interlocutors, is the energetic field that surrounds persons, places, and also activities. In the case of rituals, such as the previously described family constellations or healing *pizzica* circles, the *campo* intentionally includes the energies of the participants—visible or not, human or not. According to the ontologies of my interlocutors, the *campo* gathers, among other copresences, aspects of the selves of the different participants. Nonetheless, it is more than the sum of these individual energies. The "field" *magnifies* them, allowing for experiences of unity and expanded selfhood. For example, Fenice explained that when I felt pain in my eye before and during Luca's constellation, this was due to the *campo* we all shared together. "The energy of the *campo* is always much stronger than the one of the individual," my interlocutors claim. "This is why healing happens more powerfully and intensely when it is performed by a community of practice." Moreover, they explain that when the Sisters meet for a *pizzica* healing circle, as the one they organized for me and my grief on the occasion of the death of my mother that I described in chapter 3, the healing of one is deeply connected with the healing of every participant (including the land, other-than-human, and non-human persons) and *vice versa*. This perspective (that, I highlight once again, stems from their relational ontologies) strongly clashes with neoliberal understandings of personhood and well-being. Contrary to neoliberal technologies of the self, such a community-based understanding and practice of well-being does not align with the neoliberal moral imperative of taking responsibility—i.e., the belief that one's economic and personal well-being is the responsibility of the individual.[61] Rather, by putting *communities* of human and more-than-human persons explicitly at the center of definitions and practices of well-being, it challenges current understanding of the neoliberal subject. Therefore, different from

61 See Brown, "Sacrificial Citizenship."

"mindfulness,"[62] the adoption of the "expanded present" historicity and of the practices that stem from it, could be seen as a form of resistance to neoliberal technologies of the self.

***

The sunset is orange and pink. As Magenta invites us to notice when we share the spectacle of a sundown, there is often a green line that frames the horizon in Salento – the "idea of green" (idea del verde)*, as she calls it. This night, too, the green hue of the sky matches the color of the water at the* Cava di Bauxite*, a characteristically Salentine spot, just outside Otranto. The dirt is red, and the colors of the rocks and bushes surround the crater filled with water and marsh plants. The wind blows gently, heralding the imminent nightfall. Fiammetta and I have organized a moon ritual. It is July, and it is the last of the eclipses of one of that year's "eclipse seasons," as the women of the* cerchio *used to say. We are preparing the space with candles, incense, prayers, and crystals. Fiammetta is leading the ritual. I help her, in silence. Her mouth utters softly some prayers while her arms and finger point to the directions of the circle. I follow her fingers that, with ceremonial precision, choose specific rocks, positions, angles. I follow her fingers and place the candles at the intersections of her sacred geometry. A white, lace towel lies at the center of the circle – a Tibetan bowl, some bells, a small basket, a tiny metal container, and a disk of white candles lie on it. We are waiting for the others to arrive. They are all newcomers: a friend of the circle, her two other friends, and Carmelo – a man from Lecce I met and briefly spoke to only once before, at a family constellation at Fenice's house. Before the others arrive, we have to write on pieces of paper some of the full moon intentions that we have gathered from the other Sisters who, unfortunately, cannot be here tonight.*

Magenta is playing tonight. Her summers are full of concerts for her and her pizzica *group. She told us that she will be*

62 See Purser, *McMindfulness.*

connected with us through her music: "We'll be together after all, just not on the physical plane."

Viola is out of town, but she asked us to write her moon wishes on a piece of paper. Diligently, Fiammetta takes a pencil and a piece of paper and, with her best handwriting, writes, "for the wishes of Viola" and "for the wishes of Magenta." Then she folds the paper twice and places it with care in the small basket.

"Wishes need to be written with a pencil, you know that?" I did not, in fact, and asked for some explanation. She said that the Universe knows best what is best for us. Therefore, writing wishes with an erasable ink is a way to acknowledge and accept the wisdom of the universe over our own, and to be sure not to attract something that is not good for us, even though, right now, it really seems in our best interest. I nod and think about my own wish. Writing moon intentions is a widely adopted practice among contemporary Pagans. It is a way to tune in with the energies of the cosmos and to use them in your favor. Usually, new moons are good for "planting seeds" or desires, while full moons are good for harvesting or for pruning, for letting go of obstacles or habits that we want to get rid of. Eclipses are particularly heightened times, when the potency of the moon is magnified.

Senefera is at a concert, too, while Idrusa is busy with her family. They both left some intentions that Fiammetta meticulously transcribes on pieces of paper before punctiliously folding and placing them in the middle of the circle. I need to think about mine. It is always difficult for me to commit to one specific intention. I need to choose my words carefully. Our guests arrive; we introduce ourselves before hugging each other, in spite of the fact that, with some, we are strangers. Claudio brought some wine, Carmelo some taralli. *Claudio and Anna look a bit tense. They talk fast and giggle, asking for reassurance, "You are not witches, right?" Fiammetta laughs – with her eyes first, then with her lips. Tongue-in-cheek, she replies with an emphasized "*ca ceeeeeertu*!" (suuuure!) that was promising quite the contrary. Claudio and Anna laugh, unconvinced but charmed by the* *personality of Fiammetta. They look at me, seeking cues. I smile, change topics, and tell them that it's time to start the ritual.*

***

We are sitting on the ground, barefoot: our hands and feet are kamala red – like the dirt of Salento. I lay the palms of my hands on the ground to saturate my skin with the energy of that color: grounding, healing, balancing. We breathe in – deeply – three times. I inhale oxygen and the intoxicating smell of the Mediterranean maquis. My chest expands with memories connected to that particular smell and so does my heart. I find it moving and, for the most part, melancholic. Fiammetta opens the circle with a prayer and exhorts us to light one of the tea candles each. In the silence that accompanies the liminal time before the start of the ritual, I feel something touching my arm. It is Carmelo who, discreetly, takes off one of his necklaces and puts it in my hand. I clench my fist, instinctively, holding his pendant tightly in my hand. Then I look at Carmelo, a bit puzzled. He comes closer to me and whispers in my ear, "I bought this at the market yesterday. I feel I should give it to you now. I don't know why I need to do this, but I comply with the indications I received." I thank him with a smile and slowly open my fist. AN OLD KEY! I gasp, bewildered. Incredulous, I stare at the palm of my hand.

In a matter of seconds, the ritual begins.

Conclusions: Il Mondo/The World

[Keywords: Completion, integration, accomplishment, travel]

Figure 9. The Salento sky reflected in typical Salentinian stone paving. Photo: Giovanna Parmigiani.

In this book, I narrated the story of the *cerchio*—the circle—a southern Italian contemporary Pagan group. I described its relationships with me—an ethnographer-gone-native—other Pagan and New Age groups and practitioners in the Salento area of Italy, the more-than human and other-than-human persons that inhabit that land, and with the history and traditions of their territory. I focused on one specific aspect of their being-in-the-word, or *stare*: their "expanded presence" historicity. This particular way to experience time and temporality—otherwise called, in this book, "presence"—is characterized by the perceived *coevality* of past, present, and future in the *qui-e-ora* (here-and-now) and in the flow of linear time. It is a textured experience, and an embodied one[1]—accessed through various magical practices and, in particular, through the local traditional music and dance called *pizzica*.

The "expanded present" historicity represents, in this book, both the core descriptive device to narrate our stories and the central analytical filter to illuminate unexplored aspects not only of local understandings of *pizzica* and *tarantismo* but also of current studies in the anthropology of religion and magic, of well-being, and of history. In particular, in this book, the "expanded present" historicity is linked to what I called "presence magic." Following Ernesto de Martino, I argued that "presence magic" is a (cultural) way to establishing presence vis-à-vis the possibility of "not-being." Linked to *bellezza* and *desiderio*, it opens up possibilities of being that, figurally, transcend (uni)linear historicities and promote well-being. Moreover, I claimed that "presence magic" is obtained through what Susan Greenwood and others, in the legacy of Lévy-Bruhl, called "participatory consciousness," and that is characterized by relational ontologies, or "neo-animist" stances.

1 See Abram, *The Spell of the Sensuous*.

In a preparatory article for this book,[2] I claimed that focusing, as scholars, on the linearity and coevality of this alternative historicity could help us better understand the great variability of Pagan practices—complementing the useful "reconstructionist-eclectic" framework proposed by the scholar of religion Michael Strmiska.[3] Moreover, I added, acknowledging our own "linearity" biases in our scholarly assumptions on how we think time and history are universally experienced and understood "could potentially expand the ways we look at ourselves and at the categories we use to make sense(s) of the topics" we research.[4]

In this book, I accepted the challenge that I had posed, and asked questions such as the following: What if, as scholars or practitioners, we adopted a coeval understanding of time in the study of magic? Would this "presence-magic" show us something else about the theory of magic? What could an "expanded present" filter tell us about magic, religion, and healing? What about well-being and subjectivity?

I believe that the adoption of the "expanded present" as an analytical category, in this book, supported by my ethnographic data, allowed for the emergence of original results. In particular, concentrating on the "expanded present" allowed me to complicate and reframe anthropological understandings of magic, the links between historicities and well-being, and the connections between New-Age and Neopagan spiritualities and Neoliberal subjectivities.

The primacy of the issues about "knowing," "will," "efficacy," "psychological fulfillment," "laws," "causes and effects," and, more in general, the "logic of magic" in describing and thinking about the phenomena that characterize the history of the scholarship around this topic follows a modernist framework and, implicitly, a linear

2 See Parmigiani, "Spiritual *Pizzica*."

3 See Strmiska, "Modern Paganism in World Cultures."

4 Parmigiani, "Spiritual *Pizzica*," 72. See also Steffan Dalsgaard and Morten Nielsen, *Time and the Field* (New York: Berghahn Books, 2016).

understanding of time. Such a framework shares with the hegemonic modern thought the need to rationalize, order, enumerate the irrational along a vision of time that is, substantially, linear. This is not to say that some of this work, especially the one developed in the legacy of Lucien Lévy-Bruhl on "participation," is incorrect or unhelpful to understand magic as an embodied practice among contemporary Pagans, or elsewhere. Rather, the recognition that magic is traditionally described by a set of laws that govern the interconnectedness of the universe (the macrocosm and the microcosm), and that are mastered by the will of some through various techniques,[5] is an important element not only to describe and understand the phenomenon but also to shed some light on the implicit categories that shape the gaze of those who study said phenomenon. "Presence magic," though, linked to alternative ways to experience time and temporality and read in conversation with the work of the Italian ethnologist Ernesto de Martino, challenges these understandings by illuminating other, understudied, aspects of magic.

First, unlike the "classical" understanding of magic, "presence magic" is fundamentally ordinary. The same notion of "expanded present" makes the distinction between ordinary and non-ordinary, event and structure, rituals and everyday life simply meaningless. The multifaceted texture of the temporality of the "expanded present" is rhizomatic, multiple, and richer than the linear one and, therefore, contains different dimensions of experience *in the present*.

Moreover, in its not being necessarily associated with altered states of consciousness, the "participatory" experience of "presence magic" does not imply a particular consciousness or will, nor does it see witches as specific agents of magic—at least, not in the ways we are used to thinking about will, agency, and intention in relation to magical

5 See Magliocco, *Witching Culture*, 97–121.

practices. The experiences that the southern Italian Pagans recognize as magic are not always the result of their will, magic laws, or active agency. They are not always the outcome of knowledge seeking, relational intents, or the deliberate effects of some intentions or attempts to transform the world. Rather, they are understood and experienced as landmarks of an "active staying" in the "presence magic" of the "expanded present" of the *qui-e-ora*, where "being acted upon" is a form of action, not necessarily initiated by the individual. Clearly, this is deeply connected with the ways selfhood and personhood are lived and conceived among Pagan and New Age practitioners in Salento.

Finally, presence magic challenges the temporality of magic. The latter, in the perspective of linear time, is a set of laws of cause and effect in which the past shapes the present, and the present shapes the future. In a coeval historicity, instead, the "laws" of magic follow a different configuration: one in which every dimension of time affects and is affected by the others. Effects can precede causes, and intentions do not play a key, or necessary, role in the experience of magic.

Adopting the "expanded present" as both a descriptive and analytical category allowed us also to reframe current anthropological debates on well-being, as to include the dimension of historicities in studies on how people "live a good life." A currently neglected aspect of the academic research on well-being, the role of historicity in the pursuit of happiness is one of the fundamental contributions of this book. "Presence," in fact, is fundamentally different from "mindfulness": while the latter does not challenge a linear understanding of time, the former complements and transforms it. Through my ethnography, I proved that a non-linear experience of time, such as the "expanded present," *does* have a special role in how people both define and pursue well-being. While more transcultural research on this topic is needed, this book opens up a new direction of study.

Third, the notion of "expanded present" complicates common understandings of the relationships between contemporary New Age and Pagan spiritualities and Neoliberal subjectivity. As a matter of fact, one of the consequences of adopting the "expanded present" as an analytical category is that it allows us to shed some light on the alternative, non-hegemonic, ways to experience and conceive personhood that characterizes contemporary Paganism. This element challenges widespread assumptions and (mis)understandings of the role of the "self" in contemporary New Age and Pagan spiritualities. By looking at "presence magic" in conversation with the phenomenon of spirit possession and neo-animist (relational) ontologies, I could draw the conclusion that, contrary to Neoliberal technologies of the self, their community-based understanding and practice of well-being does not align with the neoliberal moral imperative of taking responsibility—i.e., the belief that one's economic and personal well-being is the responsibility of the individual.[6] Rather, by putting *communities* of human and more-than-human persons explicitly at the center of definitions and practices of well-being, southern Italian Pagans, here again differently from mindfulness,[7] challenge current understandings of the Neoliberal subject.

While the aforementioned insights are important additions to current scholarship, this book paves also the way for further research. What are the political implications of the adoption of the "expanded presence" historicity? Is it present elsewhere? What are the connections between non-linear historicities and well-being in other contexts? Is there an "applied" dimension to this research?

The journey of the Tarot Fool ends with the XXI *major arcanum*: the World/*Il Mondo*. This card is a symbol, at the

6 See Brown, "Sacrificial Citizenship."

7 See Purser, *McMindfulness.*

same time, of the completion of a journey and of the beginning of a new, more aware, one. *Mondo – mundus,* in Latin – and history are deeply connected: as it emerges from the work of de Martino, *mondo* is a way to refer to the various planes of history.[8] In this book, *mundus* is accessed through the textured, multifaceted, and transforming experience of the "expanded present" and of "presence magic." It is the *stare* in this particular historicity that allows for magic to happen. "After all," with the words of the Italian ethnologist, "the problem of magic is not to "know" the world, or to "change" it. Rather, it is to ensure a world in which being-here is made present."[9]

8 See de Martino, *Il Mondo Magico.*

9 *"In realtà il problema del magismo non è di 'conoscere' il mondo o di 'modificarlo,' ma piuttosto di garantire un mondo in cui l'esserci si rende presente"* (de Martino, *Il Mondo Magico,* 118–19).

Appendix: Resources on Pizzica and Tarantismo

"17/04/2020 Pizzica Salentina (Taranta) @ Lecce, Piazza Sant'Oronzo (Southern-Italy)." CareonVR. 2020. Video, 2:59. https://youtu.be/FDzPQuTRnVk

Baba, Loredana. "Ernesto De Martino a European Perspective in Italy at the Mid of the XXth Century." *Studia Europaea* 55, no. 1 (2010): 129–142.

Biagi, Laura. "Spider Dreams: Ritual and Performance in Apulian Tarantismo and Tarantella." PhD diss., New York University, 2004.

Castrignanò, Antonio. "Fomenta." 2015. Video, 4:39. https://youtu.be/4qCTJc5_23A

Castrignanò, Antonio. "Mara la fatìa," August 17, 2017. video, 5:41. https://youtu.be/z7JHiwQOnJY?si=Bs6QxbCZ71bIyLip

Castrignanò, Antonio. "Tremulaterra." 2013. video, 6:29. https://youtu.be/ZWSmQ-laJ4M

Daboo, Jerri. *Ritual, Rapture and Remorse: A Study of Tarantism and Pizzica in Salento.* Bern: Peter Lang, 2010. https://doi.org/10.3726/978-3-0353-0089-5

De Giorgi, Pierpaolo. *Tarantismo e rinascita. I riti musicali e coreutici della pizzica-pizzica e della tarantella.* Lecce: Argo, 1999.

De Giorgi, Pierpaolo. *Il Mito Del Tarantismo: dalla Terra del Rimorso alla Terra della Rinascita.* Galatina[LE]: Congedo, 2008.

De Martino, Ernesto. *La terra del rimorso. Contributo a una storia religiosa del Sud.* Milan: Il Saggiatore (1976) [1961].

Del Giudice, Luisa. "The Folk Music Revival and the Culture of Tarantismo in the Salento." In *Performing Ecstasies: Music, Dance, and Ritual in the Mediterranean*, edited by Luisa del Giudice and Nancy E. Van Deusen, 217–72. Ottawa: Institute of Mediaeval Music, 2005.

Del Giudice, Luisa. "Healing the Spider's Bite: Ballad Therapy and Tarantismo." In *The Flowering Thorn: International Ballad Studies*, edited by Thomas McKean, 23–34. Logan: Utah State University Press, 2003. https://doi.org/10.2307/j.ctt46nrm0.5

Di Nola, Annalisa. "How Critical was De Martino's 'Critical Ethnocentrism' in Southern Italy?" In *Italy's 'Southern Question': Orientalism in One Country*, edited by Jane Schneider, 157–76. Oxford: Berg, 1998.

Einaudi, Ludovico. "Mamma La Rondinella." *Taranta Project*, 2015. Video, 4:17. https://youtu.be/FT74xG5aACQ

Ferrari, Fabrizio M. *Ernesto de Martino on Religion*. Sheffield: Equinox, 2012.

Galatina. "Festa SS. Pietro e Paolo 2014". Video Wild Italia. July 2, 2014. Video, 7:33. https://youtu.be/wwyR3JTkTos

Galatina. "La guarigione delle tarantate." Dino Valente. June 29, 2014. Video, 18:43. https://youtu.be/RIkZ_uRcuAM

Gallini, Clara, and Marcello Massenzio, *Ernesto De Martino Nella Cultura Europea*. Naples: Liguori, 1997.

Inserra, Incoronata Nadia. *Global Tarantella: Reinventing Southern Italian Folk Music and Dances*. Urbana: University of Illinois Press, 2017. https://doi.org/10.5622/illinois/9780252041297.001.0001

Karanika, Andromache. "Ecstasis in Healing: Practices in Southern Italy and Greece from Antiquity to the Present." In Del Giudice and Van Deusen, eds., *Performing Ecstasies: Music, Dance, and Ritual in the Mediterranean*, 25–36.

Lanternari, Vittorio. "Tarantismo: dal medico neopositivista all'antropologo, alla etnopsichiatria di oggi." *Storia, antropologia, e scienze del linguaggio* 3 (1995): 67–92.

Lanternari, Vittorio. *La mia alleanza con Ernesto de Martino e altri saggi post-demartiniani*.Napoli: Liguori, 1997.

Lanternari, Vittorio. "Tarantismo: vecchie teorie, saperi nuovi." *Quarant'anni dopo De Martino*, ed. Gino L. Di Mitri, 199–134. Nardò: Besa, 2000.

Lapassade, Georges. *Intervista sul tarantismo*. Maglie: Madonna Oriente, 1994.

Lapassade, Georges. *Dallo sciamano al raver. Saggio sulla transe*. Milan: Apogeo edizioni, 1997.

Laviosa, Flavia. "The Frontier Apulia and its Filmmakers after 1989." *California Italian Studies Journal* 1, no. 1 (2010): 1–9. https://doi.org/10.5070/C311008885

Laviosa, Flavia. "Tarantula Myths and Music: Popular Culture and Ancient Rituals in Italian Cinema." In *Popular Italian Cinema: Culture and Politics in a Postwar Society*, ed. Flavia Brizio-Skov, 153–188. London: I.B. Tauris, 2011. https://doi.org/10.5040/9780755698295.ch-005

Lüdtke, Karen. "Dancing towards Well-Being: Reflections on the *Pizzica* in the Contemporary Salento, Italy." In *Performing Ecstasies: Music, Dance, and Ritual in the Mediterranean*, edited by Luisa del Giudice and Nancy E. Van Deusen, 37–53. Ottawa: Institute of Mediaeval Music, 2005.

Lüdtke, Karen. *Dances with Spiders: Crisis, Celebrity and Celebration in Southern Italy*. New York: Berghahn Books, 2008.

Lüdtke, Karen. *Balla Coi Ragni: La Tarantola Tra Crisi E Celebrazioni*. Bari: Edizioni Di Pagina, 2011.

Lüdtke, Karen. "'We've Got this Rhythm in our Blood': Dancing Identities in Southern Italy." In *Dancing Cultures: Globalization, Tourism and Identity in the Anthropology of Dance*, edited by Hélène Neveu Kringelbach and Jonathan Skinner, 60–74. New York: Berghahn Books, 2012. https://doi.org/10.1515/9780857455765-006

Mascarimiri. "Gitanistan." OriginalMasacarimiri. September 24, 2011. Video, 3:54. https://youtu.be/NtQZIPLQ0aA

Mascarimiri. "Lu Ballu." OriginalMascarimiri. June 28, 2013. Video, 4:30. https://youtu.be/llx1ggmrqSY

Massenzio, Marcello. "The Italian School of 'History of Religions.'" *Religion* 35, no. 4 (2005): 209–222. https://doi.org/10.1016/j.religion.2005.10.007

Mina, Gabriele, and Sergio Torsello, *La Tela Infinita. Bibliografia degli Studi sul Trantismo Mediterraneo 1945–2006*. Nardò: Besa, 2006.

Minghelli, Giuliana. "Icons of Remorse: Photography, Anthropology and the Erasure of History in 1950s Italy," *Modern Italy* 21, no. 4 (2016): 383–407. https://doi.org/10.1017/mit.2016.45

Mingozzi, Gianfranco, dir. *La Taranta*. 1961. DVD. 2008. Nardò, Italy: Besa,

Nacci, Anna. *Tarantismo e neotarantismo: musica, danza, transe: bisogni di oggi, bisogni di sempre*. Nardò: Besa, 2001.

Nacci, Anna. *Neotarantismo: pizzica, transe e riti dalle campagne alle metropoli*. Viterbo: Stampa Alternativa, Nuovi Equilibri, 2004.

Pagliara, Enza. "La Zamara." Pizzica di Torchiarolo. AnimaMundiEdizioni. November 30, 2010. Video, 7:52. https://youtu.be/RDotUjgdxA4

Pandolfi, Maria. "Boundaries Inside the Body: Women's Sufferings in Southern Peasant Italy," *Culture, Medicine and Psychiatry* 14, no. 2 (1990): 255–73. https://doi.org/10.1007/BF00046664

Parmigiani, Giovanna. "If You Dance Alone, You Cannot Be Healed": Relational Ontologies and "Epistemes of Contagion" in Salento (Italy). *California Italian Studies*, 11 no. 1 (2022). https://doi.org/10.5070/C311154536

Parmigiani, Giovanna. "Spiritual Pizzica: A Southern Italian Perspective on Contemporary Paganism." *The Pomegranate: The International Journal of Pagan Studies* 21, no. 1 (2019): 53–75. https://doi.org/10.1558/pome.37787

Pizza, Giovanni. "Tarantismi oggi: un panorama critico sulle letture contemporanee del tarantismo (1994–1998)," *Panorami* no. 7–8 (1999): 253–73.

Pizza, Giovanni. "Tarantism and the Politics of Tradition in Contemporary Salento." In *Memory, Politics and Religion: The Past Meets the Present in Europe*, ed. Idis Haukanes, 199–223 Münster, Germany: LIT, 2004.

Pizza, Giovanni. "Gramsci e de Martino: appunti per una riflessione," *Quaderni di Teoria Sociale* 13 (2013): 75–120.

Pizza, Giovanni *Il Tarantismo Oggi*. Alessano: Carocci, 2015.

Pizza, Giovanni. "Margini," *AM* 13, no. 37/39 (2016): 105–09.

Rossi, Annabella. *Lettere da una tarantata: con uno nota di Tullio De Mauro*. Lecce: Argo, 2000.

Saunders, George R. "The Crisis of Presence in Italian Pentecostal Conversion," *American Ethnologist* 22, no. 2 (1995): 324–40. https://doi.org/10.1525/ae.1995.22.2.02a00060

Seppilli, Tullio. "Ernesto de Martino e la nascita dell'etnopsichiatria italiana," *Storia, Antropologia e Scienze del Linguaggio* 10, no. 3 (1995): 147–56;

Signorelli, Amalia."Il tarantismo . . . che purtroppo non c'è più," *Studi e Materiali di Storia delle Religioni* 62, no. 20 (1996): 591–98.

Staro, Placida. "Reconstructing the Sense of Presence: Tarantula, Arlìa, and Dance." In *Performing Ecstasies: Music, Dance, and Ritual in the Mediterranean*, edited by Luisa del Giudice and Nancy E. Van Deusen, 55–70. Ottawa: Institute of Mediaeval Music, 2005.

Triace , "Pizzica 'bulgara,'" November 5, 2014, video, 2:52. https://youtu.be/XLqX4RSHrXY?si=EhHl47L-DsUqxpyU

Villani, Anna Cinzia. "Stornelli." Ninnamorella. Valentina Locchi. March 17, 2012. Video, 2:45. https://youtu.be/-EuRG3NI-Jw

Zinn, Dorothy ."An Introduction to Ernesto De Martino's Relevance for the Study of Folklore," *Journal of American Folklore* 128, no. 507 (2015): 3–17. https://doi.org/10.5406/jamerfolk.128.507.0003

Bibliography

"17/04/2020 Pizzica Salentina (Taranta) @ Lecce, Piazza Sant'Oronzo (Southern-Italy)." CareonVR. 2020. Video, 2:59. https://youtu.be/FDzPQuTRnVk

Abram, David. *The Spell of the Sensuous: Perception and Language in a More-than-Human World*. New York: Pantheon Books, 1996.

Aitamurto, Kaarina, and Scott Simpson. *Modern Pagan and Native Faith Movements in Central and Eastern Europe*. Studies in Contemporary and Historical Paganism. Durham: Acumen, 2013. https://doi.org/10.4324/9781315729008

Aitamurto, Kaarina, and Scott Simpson. "The Study of Paganism and Wicca." In *The Oxford Handbook of New Religious Movements*, 481–94. Oxford University Press, 2016. https://doi.org/10.1093/oxfordhb/9780190466176.013.36

Alighieri, Dante. *La Divina Commedia*. Edited by Natalino Sapegno. Nuova Italia Editrice. Firenze: Nuova Italia, 1955.

Andriolo, Karin. "The Twice-Killed: Imagining Protest Suicide." *American Anthropologist* 108, no. 1 (2006): 100–13. https://doi.org/10.1525/aa.2006.108.1.100

Ankhepura. https://ankheperura.weebly.com

Antica Quercia. www.anticaquercia.com

Apffel-Marglinm Frederique. *Subversive Spiritualities*. New York: Oxford University Press, 2011.

Apolito, Paolo. "I Beni DEA e il 'fare' le tradizioni." *Antrolopogia Museale* 17 (2007): 12–17.

Asad, Talal. *Genealogies of Religion*. Baltimore: Johns Hopkins University Press, 1993. https://doi.org/10.1353/book.16014

Asprem, Egil. "The Magical Theory of Politics." *Nova Religio* 23, no. 4 (2020): 15–42. https://doi.org/10.1525/nr.2020.23.4.15

Asprem, Egil. "Theosophical Attitudes Towards Science: Past and Present." In *Handbook of the Theosophical Current*, edited by Olav Hammer and Mikael Rothstein, 405–27. Leiden: Brill, 2013. https://doi.org/10.1163/9789004235977_020

Asprem, Egil, and Asbjørn Dyrendal. "Conspirituality Reconsidered: How Surprising and How New is the Confluence of Spirituality and

Conspiracy Theory?" *Journal of Contemporary Religion* 30, no. 3 (2015): 367–82. https://doi.org/10.1080/13537903.2015.1081339

Asprem, Egil, and Kennet Granholm, eds. *Contemporary Esotericism*. London: Routledge, 2013.

Auerbach, Erich. *Mimesis: The Representation of Reality in Western Literature*. New York: Doubleday, 1957.

Auerbach, Erich. *Studi su Dante*. Milano: Feltrinelli, 1967.

Augustine of Hippo. *Confessions*. Translated by James Joseph O'Donnell. Oxford; New York: Oxford University Press, 1992.

Augustine of Hippo. *Confessions*, Books 9–13. Loeb Classics Online: Harvard University Press. https://doi.org/10.4159/DLCL.augustine-confessions.1912

Aupers, Stef, and Dick Houtman. "Beyond the Spiritual Supermarket: The Social and Public Significance of New Age Spirituality." *Journal of Contemporary Religion* 21, no. 2 (2006): 201–22. https://doi.org/10.1080/13537900600655894

Baba, Loredana. "Ernesto De Martino, a European Perspective in Italy at the Mid of the XXth Century." *Studia Europaea* 55, no. 1 (2010): 129–42.

Bach Flower Remedies. "38 Bach Flower Remedies." http://www.bachflower.com/original-bach-flower-remedies/

Bacigalupo, Ana Mariella. *Thunder Shaman*. Austin, TX: University of Texas Press, 2016. https://doi.org/10.7560/308806

Badii, Michela. *Processi di patrimonializzazione e politiche del cibo*. Segrate: Morlacchi, 2012.

Bailey, Michael D. "The Meanings of Magic." *Magic, Ritual, and Witchcraft* 1, no. 1 (2006): 1–23. https://doi.org/10.1353/mrw.0.0052

Bailey, Michael D. *Magic: The Basics* (London: Routledge, 2018).

Bakhtin, M. M. *The Dialogic Imagination*. Translated by Michael Holquist and Caryl Emerson. Austin: University of Texas Press, 1981.

Ballacchino, Katia. "Per un'antropologia del patrimonio immateriale. Dalle Convenzioni Unesco alle pratiche di comunità." *Glocale* 6–7 (2013): 17–32.

Barad, Karen. "Troubling Time/s and Ecologies of Nothingness: Re-turning, Re-membering, and Facing the Incalculable." *New Formations* 92, no. 1 (2018): 56–86. https://doi.org/10.3898/NEWF:92.05.2017

Barizza, Annachiara. "Un'interpretazione fenomenologica di Agostino: Heidegger lettore del X libro delle «Confessioni»." *Annali di studi religiosi* 4 (2003): 121–44.

Barner-Barry, Carol. *Contemporary Paganism: Minority Religions in a Majoritarian America*. New York: Palgrave Macmillan, 2005.

Barnes, Linda L., and Susan Starr Sered. *Religion and Healing in America*. Oxford: Oxford University Press, 2004. https://doi.org/10.1093/acprof:oso/9780195167962.001.0001

Becket, John. "The Big Tent of Paganism," January 11, 2015. https://www.patheos.com/blogs/johnbeckett/2015/01/the-big-tent-of-paganism.html

Beeler, Dori-Michelle. *An Ethnographic Account of Reiki Practice in Britain*. Newcastle-upon-Tyne: Cambridge Scholars Publisher, 2016.

Beeler, Dori-Michelle. "Reiki as Surrender: Evidence of an External Authority." *Journal of Contemporary Religion* 32, no. 3 (2017): 465–78. https://doi.org/10.1080/13537903.2017.1362885

Beeler, Dori-Michelle. "A Reiki Sense of Well-Being." *Anthropology News* 59, no. 1 (2018): e82–e86. https://doi.org/10.1111/AN.747

Alonso Bejarano, Carolina, Lucia López Juárez, Mirian A. Mijangos García, and Daniel M. Goldstein. *Decolonizing Ethnography: Undocumented Immigrants and New Directions in Social Science*. Durham, NC: Duke University Press, 2019. https://doi.org/10.1215/9781478004547

Benjamin, Walter. *The Arcades Project*. Cambridge, MA: Harvard University Press, 1999.

Benjamin, Walter. "A Short History of Photography." *Screen* 13, no. 1 (1972): 5–26. https://doi.org/10.1093/screen/13.1.5

Benjamin, Walter. *The Work of Art in the Age of Mechanical Reproduction*. Lexington, KY: Prism Key Press, 2010.

Berger, Helen A. A *Community of Witches*. Columbia, SC: University of South Carolina Press, 1999.

Berger, Helen A. *Solitary Pagans*. Columbia, SC: University of South Carolina Press, 2019.

Berger, Helen A. *Witchcraft and Magic*. Philadelphia: University of Pennsylvania Press, 2006.

Biagi, Laura. "Spider Dreams: Ritual and Performance in Apulian Tarantismo and Tarantella." PhD diss., New York University, 2004.

Birth, Kevin K. "The Creation of Coevalness and the Danger of Homochronism." *Journal of the Royal Anthropological Institute* 14, no. 1 (2008): 3–20. https://doi.org/10.1111/j.1467-9655.2007.00475.x

Birth, Kevin K. *Time Blind: Problems in Perceiving Other Temporalities*. Cham, Switzerland: Palgrave Macmillan, 2017. https://doi.org/10.1007/978-3-319-34132-3

Blain, Jenny. *Nine Worlds of Seid-Magic*. London: Routledge, 2002.

Blain, Jenny, Douglas Ezzy, and Graham Harvey, eds. *Researching Paganisms*. Walnut Creek, CA: AltaMira Press, 2004.

Boddy, Janice. "Spirit Possession Revisited: Beyond Instrumentality." *Annual Review of Anthropology* 23, no. 1 (1994): 407–34. https://doi.org/10.1146/annurev.an.23.100194.002203

Boddy, Janice. "Spirits and Selves in Northern Sudan: The Cultural Therapeutics of Possession and Trance." *American Ethnologist* 15, no. 1 (1988): 4–27. https://doi.org/10.1525/ae.1988.15.1.02a00020

Boddy, Janice. "Subversive Kinship: The Role of Spirit Possession in Negotiating Social Place in Rural Northern Sudan." *PoLAR* 16, no. 2 (1993): 29–38. https://doi.org/10.1525/pol.1993.16.2.29

Bodini, Vittorio. *La Luna Dei Borboni e Altre Poesie, 1945–1961*. Milan: Mondadori, 1962.

Bourdieu, Pierre. *Outline of a Theory of Practice*. Cambridge: Cambridge University Press, 1977. https://doi.org/10.1007/978-3-319-34132-3

Braidotti, Rosi. "Posthuman, All Too Human. Towards a New Process Ontology." *Theory, Culture & Society* 23, nos. 7–8 (2006): 197–208. https://doi.org/10.1177/0263276406069232

Braidotti, Rosi. "We" Are in This Together, But We Are Not One and the Same." *Journal of Bioethical Inquiry* 17, no. 4 (2020): 465–69. https://doi.org/10.1007/s11673-020-10017-8

Brennan, Teresa. *The Transmission of Affect*. Ithaca, NY: Cornell University Press, 2004.

Bronzini, Giovanni Battista. "Lettura dell'Apocalisse demartiniana." *Lares* 48, no. 2 (1982): 251–61.

Brown, Wendy. "Sacrificial Citizenship: Neoliberalism, Human Capital, and Austerity Politics." *Constellations* 23, no. 1 (2016): 3–14. https://doi.org/10.1111/1467-8675.12166

Bryant, Rebecca, and Daniel M. Knight. *The Anthropology of the Future*. Cambridge: Cambridge University Press, 2019.

Butler, Jenny "The Nearest Kin of the Moon: Irish Pagan Witchcraft, Magic(k), and the Celtic Twilight." In Feraro and Doyle White, eds. *Magic and Witchery in the Modern West: Celebrating the Twentieth Anniversary of 'The Triumph of the Moon.'* 85–105. https://doi.org/10.1007/978-3-030-15549-0_5

Butler, Judith. "Bodies in Alliance and the Politics of the Street." In *Sensible Politics*, edited by Meg McLagan and Yates McKee, 117–38. New York: Zone Books, 2012.

Buyandelger, Manduhai. *Tragic Spirits*. Chicago: University of Chicago Press, 2013.

Buzekova, Tatiana. "The Shaman's Journeys Between Emic and Etic." *Anthropological Journal of European Cultures* 19, no. 1 (2010): 116–30. https://doi.org/10.3167/ajec.2010.190109

Calabrese, Joseph D. *A Different Medicine*. Oxford: Oxford University Press, 2013.

Calico, Jefferson F. *Being Viking*. Sheffield: Equinox Publishing, 2018.

Cambray, Joseph. *Synchronicity: Nature and Psyche in an Interconnected Universe*. College Station: Texas A&M University Press, 2009.

Campbell, Colin. "The Cult, the Cultic Milieu and Secularization." In *A Sociological Yearbook of Religion in Britain*, edited by Michael Hill, 119–36. London: S.C.M. Press, 1972.

Campion, Nicholas. *Astrology and Popular Religion in the Modern West: Prophecy, Cosmology and the New Age Movement*. London: Routledge, 2016. https://doi.org/10.4324/9781315568188

Caria, Cristiana. 2022. Facebook. https://www.facebook.com/CristianaCariaTeacher

Carrier, James G. *A Handbook of Economic Anthropology*. Cheltenham, UK: Edward Elgar Publishing, 2005.

Castor, N. Fadeke. 2017. *Spiritual Citizenship: Transnational Pathways from Black Power to Ifá in Trinidad*. Durham, NC: Duke University Press. https://doi.org/10.1215/9780822372585

Castor, N. Fadeke. "Subjectivity: Offerings from African Diasporic Religious Ethnography," *Fieldwork in Religion* 17, no. 1 (2022): 72–83. https://doi.org/10.1558/firn.22605

Castrignanò, Antonio. "Fomenta." 2015. Video, 4:39. https://youtu.be/4qCTJc5_23A

Castrignanò, Antonio. "Mara la fatìa." 2017. Video, 5:41. https://youtu.be/z7JHiwQOnJY

Castrignanò, Antonio. "Tremulaterra." 2013. Video, 6:29. https://youtu.be/ZWSmQ-laJ4M

Cavell, Stanley, and Russell B. Goodman. *Contending with Stanley Cavell*. Oxford: Oxford University Press, 2005.

Cerchio Druidico Italiano. "Homepage." www.cerchiodruidico.it

Champion, Françoise. "Il New Age, Una Religione Indefinita per Le Incertezze Dell'individuo Del Nostro Tempo." *Quaderni di Sociologia* 19 (1999): 23–35. https://doi.org/10.4000/qds.1446

Chireau, Yvonne Patricia. *Black Magic : Religion and the African American Conjuring Tradition*. Berkeley: University of California Press, 2003. https://doi.org/10.1525/california/9780520209879.001.0001

Ciardo, Lucio. "Xylella: il 'cancro' degli ulivi." November 18, 2014. Video, 4:26. https://youtu.be/wvPZU06Lh40

Circolo del Trivi. Associazione di Promozione Sociale. https://www.circolodeitrivi.com/

Clifton, Chas S. *Her Hidden Children: The Rise of Wicca and Paganism in America*. The Pagan Studies Series. Lanham, MD: AltaMira Press, 2006.

Clough, Patricia T., and Jean O'Malley Halley, eds. *The Affective Turn: Theorizing the Social*. Durham, NC: Duke University Press, 2007. https://doi.org/10.2307/j.ctv11316pw

Comaroff, Jean, and John L. Comaroff. "Occult Economies and the Violence of Abstraction: Notes from the South African Postcolony." *American Ethnologist* 26, no. 2 (1999): 279–303. https://doi.org/10.1525/ae.1999.26.2.279

Comunita' Odinista. www.comunitaodinista.org

Cornish, Helen. "Fashioning Magic, Fashioning History: the Past and Present of Modern Witchcraft." Magic, Ritual, and Witchcraft 16, no. 3 (2021): 389–97. https://doi.org/10.1353/mrw.2021.0048

Cornish, Helen. "Spelling Out History: Transforming Witchcraft Past and Present." *The Pomegranate: The International Journal of Pagan Studies* 11, no. 1 (2009): 14–28. https://doi.org/10.1558/pome.v11i1.14

Corti, Agustín C. "Heidegger, intérprete de San Agustín: El tiempo. Nuevas fuentes para la recepción heideggeriana de las Confesiones de San Agustín." *Revista de Filosofía* 32, no. 1 (2007): 143–63.

Crockford, Susannah. "A Mercury Retrograde Kind of Day: Exploring Astrology in Contemporary New Age Spirituality and American Social Life." *Correspondences* 6, no. 1 (2018): 47–75.

Crockford, Susannah. *Ripples of the Universe*. Chicago: University of Chicago Press, 2021. https://doi.org/10.7208/chicago/9780226778105.001.0001

Crockford, Susannah. "What Do Jade Eggs Tell Us About the Category "Esotericism"?" In *New Approaches to the Study of Esotericism*, edited by Egil Asprem and Julian Strube, 200–16. Leiden: Brill, 2020.

Crockford, Susannah, and Egil Asprem. "Ethnographies of the Esoteric. Introducing Anthropological Methods and Theories to the Study of Contemporary Esotericism," *Correspondences* 6, no. 1 (2018): 1–23.

Csordas, Thomas J. *The Sacred Self: A Cultural Phenomenology of Charismatic Healing*. Berkeley: University of California Press, 1997. https://doi.org/10.1525/9780520919068

Cvetkovich, Ann. Introduction to *Political Emotions*, edited by Janet Staiger, Ann Cvetkovich, and Ann Reynolds, 1–17. New York: Routledge, 2010.

Cvetkovich, Ann. *Mixed Feelings: Feminism, Mass Culture, and Victorian Sensationalism*. New Brunswick, N.J.: Rutgers University Press, 1992.

Cvetkovich, Ann. "Public Feelings." *South Atlantic Quarterly* 106, no. 3 (2007): 459–68. https://doi.org/10.1215/00382876-2007-004

Daboo, Jerri. Ritual, *Rapture and Remorse: A Study of Tarantism and Pizzica in Salento*. Bern: Peter Lang, 2010. https://doi.org/10.3726/978-3-0353-0089-5

Dalsgaard, Steffen, and Morten Nielsen. *Time and the Field*. New York: Berghahn Books, 2016.

Das, Veena. *Life and Words: Violence and the Descent into the Ordinary*. Berkeley: University of California Press, 2007. https://doi.org/10.1525/9780520939530

Dave, Naisargi N. "Witness: Humans, Animals, and the Politics of Becoming." *Cultural Anthropology* 29, no. 3 (2014): 433–56. https://doi.org/10.14506/ca29.3.01

De Giorgi, Pierpaolo. *Il Mito Del Tarantismo: dalla Terra del Rimorso alla Terra della Rinascita*. Galatina (LE): Congedo, 2008.

De Giorgi, Pierpaolo. *Tarantismo e rinascita. I riti musicali e coreutici della pizzica-pizzica e dellatarantella*. Lecce: Argo, 1999.

De Martino, Ernesto. *"La Fine del Mondo" Contributo All'analisi Delle Apocalissi Culturali*. Edited by Clara Gallini. Turin: Einaudi, 1977.

De Martino, Ernesto. *Il Mondo Magico: Prolegomeni a una Storia del Magismo*. Turin: Bollati Boringhieri, 1997 [1981, 1948].

De Martino, Ernesto. *Morte e pianto rituale: Dal lamento funebre antico al pianto di Maria*. Milan: Feltrinelli, 1975 [1958].

De Martino, Ernesto. *Sud e Magia*. Milan: Feltrinelli, 1980 [1959].

De Martino, Ernesto. *"La terra del rimorso." Contributo a una storia religiosa del Sud*. Milan: Il Saggiatore, 1976 [1961].

Dei, Fabio. "Da Gramsci All' UNESCO. Antropologia, Cultura Popolare e Beni Intangibili." *Parolechiave* 49, no. 1 (2013): 131–46.

Del Giudice, Luisa. "The Folk Music Revival and the Culture of Tarantismo in the Salento." In Del Giudice and Van Deusen, eds., *Performing Ecstasies: Music, Dance, and Ritual in the Mediterranean*, 217–72.

Del Giudice, Luisa. "Healing the Spider's Bite: Ballad Therapy and Tarantismo." In *The Flowering Thorn: International Ballad Studies*, edited by Thomas Mckean, 23–34. Logan: Utah State University Press, 2003. https://doi.org/10.2307/j.ctt46nrm0.5

Del Giudice, Luisa, and Nancy Van Deusen, eds. *Performing Ecstasies: Music, Dance, and Ritual in the Mediterranean*. Ottawa: Institute of Mediaeval Music 2005.

Deleuze, Gilles, and Felix Guattari. *A Thousand Plateaus: Capitalism and Schizophrenia*. Minneapolis: University of Minnesota Press, 1987.

Di Nola, Annalisa. "How Critical was De Martino's 'Critical Ethnocentrism' in Southern Italy?" In *Italy's 'Southern Question': Orientalism in One Country*, edited by Jane Schneider, 157–76. Oxford: Berg, 1998. https://doi.org/10.4324/9781003085768-10

Dior, Christian. "Dior Cruise 2021 collection." https://www.youtube.com/live/T5pBRKED0Bc

Dior, Christian. "Dior in Puglia: the Land of Cruise 2021 inspiration." https://youtu.be/A8fvoPQ2h2s

Diotallevi, Luca. *Il rompicapo della secolarizzazione: Caso italiano, teorie americane e revisione del paradigma della secolarizzazione*. Soveria Mannelli (Catanzaro): Rubbettino, 2001.

Downing, Ross. "Hashtag Heathens: Contemporary Germanic Pagan Feminine Visuals on Instagram." *The Pomegranate: The International Journal of Pagan Studies* 21, no. 2 (2020): 186–209. https://doi.org/10.1558/pome.40063

Doyle White, Ethan. "The Meaning of 'Wicca': A Study in Etymology, History, and Pagan Politics." *The Pomegranate: The International Journal of Pagan Studies* 12, no. 2 (2010): 185–207. https://doi.org/10.1558/pome.v12i2.185

Doyle White, Ethan. *Wicca: History, Belief, and Community in Modern Pagan Witchcraft*. Eastbourne, UK: Sussex Academic Press, 2016. https://doi.org/10.2307/j.ctv3029rcf

Duggan, Colin. "Perennialism and Iconoclasm: Chaos Magick and the Legitimacy of Innovation." In Asprem and Granholm, eds. *Contemporary Esotericism*, 91–112.

Durkheim, Émile. *The Elementary Forms of Religious Life*. Oxford: Oxford University Press, 2001 [1912].

Dyrendal, Asbjørn. "Hidden Knowledge, Hidden Powers: Esotericism and Conspiracy Culture." In Asprem and Granholm, eds. *Contemporary Esotericism*, 210–35.

Dyrendal, Asbjørn. "Norwegian 'Conspirituality': A Brief Sketch." In *Handbook of Nordic New Religions*, edited by James R. Lewis and Inga Bårdsen Tøllefsen, 268–90. Leiden: Brill, 2015. https://doi.org/10.1163/9789004292468_018

Eisenstein, Charles. *Sacred Economics*. Berkeley: North Atlantic Books, 2011.

Encyclopedia Britannica, s.v. "chakra." https://www.britannica.com/topic/chakra

Enodian, River. "Cultural Appropriation vs Appreciation: A Primer for Pagans, Polytheists, and Occultists." *Patheos*. January 15, 2019. https://www.patheos.com/blogs/teaaddictedwitch/2019/01/cultural-appropriation-appreciation/

Espírito Santo, Diana. "Clothes for Spirits: Opening and Closing the Cosmos in Brazilian Umbanda," HAU: Journal of Ethnographic Theory 6, no. 3 (2016): 85–106. https://doi.org/10.14318/hau6.3.010

Espírito Santo, Diana. "Divination." In Cambridge Encyclopedia of Anthropology, edited by Felix Stein and Joel Robbins. 2019. http://doi.org/10.29164/19divination

Espírito Santo, Diana and Jack Hunter. *Mattering the Invisible*. New York, NY: Berghahn Books, 2021. https://doi.org/10.2307/j.ctv2tsxjf3

Esposito, Roberto. *Pensiero Vivente: Origine E Attualità Della Filosofia Italian*. Turin: Einaudi, 2010.

Evans-Pritchard, E. E. *Witchcraft, Oracles and Magic among the Azande*. Oxford: Clarendon Press, 1937.

Ezzy, Douglas. "New Age Witchcraft? Popular Spell Books and the Re-Enchantment of Everyday Life." *Culture and Religion* 4, no. 1 (2003): 47–65. https://doi.org/10.1080/01438300302813

Ezzy, Douglas. "Practicing the Witch's Craft," in Blain, et al., eds. *Researching Paganisms*, 113–28.

Fabian, Johannes. *Time and the Other: How Anthropology Makes Its Object*. New York: Columbia University Press, 1983.

Failla, Marcelitte, "Black Tarot: African American Women and Divine Processes of Resilience." *Liturgy* (Washington) 36, no. 4 (2021): 41–51. https://doi.org/10.1080/0458063X.2021.1990665

Faivre, Antoine. *Access to Western Esotericism*. Albany: State University of New York Press, 1994.

Fedele, Anna. "From Christian Religion to Feminist Spirituality; Mary Magdalene Pilgrimages to La Sainte-Baume, France." *Culture and Religion* 10, no. 3 (2009): 243–61. https://doi.org/10.1080/14755610903279663

Fedele, Anna. *Looking for Mary Magdalene: Alternative Pilgrimage and Ritual Creativity at Catholic Shrines in France*. New York: Oxford University Press, 2013. https://doi.org/10.1093/acprof:oso/9780199898404.001.0001

Fedele, Anna. "The Metamorphoses of Neopaganism in Traditionally Catholic Countries in Southern Europe." In *Sites and Politics of Religious Diversity in Southern Europe: The Best of All Gods*, edited by José Mapril and Ruy Llera Blanes, 51–72. Leiden: Brill, 2013. https://doi.org/10.1163/9789004255241_005

Fedele, Anna, and Ruy Llera Blanes, eds. *Encounters of Body and Soul in Contemporary Religious Practices*. New York: Berghahn Books, 2011.

Federici, Silvia. *Caliban and the Witch*. London: Autonomedia, 2004.

Federici, Silvia. *Witches, Witchhunting, and Women*. Oakland: PM Press, 2018.

Feraro, Shai. "Canaanite Reconstructionism Among Contemporary Israeli Pagans." In Rountree, ed. *Cosmopolitanism, Nationalism, and Modern Paganism*, 157–77. https://doi.org/10.1057/978-1-137-56200-5_8

Feraro, Shai, and Ethan Doyle White eds., *Magic and Witchery in the Modern West*. Cham, Switzerland: Springer International Publishing AG, 2019. https://doi.org/10.1007/978-3-030-15549-0

Ferrari, Fabrizio M. *Ernesto de Martino on Religion*. Sheffield: Equinox, 2012.

Ferraro, Emilia, and Juan Pablo Sarmiento Barletti. "Placing Wellbeing." *Anthropology in Action* 23, no. 3 (2016): 1–5. https://doi.org/10.3167/aia.2016.230301

Fondazione Le Costantine. "Arte della Tessitura." https://www.lecostantine.it/larte-della-tessitura/

Ford, Phil. "Diviner's Time." *Weird Studies* podcast. February 19, 2020. https://www.weirdstudies.com/66

Frazer, James George. *The Golden Bough: A Study in Comparative Religion*. Edinburgh: Canongate, 2004 [1890].

Gaffin, Dennis. *Running with the Fairies : Towards a Transpersonal Anthropology of Religion*. Newcastle upon Tyne: Cambridge Scholars Publishing, 2012.

Gallini, Clara, and Marcello Massenzio. *Ernesto De Martino Nella Cultura Europea*. Naples: Liguori, 1997.

Il Gallo. "Xylella: la Diocesi fa il funerale agli ulivi." November 23, 2014. https://www.ilgallo.it/attualita/xylella-la-diocesi-fa-il-funerale-agli-ulivi/

Garelli, Franco. "Flexible Catholicism, Religion and the Church: The Italian Case." *Religions* 4, no. 1 (2012): 1–13. https://doi.org/10.3390/rel4010001

Garelli, Franco. *Gente Di Poca Fede: Il Sentimento Religioso Nell'Italia Incerta Di Dio*. Bologna: Il Mulino, 2020.

Garelli, Franco. *Religion Italian Style: Continuities and Changes in a Catholic Country*. London: Routledge, 2014.

Gearin Alex K. and Oscar Calavia Saez. "Altered Vision Ayahuasca Shamanism and Sensory Individualism." *Current Anthropology* 62, no. 2 (2021): 138–50. https://doi.org/10.1086/713737

Gell, Alfred. *The Anthropology of Time: Cultural Constructions of Temporal Maps and Images*. Oxford: Berg, 1992.

Gentilcore, David. *From Bishop to Witch: The System of the Sacred in Early Modern Terra D'Otranto*. Manchester: Manchester University Press, 1992.

George Maciunas Foundation. European Alternatives. "On Nomadism: Interview with Rosi Braidotti." http://dancekiosk-hamburg.de/uploads/European%20Alternatives:%20On%20nomadism%20Interview%20with%20Rosi%20Braidotti%20-%20George%20Maciunas%20Foundation%20Inc..pdf

Giancristofaro, Lia. "Rethinking Folklore as Economical Pattern: Overview of Sustainable, Creative and Popular Strategies in Italian Domestic

Life." *Human Affairs* 25, no. 2 (2015): 173–88. https://doi.org/10.1515/humaff-2015-0016

Gilmore, Lee. "Pagan and Indigenous Communities in Interreligious Contexts: Interrogating Identity, Power, and Authenticity." *The Pomegranate: The International Journal of Pagan Studies* 20, no. 2 (2018): 179–207. https://doi.org/10.1558/pome.32588.

Giordano, Cristiana. "Political Therapeutics: Dialogues and Frictions Around Care and Cure." *Medical Anthropology* 37, no. 1 (2018): 32–44. https://doi.org/10.1080/01459740.2017.1358715

Glaskin, Katie. "Anatomies of Relatedness: Considering Personhood in Aboriginal Australia." *American Anthropologist* 114, no. 2 (2012): 297–308. https://doi.org/10.1111/j.1548-1433.2012.01426.x

Glaskin, Katie. "Death and the Person: Reflections on Mortuary Rituals, Transformation and Ontology in an Aboriginal Society." *Paideuma* 52 (2006): 107–26.

Glass-Coffin, Bonnie. "Anthropology, Shamanism, and Alternate Ways of Knowing-Being in the World: One Anthropologist's Journey of Discovery and Transformation." *Anthropology and Humanism* 35, no. 2 (2010): 204–217. https://doi.org/10.1111/j.1548-1409.2010.01067.x

Gorton, Kristyn. "Theorizing Emotions and Affects: Feminist Engagements." *Feminist Theory* 8, no. 3 (2007): 333–48. https://doi.org/10.1177/1464700107082369

Gottlieb, Kathryn. "Cultural Appropriation in Contemporary Paganism and Witchcraft." PhD diss., University of Maine, 2017.

Gould, Deborah. "On Affect and Protest." In Staiger, et al., eds., *Political Emotions*, 18–39.

Gran Loggia Druidica D'Italia. http://www.druidismo.it/

Granholm, Kennet. "Post-Secular Esotericism? Some Reflections on the Transformation of Esotericism." *Scripta* 20 (2008): 50–67. https://doi.org/10.30674/scripta.67326

Granholm, Kennet. "The Secular, the Post-Secular and the Esoteric in the Public Sphere." In Asprem and Granholm, eds. *Contemporary Esotericism*, 309–29.

Gredys Harris, Grace. "Concepts of Individual, Self, and Person in Description and Analysis." *American Anthropologist* 91, no. 3 (1989): 599–612. https://doi.org/10.1525/aa.1989.91.3.02a00040

Greenhouse, Carol J. *Moment's Notice: Time Politics Across Cultures*. Ithaca, NY: Cornell University Press, 2018.

Greenwood, Susan. *The Anthropology of Magic*. Oxford: Berg, 2009.

Greenwood, Susan. *Developing Magical Consciousness*. Abington, UK: Routledge, 2019. https://doi.org/10.4324/9781315114545

Greenwood, Susan. *The Nature of Magic: An Anthropology of Consciousness*. Oxford: Berg, 2005.

Greenwood, Susan, and Erik D. Goodwyn. *Magical Consciousness*. London: Routledge, 2016. https://doi.org/10.4324/9781315719849

Gregg, Melissa, and Gregory J. Seigworth, eds. *The Affect Theory Reader*. Durham, NC: Duke University Press, 2010. https://doi.org/10.1215/9780822393047

Gregory, Chris. *Gifts and Commodities*. London: Academic Press, 1982.

Grimassi, Raven. *Ways of the Strega: Italian Witchcraft: Its Lore, Magick, and Spells*. St. Paul, MN: Llewellyn, 1995.

Gutierrez, Cathy. *Handbook of Spiritualism and Channeling*. Leiden: Brill, 2015. https://doi.org/10.1163/9789004264083

Halifax, Joan, and Julio Mario Santo Domingo. *Shaman: the Wounded Healer*. London: Thames and Hudson, 1982.

Hallowell, Alfred Irving. "Ojibwa Ontology, Behavior, and World View." In *Culture in History: Essays in Honor of Paul Radin*, edited by Stanley Diamond, 19–52. New York: Columbia University Press, 1960.

Halstead, John, ed. Introduction to *Godless Paganism: Voices of Non-Theistic Pagans*. N.p.: Lulu.com, 2016.

Hammer, Olav. *Claiming Knowledge: Strategies of Epistemology from Theosophy to the New Age*. Leiden: Brill, 2001. https://doi.org/10.1163/9789004493995

Hammer, Olav, and Mikael Rothstein, *Handbook of the Theosophical Current*. Leiden: Brill, 2013. https://doi.org/10.1163/9789004493995

Handman, Courtney. "Figures of History." *HAU: Journal of Ethnographic Theory* 6, no. 1 (2016): 237–60. https://doi.org/10.14318/hau6.1.015

Hanegraaff, Wouter J. Esotericism and the Academy: Rejected Knowledge in Western Culture. Cambridge: Cambridge University Press, 2012. https://doi.org/10.1017/CBO9781139048064

Hanegraaff, Wouter J. "The New Age Movement and Western Esotericism." In *Handbook of New Age*, edited by Daren Kemp and James R. Lewis, 25–50. Leiden: Brill, 2007. https://doi.org/10.1163/ej.9789004153554.i-484.12

Hanegraaff, Wouter J. *New Age Religion and Western Culture: Esotericism in the Mirror of Secular Thought*. Leiden: Brill, 1996. https://doi.org/10.1163/9789004378933

Hanegraaff, Wouter J. "New Age Spiritualities as Secular Religion: A Historian's Perspective." *Social Compass* 46, no. 2 (1999): 145–60. https://doi.org/10.1177/003776899046002004

Hanegraaff, Wouter J. "On the Construction of 'Esoteric Traditions.'" In *Western Esotericism and the Science of Religion*, edited by Antoine Faivre and Wouter J. Hanegraaff, 11–61. Leuven: Peeters, 1998.

Harner, Michael. *The Way of the Shaman: A Guide to Power and Healing*. New York: Bantam Books, 1982 [1980].

Harrington, Melissa. "Reflecting on Studying Wicca from within the Academy and the Craft: An Autobiographical Perspective." *The Pomegranate: The International Journal of Pagan Studies* 17, nos. 1–2 (2016): 180–93. https://doi.org/10.1558/pome.v17i1-2.28136

Harvey, Graham. Animism: Respecting the Living World. New York: Columbia University Press, 2006.

Harvey, Graham. "Bear Feasts in a Land without Wild Bears." *International Journal for the Study of New Religions* 9, no. 2 (2019): 195–213. https://doi.org/10.1558/ijsnr.37620

Harvey, Graham. *Contemporary Paganism: Listening People, Speaking Earth.* New York: New York University Press, 1997.

Harvey, Graham. *Contemporary Paganism: Religions of the Earth from Druids and Witches to Heathens and Ecofeminists.* New York: New York University Press, 2011.

Harvey, Graham. "Pagan Studies or the Study of Paganisms? A Case Study in the Study of Religions." in Blain, et al. *Researching Paganisms*, 241–55.

Heelas, Paul. *The New Age Movement: The Celebration of the Self and the Sacralization of Modernity.* Oxford: Blackwell, 1996.

Heelas, Paul. *Spiritualities of Life: New Age Romanticism and Consumptive Capitalism.* Malden, MA: Blackwell, 2008. https://doi.org/10.1002/9781444301106

Helfrich, Paul M. "The Channeling Phenomenon: A Multimethodological Assessment," *Journal of Integral Theory and Practice* 4, no. 3 (2009): 127–471.

Herzfeld, Michael. *Cultural Intimacy: Social Poetics in the Nation-State.* New York: Routledge, 2005.

Herzfeld, Michael. "The European Crisis and Cultural Intimacy." *Studies in Ethnicity and Nationalism* 13, no. 3 (2013): 491–97. https://doi.org/10.1111/sena.12060

Herzfeld, Michael. *The Poetics of Manhood: Contest and Identity in a Cretan Mountain Village.* Princeton, NJ: Princeton University Press, 1985. https://doi.org/10.1515/9780691216386

Hinderliter, Beth, William Kaizen, Vered Maimon, Jaleh Mansoor, and Seth McCormick, eds. *Communities of Sense: Rethinking Aesthetics and Politics.* Durham, NC: Duke University Press, 2009. https://doi.org/10.2307/j.ctv11smvw2

Hodges, Matt. "Reinventing 'History'?" *History and Anthropology* 26, no. 4 (2015): 515–27. https://doi.org/10.1080/02757206.2015.1074901

Hodges, Matt. "The Time of the Interval: Historicity, Modernity, and Epoch in Rural France." *American Ethnologist* 37, no. 1 (2010): 115–31. https://doi.org/10.1111/j.1548-1425.2010.01245.x

Holbraad, Martin. "The Power of Powder: Multiplicity and Motion in the Divinatory Cosmology of Cuban Ifá (or *Mana*, Again)." In *Thinking through Things: Theorising Artefacts Ethnographically*, edited by Amiria J. M. Henare, Martin Holbraad, and Sari Wastell, 189–225. London: Routledge, 2007.

Houseman, Michael, and Marie Mazzella di Bosco. "Dances of Self-Development as a Resource for Participatory Democracy." In *Ritual and Democracy: Protests, Publics and Performances*, edited by Sarah Pike, Jone Salomonsen, and Paul François Tremlett, 115–38. Sheffield: Equinox, 2020.

Howard, Michael. *Modern Wicca: A History from Gerald Gardner to the Present*. Woodbury, MN: Llewellyn, 2010.

Howell, Francesca C. *Food, Festival, and Religion: Materiality and Place in Italy*. London: Bloomsbury Academic, 2018. https://doi.org/10.5040/9781350020894

Howell, Francesca C. "The Goddess Returns to Italy: Paganism and Wicca Reborn as a New Religious and Social Movement." *The Pomegranate: The International Journal of Pagan Studies* 10, no. 1 (2008): 5–20. https://doi.org/10.1558/pome.v10i1.5

Howell, Francesca C. "Sense of Place, Heterotopia, and Community: Performing Land and Folding Time in the Badalisc Festival of Northern Italy." *Folklore* 124, no. 1 (2013): 45–63. https://doi.org/10.1080/0015587x.2013.731155

Hunter, Jack. "Engaging the Anomalous: Reflections from the Anthropology of the Paranormal." *European Journal of Psychotherapy & Counselling* 18, no. 2 (2016): 170–78. https://doi.org/10.1080/13642537.2016.1170063

Hunter, Jack, and George P. Hansen. *Engaging the Anomalous*. N.p. August Night Books, 2018).

Hutton, Ronald, "Living with Witchcraft." In Blain, et al. *Researching Paganisms*, 171–188.

Hutton, Ronald. "Modern Pagan Festivals: A Study in the Nature of Tradition." *Folklore* 119, no. 3 (2008): 251–73. https://doi.org/10.1080/00155870802352178

Hutton, Ronald. "Neo-Paganism, Paganism and Christianity." *Religion Today* 9, no. 3 (1994): 29–32. https://doi.org/10.1080/13537909408580718

Hutton, Ronald. *The Stations of the Sun*. Oxford: Oxford University Press, 1996. https://doi.org/10.1093/acprof:oso/9780198205708.001.0001

Hutton, Ronald. *The Triumph of the Moon: A History of Modern Pagan Witchcraft*. Oxford: Oxford University Press, 1999. https://doi.org/10.1093/acprof:oso/9780198207443.001.0001

Ibrahim, Awad. *The Rhizome of Blackness*. New York: Peter Lang, 2014. https://doi.org/10.3726/978-1-4539-1276-8

Il Giardino degli Illuminati. 2022. Facebook. https://www.facebook.com/Ilgiardinodegliilluminati

Ingold, Timothy. *The Perception of the Environment: Essays in Livelihood, Dwelling and Skill*. London: Routledge, 2000.

Inserra, Incoronata Nadia. *Global Tarantella: Reinventing Southern Italian Folk Music and Dances*. Urbana: University of Illinois Press, 2017. https://doi.org/10.5622/illinois/9780252041297.001.0001

Insubriapress. "Noi Siamo Rivoluzionari." April 2, 2013. https://insubriapress.wordpress.com/tag/doma-nunch/

Itzhak, Nofit. "Making Selves and Meeting Others in Neo-Shamanic Healing." *Ethos* 43, no. 3 (2015): 286–310. https://doi.org/10.1111/etho.12086

Johnston, Jay. "Theosophical Bodies: Colour, Shape and Emotion from Modern Aesthetics to Healing Therapies," in *Handbook of*

New Religions and Cultural Production Vol. 4, edited by Carole M. Cusack and Alex Norman, 153–170. Leiden: Brill, 2012. https://doi.org/10.1163/9789004226487_008

Jonuks, Tõnno, and Tiina Äikäs. "Contemporary Deposits at Sacred Places: Reflections on Contemporary Paganism in Estonia and Finland." *Folklore* 75, no. 75 (2019): 7–46. https://doi.org/10.7592/FEJF2019.75.jonuks_aikas

Jordheim, Helge. "Against Periodization: Koselleck's Theory of Multiple Temporalities." *History and Theory* 51, no. 2 (2012): 151–71. https://doi.org/10.1111/j.1468-2303.2012.00619.x

Jorgensen, Danny L. *The Esoteric Scene, Cultic Milieu, and Occult Tarot*. Cults and Nonconventional Religious Groups. New York: Garland, 1992.

Josephson-Storm, Jason Ānanda. 2021. *Metamodernism: The Future of Theory*. Chicago: The University of Chicago Press.

Jung, Carl. *Synchronicity: An Acausal Connecting Principle*. Princeton: Princeton University Press, 2010 [1960]. https://doi.org/10.1515/9781400839162

Kahn-John, Michelle. "Concept Analysis of Diné Hózhó." *Advances in Nursing Science* 33, no. 2 (2010): 113–25. https://doi.org/10.1097/ans.0b013e3181dbc658

Kahn-John, Michelle. "The Path to Development of the Hózhó Resilience Model for Nursing Research and Practice." *Applied Nursing Research* 29 (2016): 144–47. https://doi.org/10.1016/j.apnr.2015.02.010

Karanika, Andromache. "Ecstasis in Healing: Practices in Southern Italy and Greece from Antiquity to the Present." In Del Giudice and Van Deusen, eds., *Performing Ecstasies: Music, Dance, and Ritual in the Mediterranean*, 25–36.

Kavedžija, Iza. *Values of Happiness: Toward an Anthropology of Purpose in Life*. Chicago: HAU Books, 2016.

Keen, Ian. "Ancestors, Magic, and Exchange in Yolngu Doctrines: Extensions of the Person in Time and Space." *Journal of the Royal Anthropological Institute* 12, no. 3 (2006): 515–30. https://doi.org/10.1111/j.1467-9655.2006.00350.x

Kehoe, Alice Beck. *Shamans and Religion: An Anthropological Exploration in Critical Thinking*. Prospect Heights, IL: Waveland Press, 2000.

Kirtsoglou, Elisabeth, and Bob Simpson. *The Time of Anthropology: Studies of Contemporary Chronopolitics*. Abington, UK: Routledge, 2020. https://doi.org/10.4324/9781003087199

Klin-Oron, Adam. "How I Learned to Channel: Epistemology, Phenomenology, and Practice in a New Age Course." *American Ethnologist* 41, no. 4 (2014): 635–47. https://doi.org/10.1111/amet.12102

Konkolÿ Thege, Barna, Carla Petroll, Carlos Rivas, and Salome Scholtens. "The Effectiveness of Family Constellation Therapy in Improving Mental Health: A Systematic Review." *Family Process* 60, no. 2 (2021): 409–23. https://doi.org/10.1111/famp.12636

Koss-Chioino, Joan, David J. Hufford, Bruce Greyson, Antonia Mills, Evgenia Fotiou, Bonnie Glass-Coffin, Edith Turner, Laura Biagi, Todd Ochoa, and Sienna Craig. "Do Spirits Exist? Ways to Know." *Anthropology and Humanism* 35, no. 2 (2010): 131–226. https://doi.org/10.1111/j.1548-1409.2010.01062.x

Kraemer, Christine Hoff. "Gender and Sexuality in Contemporary Paganism." *Religion Compass* 6, no. 8 (2012): 390–401. https://doi.org/10.1111/j.1749-8171.2012.00367.x

Krueger, Oliver. "The Internet as Distributor and Mirror of Religious and Ritual Knowledge." *Asian Journal of Social Science* 32, no. 2 (2004): 183–197. https://doi.org/10.1163/1568531041705077

Kryon Lee Carroll. 2022. Facebook. https://www.facebook.com/KryonLeeCarroll

Lambek, Michael. "The Anthropology of Religion and the Quarrel between Poetry and Philosophy." *Current Anthropology* 41, no. 3 (2000): 309–20. https://doi.org/10.1086/300143

Lambek, Michael. "The Continuous and Discontinuous Person: Two Dimensions of Ethical Life." *Journal of the Royal Anthropological Institute* 19, no. 4 (2013): 837–58. https://doi.org/10.1111/1467-9655.12073

Lambek, Michael. "The Interpretation of Lives or Life as Interpretation: Cohabiting with Spirits in the Malagasy World." *American Ethnologist* 41, no. 3 (2014): 491–503. https://doi.org/10.1111/amet.12089

Lambek, Michael. *Knowledge and Practice in Mayotte: Local Discourses of Islam, Sorcery, and Spirit Possession*. Toronto: University of Toronto Press, 1993. https://doi.org/10.3138/9781442676534

Lambek, Michael, ed. *Ordinary Ethics*. New York: Fordham University Press, 2010.

Lambek, Michael. *The Weight of the Past: Living with History in Mahajanga, Madagascar*. New York: Palgrave Macmillan, 2002. https://doi.org/10.1007/978-1-349-73080-3

Lanternari, Vittorio. "Ernesto De Martino fra storicismo e ontologismo." *Studi Storici* 19, no. 1 (1978): 187–200.

Lanternari, Vittorio. *La mia alleanza con Ernesto de Martino e altri saggi post-demartiniani*. Naples: Liguori, 1997.

Lanternari, Vittorio. "Tarantismo: dal medico neopositivista all'antropologo, alla etnopsichiatria di oggi." *Storia, antropologia, e scienze del linguaggio* 3 (1995): 67–92.

Lanternari, Vittorio. "Tarantismo: vecchie teorie, saperi nuovi." In *Quarant'anni dopo De Martino*, edited by Gino L. Di Mitri, 119–34. Nardò: Besa, 2000.

Lapassade, Georges. *Dallo sciamano al raver: Saggio sulla transe*. Milan: Apogeo edizioni, 1997.

Lapassade, Georges. *Intervista sul tarantismo*. Maglie: Madona Oriente, 1994.

La Soffitta delle Streghe. 2022. Facebook. https://www.facebook.com/soffittadellestreghe

Lau, Kimberly. *New Age Capitalism: Making Money East of Eden*. Philadelphia: Philadelphia University Press, 2000. https://doi.org/10.9783/9781512820010

Lavin, Melissa F. "On Spiritualist Workers: Healing and Divining through Tarot and the Metaphysical." *Journal of Contemporary Ethnography* 50, no. 3 (2020): 317–40. https://doi.org/10.1177/0891241620964951

Laviosa, Flavia. "The Frontier Apulia and its Filmmakers after 1989." *California Italian Studies Journal* 1, no. 1 (2010): 1–9. https://doi.org/10.5070/C311008885

Laviosa, Flavia. "Tarantula Myths and Music: Popular Culture and Ancient Rituals in Italian Cinema." In *Popular Italian Cinema: Culture and Politics in a Postwar Society*, edited by Flavia Brizio-Skov, 153–88. London: I. B. Tauris, 2011. https://doi.org/10.5040/9780755698295.ch-005

Leadbeater, Charles W. *The Chakras: An Introduction*. New Delhi: Cosmo Books, 2003 [1927].

Leland, Charles Godfrey. *Aradia, or, The Gospel of the Witches: A New Translation*. Edited and translated by Mario Pazzaglini and Dina Pazzaglini. Blaine, WA: Phoenix Publishing, 1998.

Lepselter, Susan Claudia. *Resonance of Unseen Things: Poetics, Power, Captivity, and UFOs in the American Uncanny*. Ann Arbor. University of Michigan Press, 2016. https://doi.org/10.3998/mpub.7172850

Lévy-Bruhl, Lucien. *La Mentalité Primitive*. Paris: Librairie Félix Alcan, 1922.

Lévi-Strauss, Claude. *The Savage Mind*. Chicago: University of Chicago Press, 1966.

Lévi-Strauss, Claude. *Tristes Tropiques*. Translated by John and Doreen Weightman. New York: Atheneum, 1981 [1955].

Lewis, James R. "Approaches to the Study of the New Age Movement." *In Perspectives on the New Age*, edited by James R. Lewis and J. Gordon Melton, 1–12. Albany: State University of New York Press, 1992.

Le 4 facce della Luna. 2022. Facebook. https://www.facebook.com/Le-4-facce-della-Luna-499633193481219

Lindroos, Kia. *Now-Time Image-Space: Temporalization of Politics in Walter Benjamin's Philosophy of History and Art*. Jyväskylä, Finland: University of Jyväskylä, 1998.

Lippy, Charles H., and Peter W. Williams. "Neo-paganism." In *Encyclopedia of Religion in America*, 1539–1541. Washington: CQ Press, 2010.

Lüdtke, Karen. *Balla Coi Ragni: La Tarantola Tra Crisi E Celebrazioni*. Bari: Edizioni Di Pagina, 2011.

Lüdtke, Karen. *Dances with Spiders: Crisis, Celebrity and Celebration in Southern Italy*. New York: Berghahn Books, 2008.

Lüdtke, Karen. "Dancing towards Well-Being: Reflections on the Pizzica in the Contemporary Salento, Italy." In Del Giudice and Van Deusen, eds., *Performing Ecstasies: Music, Dance, and Ritual in the Mediterranean*, 37–53.

Lüdtke, Karen. "'We've Got this Rhythm in our Blood': Dancing Identities in Southern Italy." In *Dancing Cultures: Globalization, Tourism and Identity in the Anthropology of Dance*, edited by Hélène Neveu Kringelbach and

Jonathan Skinner, 60–74. New York: Berghahn Books, 2012. https://doi.org/10.1515/9780857455765-006

Luhrmann, Tanya. *Persuasions of the Witch's Craft: Ritual Magic in Contemporary England*. Cambridge, MA: Harvard University Press, 1989.

Luhrmann, Tanya. *How God Becomes Real*. Princeton, NJ: Princeton University Press, 2020. https://doi.org/10.1515/9780691211985

Lyra. http://chi-lyra.com

Magliocco, Sabina."Beyond Belief: Context, Rationality and Participatory Consciousness." *Western Folklore* 71, no. 1 (2012): 5–24.

Magliocco, Sabina. "Italian Cunning Craft: Some Preliminary Observations." *Journal of the Academic Study of Magic* 5 (2009): 103–33.

Magliocco, Sabina. "New Age and Neopagan Magic." In *The Cambridge History of Magic and Witchcraft in the West*, edited by David J. Collins, 635–64. Cambridge: Cambridge University Press, 2015. https://doi.org/10.1017/CHO9781139043021.027

Magliocco, Sabina. "Reconnecting to Everything: Fairies in Contemporary Paganism," In *Fairies, Demons, and Nature Spirits*, edited by Michael Ostling, 325–47. London: Palgrave Macmillan UK, 2017. https://doi.org/10.1057/978-1-137-58520-2_14

Magliocco, Sabina. "The Taming of the Fae: Literary and Folkloric Fairies in Modern Paganisms," In Feraro and Doyle White, eds., *Magic and Witchery in the Modern West: Celebrating the Twentieth Anniversary of 'The Triumph of the Moon,'* 107–30. https://doi.org/10.1007/978-3-030-15549-0_6

Magliocco, Sabina. "Witchcraft as Political Resistance." *Nova Religio* 23, no. 4 (2020): 43–68. https://doi.org/10.1525/nr.2020.23.4.43

Magliocco, Sabina. "Witchcraft, Healing and Vernacular Magic in Italy." In *Witchcraft Continued: Popular Magic in Modern Europe*, edited by Willelm de Blécourt and Owen Davies, 151–3. Manchester: Manchester University Press, 2004.

Magliocco, Sabina. *Witching Culture: Folklore and Neo-Paganism in America*. Philadelphia: University of Pennsylvania Press, 2004. https://doi.org/10.9783/9780812202700

Magnified Healing. https://www.magnifiedhealing.com/

Mahmud, Lilith. "In the Name of Transparency: Gender, Terrorism, and Masonic Conspiracies in Italy." *Anthropological Quarterly* 85, no. 4 (2012): 1177–1207. https://doi.org/10.1353/anq.2012.0054

Mahmud, Lilith. "The World Is a Forest of Symbols': Italian Freemasonry and the Practice of Discretion." *American Ethnologist* 39, no. 2 (2012): 425–38. https://doi.org/10.1111/j.1548-1425.2012.01373.x

Malara, Diego Maria. "Sympathy for the Devil: Secrecy, Magic and Transgression Among Ethiopian Orthodox Debtera." *Ethnos* 87, no. 3 (2022): 444–62. https://doi.org/10.1080/00141844.2019.1707255

Malinowski, Bronislaw, and Robert Redfield. *Magic, Science and Religion, and Other Essays*. Boston: Beacon Press, 1948.

Mapril, José, and Ruy Llera Blanes, eds. *Sites and Politics of Religious Diversity in Southern Europe: The Best of All Gods*. Leiden: Brill, 2013.

Marrè, Davide. "La tradizione molteplice: viaggio nel tradizionalismo romano." *Athame*. www.athame.it/la-tradizione-molteplice-viaggio-nel-tradizionalismo-romano

Martello, Leo Louis. *Witchcraft: The Old Religion*. Secaucus, NJ: University Books, 1973.

Martino, Simone, and Roberto Scalon. *Cattolicesimi nell'Europa-post secolare Uno sguardo comparato*. Rome: Carocci, 2018.

Mascarimiri. "Gitanistan." OriginalMasacarimiri. September 24, 2011. Video, 3:54. https://youtu.be/NtQZIPLQ0aA

Mascarimiri. "Lu Ballu." OriginalMascarimiri. June 28, 2013. Video, 4:30. https://youtu.be/llx1ggmrqSY

Massenzio, Marcello. "The Italian School of 'History of Religions.'" *Religion* 35, no. 4 (2005): 209–22. https://doi.org/10.1016/j.religion.2005.10.007

Massumi, Brian. "The Autonomy of Affect." In *Parables for the Virtual: Movement, Affect, Sensation*, edited by Brian Massumi, 23–45. Durham, NC: Duke University Press, 2002. https://doi.org/10.2307/j.ctv11smvr0.5

Mathews, Gordon, and Carolina Izquierdo. *Pursuits of Happiness: Well-being in Anthropological Perspective*. New York: Berghahn Books, 2009.

Mauss, Marcel. *The Gift: Forms and Functions of Exchange in Archaic Societies*. Translated by Ian Cunnison. New York: Norton, 1967 [1925].

Mauss, Marcel, Henri Hubert, and Robert Hertz. *Saints, Heroes, Myths, and Rites*. Edited by Alexander Riley, Sarah Daynes, and Cyril Isnart. New York: Routledge, 2016. https://doi.org/10.4324/9781315632292

Mazzarella, William. *Shoveling Smoke: Advertising and Globalization in Contemporary India*. Durham, NC: Duke University Press, 2003. https://doi.org/10.1515/9780822385196

Mazzarella, William. "Culture, Globalization, Mediation." *Annual Review of Anthropology* 33, no. 1 (2004): 345–67. https://doi.org/10.1146/annurev.anthro.33.070203.143809

Mazzarella, William. "Affect: What is it Good For?" In *Enchantments of Modernity: Empire, Nation, Globalization*, edited by Saurabh Dube, 291–309. London: Routledge, 2009. https://doi.org/10.1201/9781003071020-13

McCall, John C. *Dancing Histories: Heuristic Ethnography with the Ohafia Igbo*. Ann Arbor: University of Michigan Press, 2000. https://doi.org/10.3998/mpub.15520

McRoberts, Omar M. "Beyond Mysterium Tremendum: Thoughts toward an Aesthetic Study of Religious Experience." *Annals of the American Academy of Political and Social Science* 595, no. 1 (2004): 190–203. https://doi.org/10.1177/0002716204267111

Meyer, Birgit, and Peter J. Pels. *Magic and Modernity*. Stanford: Stanford University Press, 2003. https://doi.org/10.1515/9781503620056

Micieli, Raùl-Metafisica Saint Germain. 2022. Facebook. https://www.facebook.com/Raúl-Micieli-Metafisica-Saint-Germain-1745187245808695

Miles-Watson, Jonathan. "Teachings of Tara: Sacred Place and Human Wellbeing in the Shimla Hills." *Anthropology in Action* 23, no. 3 (2016): 30–42. https://doi.org/10.3167/aia.2016.230304

Miller, Bruce G., and Jean-Guy Goulet eds., *Extraordinary Anthropology: Transformations in the Field*. Lincoln: University of Nebraska Press, 2007.

Mina, Gabriele, and Sergio Torsello. *La tela infinita: bibliografia degli studi sul trantismo mediterraneo 1945–2006*. Nardò: Besa, 2006.

Minghelli, Giuliana. "Icons of Remorse: Photography, Anthropology and the Erasure of History in 1950s Italy." *Modern Italy* 21, no. 4 (2016): 383–407. https://doi.org/10.1017/mit.2016.45

Mingozzi, Gianfranco, dir. *La Taranta*. 1961. DVD. 2008. Nardò, Italy: Besa,

Molgaard, Craig, Elizabeth Byerly, and Charles Snow. "Bach's Flower Remedies: A New Age Therapy." *Human Organization* 38, no. 1 (1979): 71–74. https://doi.org/10.17730/humo.38.1.h47345t142153v47

Muehlebach, Andrea. "On Affective Labor in Post-Fordist Italy." *Cultural Anthropology* 26, no. 1 (2011): 59–82. https://doi.org/10.1111/j.1548-1360.2010.01080.x

Muir, Stewart. "The Good of New Age Goods." *Culture and Religion* 8, no. 3 (2007): 233–53. https://doi.org/10.1080/14755610701649893

Nacci, Anna. *Neotarantismo: pizzica, transe e riti dalle campagne alle metropoli. Viterbo: Stampa alternative*, Nuovi equilibri, 2004.

Nacci, Anna. *Tarantismo e neotarantismo: musica, danza, transe: bisogni di oggi, bisogni di sempre*. Nardò: Besa, 2001.

Napolitano, Valentina. "The Virgin of Guadalupe: A Nexus of Affect." *Journal of the Royal Anthropological Institute* 15, no. 1 (2009): 96–112. https://doi.org/10.1111/j.1467-9655.2008.01532.x

Navaro-Yashin, Yael. "Affective Spaces, Melancholic Objects: Ruination and the Production of Anthropological Knowledge." *Journal of the Royal Anthropological Institute* 15, no. 1 (2009): 1–18. https://doi.org/10.1111/j.1467-9655.2008.01527.x

Navaro-Yashin, Yael. *The Make-Believe Space: Affective Geography in a Postwar Polity*. Durham, NC: Duke University Press, 2012.

Nhat Hanh, Thich. *Bells of Mindfulness*. Berkeley: Parallax Press, 2013.

Nock, J.A. *Provenance Press's Guide to the Wiccan Year: A Year-Round Guide to Spells, Rituals, and Holiday Celebrations*. Avon, MA: Provenance Press, 2007.

OBOD: Ordine Bardi, Ovati e Druidi. www.druidry.it

Oliveira, Amurabi. "Umbanda as Syncretistic Shamanism in Barcelona." *International Journal of Latin American Religions* 4, no. 1 (2020): 123–36. https://doi.org/10.1007/s41603-020-00097-0

Otto, Bernd-Christian, and Michael Stausberg. *Defining Magic: A Reader*. London: Routledge, 2012.

Otto, Rudolf. *The Idea of the Holy: An Inquiry into the Non-Rational Factor in the Idea of the Divine and Its Relation to the Rational*. New York: Oxford University Press, 1958.

Pace, Enzo. "La Pocket-religion. Il New Age Nel Sistema Religioso Italiano." *Quaderni di Sociologia* 19 (1999): 36–54. https://doi.org/10.4000/qds.1616

Pace, Enzo, ed. *Le religioni nell'Italia che cambia*. Rome: Carocci, 2013.

Pagliara, Enza. "La Zamara." Pizzica di Torchiarolo. AnimaMundiEdizioni. November 30, 2010. Video, 7:52. https://youtu.be/RDotUjgdxA4

Palmié, Stephan. "Fascinans or Tremendum? Permutations of the State, the Body, and the Divine in Late-Twentieth-Century Havana." *Nieuwe West-Indische Gids* 78, nos. 3–4 (2004): 229–68. https://doi.org/10.1163/13822373-90002513

Palmié, Stephan. "Historicist Knowledge and Its Conditions of Impossibility." In *The Social Life of Spirits*, edited by Ruy Blanes and Diana Espírito Santo, 218–39. Chicago: University of Chicago Press, 2013.

Palmié, Stephan, and Charles Stewart. "Introduction: For an Anthropology of History." *HAU: Journal of Ethnographic Theory* 6, no. 1 (2016): 207–36. https://doi.org/10.14318/hau6.1.014

Palmisano, Stefania, and Nicola Pannofino. *Contemporary Spiritualities*. London: Routledge, 2021. https://doi.org/10.4324/9780429019722

Palumbo, Berardino. "Iperluogo." *Antropologia Museale* 14 (2006): 45–47.

Palumbo, Berardino. *L'Unesco e il Campanile*. Rome: Meltemi, 2003.

Panagia, Davide. *The Political Life of Sensation*. Durham, NC: Duke University Press, 2009.

Pandolfi, Maria. "The Expanded Body and the Fragmented Body: Inside and Beyond Narrative." *Surfaces* 2 (1992). https://doi.org/10.7202/1065231ar

Pandolfi, Mariella. "Boundaries Inside the Body: Women's Sufferings in Southern Peasant Italy." *Culture, Medicine and Psychiatry* 14, no. 2 (1990): 255–73.

Parmigiani, Giovanna. "Femminicidio and the Emergence of a 'Community of Sense' in Contemporary Italy." *Modern Italy* 23, no. 1 (2018): 19–34. https://doi.org/10.1017/mit.2017.67

Parmigiani, Giovanna. Feminism, Violence and Representation in Modern Italy: "We Are Witnesses, Not Victims." Bloomington: Indiana University Press, 2019.

Parmigiani, Giovanna. "If You Dance Alone, You Cannot Be Healed": Relational Ontologies and "Epistemes of Contagion" in Salento (Italy). *California Italian Studies* 11, no. 1 (2022). http://dx.doi.org/10.5070/C311154536

Parmigiani, Giovanna. "Magic and Politics: Conspirituality and Covid-19." *Journal of the American Academy of Religion* 89, no. 2 (2021): 506–29. https://doi.org/10.1093/jaarel/lfab053

Parmigiani, Giovanna. "Spiritual Pizzica: A Southern Italian Perspective on Contemporary Paganism." *The Pomegranate: The International Journal of Pagan Studies* 21, no. 1 (2019): 53–75. https://doi.org/10.1558/pome.37787

Parmigiani, Giovanna. "'The Witness Is Passing By': Femminicidio and the Politics of Representation in Italy." *Italian Culture* (2020): 1–19. https://doi.org/10.1080/01614622.2020.1834725

Partridge, Christopher. *The Re-Enchantment of the West: Vol. 1*. London; New York: T&T Clark, 2004.

Partridge, Christopher. *The Re-Enchantment of the West: Vol. 2*. London; New York T&T Clark, 2005.

Partridge, Christopher. "Occulture is Ordinary." In Asprem and Granholm, eds. *Contemporary Esotericism*, 113–33.

Pearce, Cathie, Debora Kidd, Rebecca Patterson, and Una Hanley. "The Politics of Becoming." *Qualitative Inquiry* 18, no. 5 (2012): 418–26.

Pederzoli, Luciano, Patrizio Tressoldi, and Helané Wahbeh, "Channeling: A Non-Pathological Possession and Dissociative Identity Experience or Something Else?" *Culture, Medicine and Psychiatry* 46, no. 2 (2021): 161–169. https://doi.org/10.1007/s11013-021-09730-9

Pellegrino, Manuela. "'Dying Language' or 'Living Monument'? Language Ideologies, Policies and Practices in the Case of Griko." PhD diss., University College London, 2013.

Pellegrino, Manuela. "I Glossa Grika: Itte C'è Avri: La Lingua GrecoSalentina tra Passato e Futuro." In *Raccontare la Grecìa,* edited by Giovanni Azzaroni and Matteo Casari, 1–33. Martano: Kurumuny, 2015.

Pellegrino, Manuela. "Performing Griko beyond Death." *Palaver* 5, no. 1 (2016): 137–62.

Pellegrino, Manuela. *Greek Language, Italian Landscape: Griko and the Re-Storying of a Linguistic Minority*. Hellenic Studies Series 89. Washington, DC: Center for Hellenic Studies, 2020.

Pels, Peter. Introduction to *Magic and Modernity*, edited by Birgit Meyer and Peter J. Pels, 1–38. Stanford: Stanford University Press, 2003.

Pensky, Max. "Method and Time: Benjamin's Dialectical Images." In *The Cambridge Companion to Walter Benjamin*, edited by David S. Ferris, 177–98. Cambridge: Cambridge University Press, 2004.

Pérez, Elizabeth. *Religion in the Kitchen*. New York: New York University Press, 2016.

Perocco, Fabio. "Il New Age Come Paradigma Sociale." *Quaderni di Sociologia* 19 (1999): 55–70. https://doi.org/10.4000/qds.1450

Pike, Sarah M. *Earthly Bodies, Magical Selves: Contemporary Pagans and the Search for Community*. Berkeley: University of California Press, 2001.

Pike, Sarah M. *New Age and Neopagan Religions in America*. New York: Columbia University Press, 2004.

Pizza, Giovanni. "Gramsci e de Martino: appunti per una riflessione." *Quaderni di Teoria Sociale* 13 (2013): 75–120.

Pizza, Giovanni. "Margini." *AM* 13, no. 37/39 (2016): 105–109.

Pizza, Giovanni. "Tarantism and the Politics of Tradition in Contemporary Salento." In *Memory, Politics and Religion: The Past Meets the Present in Europe*, edited by Idis Haukanes, 119–223. Münster, Germany: LIT, 2004.

Pizza, Giovanni. "Tarantismi oggi: un panorama critico sulle letture contemporanee del tarantismo (1994–1998)." *Panorami* 7–8 (1999): 253–73.

Pizza, Giovanni. *Il Tarantismo Oggi*. Alessano: Carocci, 2015.

Pizza, Murphy, and James R. Lewis. *Handbook of Contemporary Paganism*. Brill Handbooks on Contemporary Religion. Leiden: Brill, 2009.

Pliny the Elder. *Natural History*.

Possamaï, Adam. "Cultural Consumption of History and Popular Culture in Alternative Spiritualities." *Journal of Consumer Culture* 2, no. 2 (2002): 197–218. https://doi.org/10.1177/146954050200200203

Prince, Ronna. *Aura-Soma*. Accessed 05/06/2021. https://www.ronnaprince.com/aura-soma/

Puca, Angela. "'Witch' and 'Shaman: Discourse Analysis of the Use of Indigenizing Terms in Italy." *International Journal for the Study of New Religions* 9, no. 2 (2018): 271–84. https://doi.org/10.1558/ijsnr.37624

Puca, Angela. "The Tradition of Segnature. Underground Indigenous Practices in Italy." *Journal of the Irish Society for the Academic Study of Religions* 7 (2019): 104–24.

Purkiss, Diane. "Getting It Wrong: The Problems with Reinventing the Past." *The Pomegranate : The International Journal of Pagan Studies* 21, no. 2 (2019): 256–77. https://doi.org/10.1558/pome.39116

Purser, Ronald. *McMindfulness: How Mindfulness Became the New Capitalist Spirituality*. London: Repeater, 2019.

Rancière, Jacques. *Disagreement: Politics and Philosophy*. Minneapolis: University of Minnesota Press, 1999.

Rancière, Jacque. "The Politics of Literature." *SubStance* 33, no. 1 (2004): 10–24. https://doi.org/10.2307/3685460

Reid, Síân, and Lee MacDonald. *Between the Worlds: Readings in Contemporary Neopaganism*. Toronto: Canadian Scholars' Press, 2006.

La Repubblica. "Salento, Diocesi promuove processione e funerali per la peste degli ulivi." November 22, 2014. Video, 3:39. https://video.repubblica.it/edizione/bari/salento-diocesi-promuove-processione-e-funerali-per-la-peste-degli-ulivi/184239/183089

Ricco, Isabella. "Searching for a 'new Magical World': The Contradictions of CAM and New Age Therapies in the West." *Anthropology & Medicine* 27, no. 1 (2020): 96–109. https://doi.org/10.1080/13648470.2018.1544605

Rindfleish, Jennifer. "Consuming the Self: New Age Spirituality as 'Social Product' in Consumer Society." *Consumption Markets & Culture* 8, no. 4 (2005): 343–60. https://doi.org/10.1080/10253860500241930

Robertson, David G., Egil Asprem, and Asbjørn Dyrendal. "Introducing the Field: Conspiracy Theory in, about, and as Religion." In *Handbook of Conspiracy Theory and Contemporary Religion*, edited by Egil Asprem, Asbjørn Dyrendal, and David G. Robertson, 1–18. Leiden: Brill, 2018.

Robbins, Joel. "On Happiness, Values, and Time." *HAU Journal of Ethnographic Theory* 5, no. 3 (2015): 215–33.

Robertson, Robin. "Divination." *Psychological Perspectives* 61, no. 2 (2018): 170–93. https://doi.org/10.1080/00332925.2018.1461501

Rodgers, Charlotte. "High Glamour: Magical Clothing and Talismanic Fashion." *The Pomegranate: The International Journal of Pagan Studies* 21, no. 2 (2020): 172–85. https://doi.org/10.1558/pome.41521

Rossi, Annabella. *Lettere da una tarantata: con uno nota di Tullio De Mauro.* Lecce: Argo, 2000.

Rouget, Gilbert. *La musique et la transe: esquisse d'une théorie générale des relations de la musique et de la possession.* Paris: Gallimard, 1980.

Rountree, Kathryn, ed. *Contemporary Pagan and Native Faith Movements in Europe: Colonialist and Nationalist Impulses.* New York: Berghahn Books, 2015.

Rountree, Kathryn, ed. *Cosmopolitanism, Nationalism, and Modern Paganism.* New York: Palgrave Macmillan, 2016.

Rountree, Kathryn. Crafting Contemporary Pagan Identities in a Catholic Society. Farnham, UK: Ashgate Pub, 2010.

Rountree, Kathryn. "Localizing Neo-Paganism: Integrating Global and Indigenous Traditions in a Mediterranean Catholic Society." *Journal of the Royal Anthropological Institute* 17, no. 4 (2011): 846–72. https://doi.org/10.1111/j.1467-9655.2011.01722.x

Rountree, Kathryn. "Neo-Paganism, Native Faith and Indigenous Religion: A Case Study of Malta within the European Context." *Social Anthropology/Anthropologie Sociale* 22, no. 1 (2014): 81–100. https://doi.org/10.1111/1469-8676.12063

Rutherford, Danilyn. "Commentary: What Affect Produces." *American Ethnologist* 39, no. 4 (2012): 688–91. https://doi.org/10.1111/j.1548-1425.2012.01388.x

Salazar Parreñas, Rheana "Juno". "Producing Affect: Transnational Volunteerism in a Malaysian Orangutan Rehabilitation Center." *American Ethnologist* 39, no. 4 (2012): 673–87. https://doi.org/10.1111/j.1548-1425.2012.01387.x

Salomonsen, Jone. *Enchanted Feminism: Ritual, Gender and Divinity among the Reclaiming Witches of San Francisco.* London: Routledge, 2002. https://doi.org/10.4324/9780203160282

Salomonsen, Jone. "Methods of Compassion or Pretension? Conducting Anthropological Fieldwork in Modern Magical Communities." *The Pomegranate: The International Journal of Pagan Studies* 8 (1999): 4–13. https://doi.org/10.1558/pome.v13i8.4

Sanga, Glauco. "L'etnografo impaziente." *La Ricerca Folklorica* 67–68 (2013): 35–43.

Sartwell, Crispin. *Six Names of Beauty.* London: Routledge, 2004.

Saunders, George R. "The Crisis of Presence in Italian Pentecostal Conversion." *American Ethnologist* 22, no. 2 (1995): 324–40. https://doi.org/10.1525/ae.1995.22.2.02a00060

Schatzki, Theodore R. *The Timespace of Human Activity: On Performance, Society, and History as Indeterminate Teleological Events.* Lanham, MD: Lexington Books, 2010.

Scheper-Hughes, Jennifer. "Mysterium Materiae: Vital Matter and the Object as Evidence in the Study of Religion." *Bulletin for the Study of Religion* 41, no. 4 (2012): 16–24. https://doi.org/10.1558/bsor.v41i4.16

Schneider, Jakob Robert. *Family Constellations: Basic Principles and Procedures.* Heidelberg: Carl-Auer, 2009.

Schneider-Mayerson, Matthew, Brent Ryan Bellamy, and Project Muse. *An Ecotopian Lexicon*. Minneapolis: University of Minnesota Press, 2019. https://doi.org/10.5749/j.ctvthhdbm

Screti, Antonella. *La Storia di Rahida e la Chiesetta.* Neviano: Musicaos Editore, 2015.

Seligman, Rebecca. *Possessing Spirits and Healing Selves: Embodiment and Transformation in an Afro-Brazilian Religion.* New York: Palgrave Macmillan, 2014. https://doi.org/10.1057/9781137409607

Senvaityte, Dalia. "The Hunt for Lost Identity: Native Faith Paganism in Contemporary Lithuania." *The Pomegranate: The International Journal of Pagan Studies* 20, no. 2 (2018): 234–60. https://doi.org/10.1558/pome.34718

Seppilli, Tullio. "Ernesto de Martino e la nascita dell'etnopsichiatria italiana." *Storia, Antropologia e Scienze del Linguaggio* 10, no. 3 (1995): 147–56.

Sibaldi, Igor. *Resuscitare: L'arte di riportare in vita ciò che credevamo perduto.* Milan: Mondadori, 2018.

Signorelli, Amalia. "Il tarantismo. . . che purtroppo non c'è più." *Studi e Materiali di Storia delle Religioni* 62, no. 20 (1996): 591–98.

Signorelli, Amalia. "La destorificazione del negativo in Ernesto de Martino." *L'analisi e la classe.* January 8, 2017. http://ferdinandodubla.blogspot.com/2017/01/la-destorificazione-del-negativo-in.html

Simpson, Scott. "Only Slavic Gods: Nativeness in Polish Rodzimowierstwo." In Kathryn Rountree, ed. *Cosmopolitanism, Nationalism, and Modern Paganism*, 65–86. https://doi.org/10.1057/978-1-137-56200-5_4

Simpson, Scott. "The Study of Paganism and Wicca." In *The Oxford Handbook of New Religious Movements*, edited by James R. Lewis and Inga Tøllefsen, 482–94. Oxford: Oxford University Press, 2016.

Staiger, Janet, Ann Cvetkovich, and Ann Reynolds. *Political Emotions.* London: Routledge, 2010. https://doi.org/10.4324/9780203849538

Stang, Charles M. "Reading Plato's Many Doubles." In *Our Divine Double.* Cambridge, MA: Harvard University Press, 2016. https://doi.org/10.4159/9780674970168-002

Staro, Placida. "Reconstructing the Sense of Presence: Tarantula, Arlìa, and Dance." In Del Giudice and Van Deusen, eds., *Performing Ecstasies: Music, Dance, and Ritual in the Mediterranean*, 55–70.

Steedman, Ian, John R. Atherton, and Elaine Graham, eds. *The Practices of Happiness.* London: Routledge, 2010. https://doi.org/10.4324/9780203846902

Stewart, Charles. *Dreaming and Historical Consciousness in Island Greece.* Cambridge, MA: Harvard University Press, 2012.

Stewart, Charles. "Historicity and Anthropology." *Annual Review of Anthropology* 45 (2016): 79–94. https://doi.org/10.1146/annurev-anthro-102215-100249

Stewart, Kathleen. *Ordinary Affects*. Durham, NC: Duke University Press, 2007.

Stoller, Paul. "Ethnography/Memoir/Imagination/Story." *Anthropology and Humanism* 32, no. 2 (2007): 178–91. https://doi.org/10.1525/ahu.2007.32.2.178

Strathern, Marilyn. *The Gender of the Gift*. Berkeley: University of California Press, 1988.

Strmiska, Michael. "Modern Latvian Paganism: Some Introductory Remarks." *The Pomegranate: The International Journal of Pagan Studies* 14, no. 1 (2013): 22–30. https://doi.org/10.1558/pome.v14i1.22

Strmiska, Michael. "Modern Paganism in World Cultures: Comparative Perspectives." In *Modern Paganism in World Cultures: Comparative Perspectives*, edited by Michael Strmiska, 1–53. Santa Barbara, CA: ABC-Clio, 2005.

Stuckrad, Kocku von. *Western Esotericism: A Brief History of Secret Knowledge*. London: Equinox, 2005. https://doi.org/10.1016/j.religion.2005.07.002

Stuckrad, Kocku von. "Western Esotericism: Towards an Integrative Model of Interpretation." *Religion* 35, no. 2 (2005): 78–97. https://doi.org/10.1016/j.religion.2005.07.002

Stuckey, Priscilla. "Being Known by a Birch Tree: Animist Refigurings of Western Epistemology." *Journal for the Study of Religion, Nature and Culture* 4, no. 3 (2010): 182–205. https://doi.org/10.1558/jsrnc.v4i3.182

Sutcliffe, Steven J., and Ingvild Saelid Gilhus. *New Age Spirituality: Rethinking Religion*. London: Routledge, 2014. https://doi.org/10.4324/9781315729541

Tafjord, Bjorn Ola. "Modes of Indigenizing: Remarks on Indigenous Religion as a Method." *International Journal for the Study of New Religions* 9, no. 2 (2018): 303–27. https://doi.org/10.1558/ijsnr.37626

Tambiah, Stanley. *Magic, Science, Religion, and the Scope of Rationality*. Cambridge: Cambridge University Press, 1990.

Tanaka, Stefan. "History without Chronology." *Public Culture* 28, no. 1 (2016): 161–86. https://doi.org/10.1215/08992363-3325064

Taussig, Michael. "History as Sorcery." *Representations* 7 (1984): 87–109. https://doi.org/10.2307/2928457

Taussig, Michael. *The Magic of the State*. London: Routledge, 1997.

Taussig, Michael. *Mimesis and Alterity: A Particular History of the Senses*. New York: Routledge, 1993.

Taylor, Bron R., *Dark Green Religion: Nature Spirituality and the Planetary Future*. Berkeley: University of California Press, 2010. https://doi.org/10.1525/9780520944459

Taylor, Bron R. "Bounding Paganism: Who and What Is In and Out, and What Does This Reveal about Contemporary Kinship-Entangled Nature

Spiritualities?", *Journal for the Study of Religion, Nature and Culture*, forthcoming.

Teisenhoffer, Viola. "Assessing Ritual Experience in Contemporary Spiritualities: The Practice of 'Sharing' in a New Age Variant of Umbanda." *Religion and Society* 9 (2018): 131–44. https://doi.org/10.3167/arrs.2018.090110

Thrift, Nigel. "Intensities of Feeling: Towards a Spatial Politics of Affect." Geografiska Annaler: Series B, *Human Geography* 86, no. 1 (2004): 57–78. https://doi.org/10.1111/j.0435-3684.2004.00154.x

Thrift, Nigel. *Non-Representational Theory: Space, Politics, Affect*. London: Routledge, 2008. https://doi.org/10.4324/9780203946565

Tolle, Eckhart. *A New Earth: Awakening to Your Life's Purpose*. New York: Penguin Group, 2005.

Tolle, Eckhart. *The Power of Now: A Guide to Spiritual Enlightenment*. Vancouver, BC: Namaste Publishing, 2004.

Triace. "Pinguli Pinguli." S'Ardmusic. May 17, 2012. Video, 5:30. https://youtu.be/CCJMVxuWCQ0

Triace. "Pizzica 'Bulgara.'" The Orchard Enterprises. November 5, 2014. Video, 2:52. https://youtu.be/XLqX4RSHrXY

Turner, Victor W. *The Forest of Symbols: Aspects of Ndembu Ritual*. Ithaca, NY: Cornell University Press, 1967.

L'UCN: L' Unione delle Comunità Neopagane. www.neopaganesimo.it

UNESCO. "World Heritage List." http://whc.unesco.org/en/list/

Vanni, Ilaria. "'Oggetti Spaesati', Unhomely Belongings Objects, Migrations and Cultural Apocalypses." *Cultural Studies Review* 19, no. 2 (2013), 162–63. https://doi.org/10.5130/csr.v19i2.2848

Vitullo, Alessandra. "New Age Goes Online: Relocating Spirituality in Virtual Spaces. The Study of Damanhur Community." *Methaodos: Revista de Ciencias Sociales* 4, no. 2 (2015): 339–48. https://doi.org/10.17502/m.rcs.v4i2.125

Viveiros de Castro, Eduardo. "The Gift and the Given: Three Nano-Essays on Kinshipand Magic." In *Kinship and Beyond: The Genealogical Model Reconsidered*, edited by Sandra Bamford and James Leach, 237–68. New York: Berghahn Books, 2009. https://doi.org/10.1515/9781845458966-012

Waldram, James B. "The Efficacy of Traditional Medicine: Current Theoretical and Methodological Issues." *Medical Anthropology Quarterly* 14, no. 4 (2000): 603–25. https://doi.org/10.1525/maq.2000.14.4.603

Wallis, Robert J. "Between the Worlds: Autoarchaeology and Neo-Shamans." Blain, et al. *Researching Paganisms*, 191–216.

Wallis, Robert J. "Journeying the Politics of Ecstasy: Anthropological Perspectives on Neoshamanism." *The Pomegranate: The International Journal of Pagan Studie*s 13, no. 6 (2012): 20–28. https://doi.org/10.1558/pome.v13i6.20

Ward, Charlotte, and David Voas. "The Emergence of Conspirituality." *Journal of Contemporary Religion* 26, no. 1 (2011): 103–21. https://doi.org/10.1080/13537903.2011.539846

Warren, Áine. "The Morrigan as a 'Dark Goddess': A Goddess Re-Imagined Through Therapeutic Self-Narration of Women on Social Media." *The Pomegranate: The International Journal of Pagan Studies* 21, no. 2 (2019): 237–55. https://doi.org/10.1558/pome.37967

Weiner, Annette B. *Inalienable Possessions: The Paradox of Keeping-While-Giving*. Berkeley: University of California Press, 1992. https://doi.org/10.1525/california/9780520076037.001.0001

Weinhold, Jan, Christina Hunger, Annette Bornhäuser, Leoni Link, Justine Rochon, Beate Wild, and Jochen Schweitzer. "Family Constellation Seminars Improve Psychological Functioning in a General Population Sample: Results of a Randomized Controlled Trial." *Journal of Counseling Psychology* 60, no. 4 (2013): 601–09. https://doi.org/10.1037/a0033539

Werito, Vincent. "Understanding HóZhǫ́ to Achieve Critical Consciousness: A Contemporary Diné Interpretation of the Philosophical Principles of HóZhǫ́." In *Diné Perspectives: Revitalizing and Reclaiming Navajo Thought*, edited by LLoyd L. Lee, 25–38. Tucson: University of Arizona Press.

Wernitznig, Dagmar. *Going Native or Going Naive?: White Shamanism and the Neo-Noble Savage*. Lanham, MD: University Press of America, 2003.

Willeto, Angela A.A. "Happiness in Navajos (Diné Ba' HóZhó)." In *Happiness Across Cultures*, by Helaine Selin, 377–86. Dordrech: Springer, 2012. https://doi.org/10.1007/978-94-007-2700-7_25

Winnicott, Donald W. *Home is Where We Start From*. New York: Norton, 1986.

Wirtz, Kristina. "The Living, the Dead, and the Immanent." *HAU: Journal of Ethnographic Theory* 6, no. 1 (2016): 343–69. https://doi.org/10.14318/hau6.1.019

Witmore, Christopher L. "Vision, Media, Noise and the Percolation of Time." *Journal of Material Culture* 11, no. 3 (2006): 267–92. https://doi.org/10.1177/1359183506068806

Witmore, Christopher L. "Landscape, Time, Topology: An Archaeological Account of the Southern Argolid, Greece." In *Envisioning Landscape: Situations and Standpoints in Archaeology and Heritage*, edited by Dan Hicks, Laura McAtackney, and Graham Fairclough, 194–225. Walnut Creek, CA: Left Coast, 2007.

Wu, Hong-An. "Tarot as a Technology." *Journal of Cultural Research in Art Education* 37, no. 1 (2020): 193–218. https://doi.org/10.2458/jcrae.4760

"Xyella: il 'cancro' degli ulivi." Directed by Antonio Scarcella and Michele Rizzo. Lucio Ciardo. November 18, 2014. video, 4:26. https://youtu.be/wvPZU06Lh40

Yang, Xunxian. "The Gift and Gift Economy." In *A Handbook of Economic Anthropology*, edited by James G. Carrier, 246–61. Cheltenham, UK. Edward Elgar, 2005. https://doi.org/10.4337/9781845423469.00027

York, Michael. "New Age Commodification and Appropriation of Spirituality." *Journal of Contemporary Religion* 16, no. 3 (2001): 361–72. https://doi.org/10.1080/13537900120077177

York, Michael. *Pagan Theology: Paganism as a World Religion*. New York: New York University Press, 2003.

Zakroff, Laura Tempest. "A Witch's Dance of Healing." *Patheos*. May 11, 2020. https://www.patheos.com/blogs/tempest/2020/05/a-witchs-dance-of-healing.html

Zeitlyn, David. "Haunting, Dutching, and Interference Provocations for the Anthropology of Time." *Current Anthropology* 61, no. 4 (2020): 495–513. https://doi.org/10.1086/710105

Ziarek, Ewa. *An Ethics of Dissensus: Postmodernity, Feminism, and the Politics of Radical Democracy*. Stanford: Stanford University Press, 2001. https://doi.org/10.1515/9780804780360

Ziarek, Ewa. *Feminist Aesthetics and the Politics of Modernism*. New York: Columbia University Press, 2012. https://doi.org/10.7312/ziar16148

Zinn, Dorothy. "An Introduction to Ernesto De Martino's Relevance for the Study of Folklore." *Journal of American Folklore* 128, no. 507 (2015): 3–17. https://doi.org/10.5406/jamerfolk.128.507.0003

Index

www.ingramcontent.com/pod-product-compliance
Lightning Source LLC
Chambersburg PA
CBHW070607270326
41926CB00013B/2454